£2·50

Stepney:
Profile of a London Borough from the Outbreak of the First World War to the Festival of Britain, 1914-1951

Stepney:
Profile of a London Borough from the Outbreak of the First World War to the Festival of Britain, 1914-1951

By

Samantha L. Bird

CAMBRIDGE
SCHOLARS
P U B L I S H I N G

Stepney: Profile of a London Borough from the Outbreak of the First World War
to the Festival of Britain, 1914-1951,
by Samantha L. Bird

This book first published 2011

Cambridge Scholars Publishing

12 Back Chapman Street, Newcastle upon Tyne, NE6 2XX, UK

British Library Cataloguing in Publication Data
A catalogue record for this book is available from the British Library

ISBN (10): 1-4438-2582-4, ISBN (13): 978-1-4438-2582-5

TABLE OF CONTENTS

LIST OF ILLUSTRATIONS

LIST OF TABLES

PREFACE

The motto for Stepney was *a magnis ad maiora* (from great things to greater) and this book attempts to assess how far the area achieved such improvements, and against what odds, during the first half of the 20th Century.

The First World War is the starting point of this book as it was to have long-term implications for Stepney. Arthur Foley Winnington-Ingram, Bishop of London, in his Easter sermon of 1918 first used the slogan "They Shall Not Pass". For Stepney, this was to become a significant slogan during the Battle of Cable Street, eighteen years later, in 1936. Another event in the First World War, which was to have an affect on the country's preparations for the Second World War, was the death of 18 schoolchildren when Upper North Street School was directly struck during a zeppelin raid. This event was one of the main reasons, according to Philip Ziegler, for the later evacuation of schoolchildren from cities across the country.

The overall theme for this book is the politics of the broader labour movement as represented by both the Labour and Communist parties and the Trade Union during the first half of the 20th Century. What makes Stepney distinctive during this period is its political diversity with the rise of the Labour, Communist and Fascist parties. The politics of the labour movement are addressed through relevant local issues such as housing and ethnicity. Stepney also had a diverse community. During the First and Second World War tensions were heightened within the area due to the internment of military aged "alien" males. However in the inter-war years there was the significance of the integration of the Jewish community, in particular, into the politics of the labour movement. For Stepney, housing was also an ever-present issue. Poor quality housing characterised Stepney.

Throughout the period covered by this book, housing was a persistent issue on the borough council. Both the First and Second World War saw a halt to building work, and the subsequent post-war periods saw election campaigns promising that the housing issue would be effectively addressed. A test of the promises in the 1945 election campaign was the Live Architectural Exhibition for the Festival of Britain, which saw the Lansbury estate presented as a pioneering example of modern architecture.

This book aims to address two further issues which have generally been overlooked by other historians. The first is the tendency of historians to try and encompass the entire East End, which is often undefined, or vague, in their work. This book is focused on a specific study of the Stepney area. Secondly historians have often concentrated on the late 19th Century up to the outbreak of the First World War. This research begins with the First World War and climaxes with the Festival of Britain thus aiming to add to our collective knowledge.

ACKNOWLEDGEMENTS

I would like to thank a number of people who have been vital in writing this book. Firstly, my sincere thanks go to Professor Denis Judd who has enthusiastically supported me throughout. My thanks also go to Carol Koulikourdi for commissioning this book. Over the many years that, as a part-time student, this originally took to complete as a PhD I encountered many librarians at the various archives and institutes where I sourced material. I thank you all for your knowledge and help in finding material and particularly staff at the Bancroft Local History Archive (Tower Hamlets). Finally, but most importantly, my thanks go to my family, who have made this all possible. To Mum and Janet, thank you both for many Wednesday night's tea and chocolate cake that went into this. To Hooch, thank you for bravely supporting me throughout and taking me to numerous farm sales. For you this is the ultimate bed-time read. For me this book is the result of my many years of enjoyment poking around in the archives.

ABBREVIATIONS

ARP	Air Raid Precautions
BBL	British Brothers League
BSP	British Socialist Party
BUF	British Union of Fascists
CPGB	Communist Party of Great Britain
ELFS	East London Federation of the Suffragettes
ILD	International Labour Defence
ILP	Independent Labour Party
LCC	London County Council
MP	Member of Parliament
MFGB	Miners' Federation of Great Britain
NAFTA	National Amalgamated Furnishing Trades Association
NDP	National Democratic Party
NIA	Non-Intervention Agreement
NIC	Non-Intervention Committee
NSS	National Shop Stewards
NTWF	National Transport Workers' Federation
NUR	National Union of Railwaymen
NUTGW	National Union of Tailors and Garment Workers
NUWM	National Union of Workers Movement
RA	Ratepayers Association
SLP	Social Liberal Party
STDL	Stepney Tenants' Defence League
TGWU	Transport and General Workers Union
TUC	Trades Union Congress
USR	Union of Stepney Ratepayers
WC	Water Closet
WCM	Workers' Committee Movement
WSF	Workers' Suffrage Federation
WSPU	Women's Social and Political Union
WVS	Women's Voluntary Service
YCL	Young Communist League

INTRODUCTION

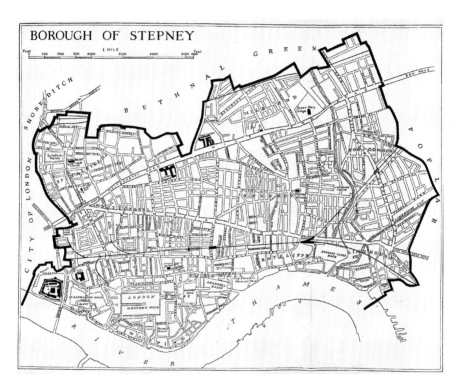

Fig. 0-1 Map of the Borough of Stepney based on 1899 London Government Act
(Tower Hamlets Local History Library and Archives)

Stepney, as shown in the map above, was bordered to the west by the
City. To the north it was bordered by Bethnal Green, to the east by Poplar
and to the south by the River Thames. According to the terms of the
London Government Act of 1899 the borough of Stepney comprised "the
area including the parishes of Mile End Old Town and St George's-in-the-
East and the districts of the Limehouse and the Whitechapel Boards of

Works, including the Tower of London and the Liberties thereof".[1] The
new Stepney which was created in 1899 consisted of 20 wards with 60
councillors and 10 Aldermen. The borough was divided into three
Parliamentary constituencies: Limehouse, Mile End and Whitechapel & St
George's. A number of wards made up each of these constituencies, as
shown in the breakdown of Borough election results in the appendix.

   As an area Stepney had developed without much planning or control,
and its growth had brought much overcrowding, disease and misery.
Toynbee Hall classified Stepney as the heart of the East End because it
was "where many races mix and life is colourful and varied".[2] Since
medieval times the east side of the City had been regarded by many as
London's backyard, with workshops and shipyards, bakeries and mills,
breweries and distilleries interspersed with allotments and market gardens.
According to the Tax records from the time of Samuel Pepys, half the
residents of the East of London were classified as poor.[3] Therefore, one
can gather that the East End had had a long tradition of poverty. According
to the Stepney Reconstruction Group, the East End of 1945 had come
"into being when the docks were built in the early 19th century". The group
stated that "by 1870 the whole of Stepney was built up".[4]

   The haphazard growth of the area is well illustrated by the example of
the laying of the Fenchurch Street to Tilbury railway line in 1854. No
consideration was shown for the East End people living nearby. The tracks
ran so close to many of their houses that they had to keep their windows
closed when trains passed lest their bedding catch fire from the sparks.
Between 1780 and 1830, prior to the arrival of the railways, the population
had more than doubled to over a quarter of a million. During this time,
houses had shot up for the new arrivals, with very little thought given to
planning.[5] By the time of the 1911 Census the population stood at
279,804. Stepney comprised 1,766 acres, so the density of the population
was 158 persons per acre. Throughout the period of this book this was to
decline, and by 1951 the density was at a record low of 56 persons per
acre.[6] This book will establish the reasons behind such a decline,
particularly the destruction of the area during the Blitz. Also, the turbulent

---

[1] Stepney Borough Council, *The Metropolitan Borough of Stepney, Official Guide,
10th Edition* (1962)
[2] Toynbee Hall, *Living in Stepney: Past, Present and Future* (1943) p2
[3] Cox, Jane, *London's East End: Life and Traditions* (1994) p9
[4] Stepney Reconstruction Group, *Living in Stepney: Past, present and future*
(1945) p11
[5] Wyld, Peter, *Stepney Story: A thousand years of St Dunstans* (1952) p510
[6] *Census of England & Wales 1921 & 1951*

politics of Stepney will be considered by looking at the rise of both the Communist and Fascist Parties and examining the consequences of their influence, and their rivalry, upon the area.

In the popular imagination, the notoriety of the East End is well established. Such notoriety was created by events like the Houndsditch Murders, and the subsequent Siege of Sidney Street, which according to the television programme *Scenes of Crime,* was "a great event of the 20th Century for the East End".[7] Depictions of shocking crimes have become part of the folk-law of the nation's perspective of the East End and Stepney. The Houndsditch Murders of December 1910 centred on the murder of three policemen by East European immigrants. For the police these murders served to highlight the fact that the community in the Stepney area had a large and potentially turbulent foreign element. Having no Russian or Lettish, and virtually no Yiddish language skills, the detectives could make little progress in their investigations. Another problem for them was the disconcerting number of vagabond people who seemed able to appear or disappear at will. The murders at Houndsditch had occurred after a group of Lettish men attempted to rob H. S. Harris the Jewellers. The robbers made so much noise drilling a tunnel through from a neighbouring property, that neighbours notified the authorities. The police then made a forceful entrance, which was to have disastrous consequences. Along with the three policemen who were killed, one of the robbers also died. The nation mourned the deaths of the three policemen and was also shocked by the evidence that anarchists from Europe appeared to be invading England. On 3 January 1911, it was reported that two of the suspects from the Hounsditch Murders had besieged 100 Sidney Street. Winston Churchill, the Home Secretary, went to Sidney Street to observe. The police and army were called in and a gun battle ensued. The affair drew to a close when the house caught fire and began to burn down, with the suspects still in it. In the aftermath of this dramatic incident, Churchill was criticized for not bringing out the men alive. These events have been described as "London's biggest hue-and-cry since the 'Jack the Ripper' murders in 1888".[8]

The East End therefore, can appear to be a mini-world of its own or even "a complete city in itself",[9] with so many different cultures all living on top of each other and a sense of potential drama, that has made the area

---

[7] Television Programme, *Scenes of Crime* broadcast on 15 November 2001 ITV1 Carlton
[8] Rogers, Colin, *The Battle of Stepney. The Sidney Street Siege: Its causes and consequences* (1989) p66
[9] Keating, P. J., *The Working Class in Victorian Fiction* (1971) p124

distinctive from the rest of London. It developed as a controversial nucleus, which the rest of London strives to know and understand.

There have been a number of general studies by historians which have included an investigation into Stepney's history. For example, Charles Booth's *Survey of London* looks at all aspects of London life in the late 19th Century. Research on Stepney has often been a part of broader surveys of London's history. Examples of such work include Jerry White's *London in the 20th Century,* Stephen Inwood's *A History of London* and the novelist Peter Ackroyd's *London: The Biography*.[10] In *London in the 20th Century,* White chooses to divide his book into themes and more or less adheres to a chronological approach to each thematic section.[11] In this book, the overall theme is the development and influence of the labour movement, through relevant local issues, such as housing and ethnicity which are considered throughout the book.

Several historians have studied the "East End": William Fishman with *East End Jewish Radicals 1875-1914* and Julia Bush in her PhD "Labour Politics and Society in East London during the First World War". One difficulty in studying the "East End", however, is that it can be a very loose term, covering any part of the east of London. This book is inevitably constrained by the boundaries of the borough of Stepney, which are clearly defined in the map at the beginning of this introduction. It appears that little research has been done on this area during the 1914 to 1951 period. There have been only specific studies such as Jerry White's *Rothschild buildings: Life in an East End Tenement Block 1887-1920.* Other works on parts of the area have been produced to mark anniversaries. For instance, with the 50th anniversary of the Battle of Cable Street, much work was done to commemorate the event, and the Cable Street Group published a pamphlet called *The Battle of Cable Street 1936.*[12] Perhaps more significantly a permanent reminder was commissioned, by the Tower Hamlets Arts Project, in the area. This was a mural, painted in the 1980s to mark the 50th anniversary of the event, on the west wall of St George's town hall, Cable Street, which still exists today (see illustration below). But, these are studies of one particular event rather than a profile of the area.

The objective of this book is to assess the development of Stepney in the first half of the 20th Century, in particular, through a study of the labour

---

[10] White, Jerry, *London in the 20th Century* (2001); Inwood, Stephen, *A History of London* (1998); Ackroyd, Peter, *London: The Biography* (2001)
[11] White, op. cit. pxiii
[12] Cable Street Group, *The Battle of Cable Street* (1995)

Fig. 0-2 Mural of the Battle of Cable Street (Tower Hamlets Local History Library and Archive)

movement. This has been carried out through addressing relevant local issues such as housing and ethnicity. Many different sources have been used, such as the papers of the Bishops of Stepney and the LCC Government Evacuation Scheme's Directory of London Schools in Reception Areas, alongside MEPO 3/2501 Evacuation of Schoolchildren on the first day of evacuation. In using such sources, the aim has been to write about apparently well covered events and yet bring fresh and important additions to our knowledge.

By focusing on specific studies of the Stepney area between 1914 and 1951 similarities and links can be made. For example, during the First World War, the destruction of Upper North Street School caused the death of 18 schoolchildren. The death of so many schoolchildren became one of the main reasons (according to Philip Ziegler) for the carefully planned evacuation of children during the Second World War.[13] Another significant event during the First World War was a much earlier reference to the slogan "they shall not pass". This was first uttered by Arthur Foley Winnington-Ingram, the Bishop of London, in his Easter sermon of

---

[13] Ziegler, Philip, *London at War 1939-1945* (Great Britain, 1995) p9

1918.[14] This was a slogan used nearly 20 years later in Stepney at the Battle of Cable Street in 1936. Also, after the First World War and the surrender of Germany in the Second World War, the election campaigns focused upon the issue of housing, promising major improvements. Throughout the inter-war years and again after the Second World War, poor housing was a serious issue with improvements being demanded and striven for. However, during the late 1930s, the Stepney Tenants Defence League (STDL) took direct action for improvements through rent strikes, which were specific to Stepney. This was a community based group, actively seeking improvements, and with a Communist core. The STDL worked tirelessly on housing issues until the outbreak of the Second World War. After this, the group transferred its work to that of wartime issues and predominantly the use of deep-shelters. Without the demonstrations of the STDL the use of the underground stations, which typify the London experience of the Second World War, would have remained prohibited. Again activities in Stepney had a direct impact upon many other areas and upon government policy.

It was partly due to these campaigns that in the 1945 General Election Stepney saw its first (and only) Communist Member of Parliament elected, Phil Piratin. This was due to the personal campaigning of Piratin alongside the intensely community-based work that the party had done over the past twenty-five year. This election also saw long standing Stepney MP, Clement Attlee, become the Prime Minister of Labour's first majority government.

Since the Stepney Labour Party's foundation in 1918 the party had helped to unify the community and to a considerable extent brought together the Jewish and Irish population, the two dominant groups in Stepney. From 1918 onwards, many of the people of the area realised that they could have a direct impact upon their surroundings, through working together in politics. The Labour party became established as the most powerful party in the elections, as can be seen from the election results in the appendix. However, this period also saw the rise of the Communist and Fascist parties. Although generally weak, these parties were influential in the area. For Stepney, the Fascists were an invasive force as the party had a stronghold in neighbouring Bethnal Green. Fascism, according to the majority of the people of Stepney, had to be stopped, and thus the slogan "they shall not pass" was adopted. The Battle of Cable Street is one

---

[14] "They Shall Not Pass" A Sermon preached by Rev Arthur Foley Winnington-Ingram DD Bishop of London, St Paul's Cathedral, Easter Day 1918 (1918) p15

significant incident for an area that experienced many dramatic scenes between 1914 and 1951.

Above all, by examining the themes described, and by scrutinising such incidents and events, this book attempts to provide a fresh and important addition to our knowledge of the Borough of Stepney.

CHAPTER ONE

ASPECTS OF THE IMPACT OF THE FIRST WORLD WAR UPON STEPNEY: WITH PARTICULAR REFERENCE TO THE ROLE OF THE BISHOPS OF STEPNEY AND LONDON

Old Lady. "Ah, it'll take more than *preaching* to make them Zeppelins repent!"

Fig. 1-1 Old Lady *Punch*, 23 Feb 1916 p142. (Reproduced with permission of Punch Ltd)

The First World War saw the dawning of a new era in warfare: attack from the air. This new warfare "threatened to blur the traditional distinction between soldier and civilian, front and home. Air raids made clear that the Front was wherever the enemy chose to strike".[1] For Stepney, possessing a prime target within its boundaries: the docks, the war had a direct impact on the civilian population. This chapter will assess the impact of air raids upon Stepney, which was to have future implications for Stepney and Britain in the planning for civilian safety during the Second World War. Another important issue for Stepney during the war was the Jewish population. Many Jewish people were still not British citizens and therefore classified as "aliens". During the war "alien" men of military age were interned. For the remaining men of military age the aim was to encourage them to be recruited into the forces. Arthur Foley Winnington-Ingram was a significant figure in encouraging recruits, but also as a Bishop of Stepney, his writings have provided a valuable and different source in understanding the war, especially its impact upon Stepney.

The wealth of material written on the domestic impact of the First World War, the majority of which is concerned with its political, strategic or economic aspects, has paid little attention to the war's larger social and cultural context. Amongst these works two schools of thought have come to the foreground. Some historians, like Arthur Marwick, whose work *The Deluge* "initiated a wave of pioneering work on the social history of the war",[2] saw war as a catalyst for change. "The very title, *The Deluge*, imagines the war as a catalytic flood which swept away much of Victorian culture and inaugurated a more modern world".[3] Modris Eksteins emphasises this by asserting that:

> For our preoccupation with speed, newness, transience, and inwardness – with life lived, as the jargon puts it, 'in the fast lane' – to have taken hold, an entire scale of values and beliefs had to yield pride of place, and the Great War was … the single most significant event in that development.[4]

On the other hand, revisionist historians have emphasised the conservatism of British culture which acted as a constraint or an absorber of change. For example, Gerard J. DeGroot concludes:

---

[1] Robb, George, *British Culture and the First World War* (Hampshire, 2002) p200
[2] Ibid. p1
[3] Ibid. pp2–3
[4] Eksteins, Modris, *Rites of Spring: The Great War and the Birth of the Modern Age* (1989) pxiv

War was tragic, in some cases catastrophic. But for most people it was an extraordinary event of limited duration which as much as it brought change, also inspired a desire to reconstruct according to cherished patterns. If war is the locomotive of history, the rolling stock in this case, was typically British: slow, outmoded and prone to delay and cancellation.[5]

But the debate over whether the war promoted "tradition" or "modernity" is rather sterile according to Susan Kingsley-Kent who has claimed it does not help one to a "deeper understanding of the conflict".[6] What is called for is an understanding of what it meant for an entire society to undergo total war. This chapter will engage in a debate along the line of Marwick. The effects of total war upon Stepney will be discussed partly through the role of the Bishop of Stepney. By looking at such ephemeral material as sermons, pamphlets and newspapers, which have rarely been studied by historians, "an invaluable means of enlarging and broadening our view of British society and culture during the war"[7] can be achieved.

Through this book, the discourse on the impact of the air raids on Stepney during the First and Second World War, illustrates how people's views of air raids as a type of warfare changed between the wars. During the First World War, church crypts along with other public buildings were opened for people to use as shelters if they so desired, although many preferred to stay at home and be like one stout-hearted lady of Stepney who said she would "rather die among me own pots and pans".[8] By the Second World War there were many more designated, and supposedly bomb-proofed, places to shelter from the Blitz. And for those who chose to remain at home, protection was provided by the government in the form of Anderson or Morrison shelters. For Stepney, during both wars, there were a few notorious shelters: in the First World War it was the Bishopsgate Goods Station and in the Second World War it was the Tilbury Shelter.

The church played an active role in the war, both at home and at the front. At home the church provided vital support for significant numbers of Stepney people. Church crypts were used as shelters during the air raids. The East End churches were amongst the first to have "children's

---

[5] DeGroot, Gerard J., *Blighty: British Society in the Era of the Great War* (1996) p311
[6] See Kingsley-Kent, Susan, review "Remembering the Great War" *Journal of British Studies* 37 (January 1998) pp105–10
[7] Robb, op. cit. p1
[8] Paget, The Right Rev Henry Luke DD Bishop of Stepney (ed.) *Records of the Raids* (1918) p6

corners", for the children to be able to remember men at the Front. It was not uncommon to see 70 or 80 children there every day praying for fathers, brothers or friends.[9] Also, war shrines appeared in the back streets of Stepney. They sprang up spontaneously as Elma K. Paget remarks: "no one seems to have planned them: they were entirely of the people, imagined, carried out and paid for by them".[10] They were, she writes, simple shrines "recording the names of all who had gone out from the street to serve the Colours".[11] These memorials go some way in showing "how far the traditional bonds of community in the East London area were applied to the scale of human loss".[12]

In the 1880s practiced religion in the East of London according to Bishop Walsham How belonged "to a wholly different class from themselves"[13] and was therefore associated with prosperity and luxury - which was resented. According to Paul Thompson, in the East End boroughs less than fifteen per cent of the population attended any place of worship.[14] This religious indifference was inevitable due to a long period of neglect by the Anglican Church, which had failed to adapt to the changing structure of London after 1600. The nonconformists were even weaker in London than the Church of England. For example, the Salvation Army, begun in Whitechapel, had an attendance in 1886 of only 53,000 out of 367,000 non conformists or 14 per cent.[15] As we shall discover in this book political clubs tended to be more influential than religion. This was particularly the case in the inter-war years for the Jewish population. However, missionaries did have an influence, as Arthur Foley Winnington-Ingram did in his mission to gain recruits. The clergy also had a role in social work in slum areas such as Stepney. For example, Henry Luke Paget was to open his crypts to the people of Stepney during air raids.

In Stepney, there was also the influence of other religions: Judaism and Roman Catholicism. The main influx of Irish into London was from the 1830s to the 1870s. Many crowded into the slum areas by the riverside such as St George's-in-the-East but as the census returns give no

---

[9] *The Times* 1 July 1916

[10] Paget, Elma K., *Henry Luke Paget: Portrait and Frame* (1939) p197

[11] Ibid. p197

[12] Connelly, M. L., *The Commemoration of the Great War in the City and East London 1916–1939* PhD thesis (1995) p2

[13] *Church Congress Report* (1880) pp94-95

[14] Thompson, Paul, *Socialists, Liberals and Labour: The Struggle for London 1885-1914* (1967) p17

[15] Ibid. pp18-19

indication of the growth of the Irish presence and the religious surveys do not distinguish Irish from other Catholics it is impossible to give a precise number of Irish residents. However, religious surveys estimate that in Stepney, Catholics accounted for between 11 and 15 per cent of total church attendance.[16]

The Jewish settlement in the East End had begun with the arrival of the Spanish and Portuguese Jews in the 17th century. They were followed in the mid 19th century by German Jews and finally in 1881-2 and the early 1900s by large numbers of Russian and Polish Jews. In the 1870's the Jewish area had been between Houndsditch and Whitechapel High Street, but by 1900 had spread southwards to Cable Street. This formed a frontier with the Irish in St George's.[17] The area was compact, with most streets having over 75 per cent Jewish population.[18] In such circumstances, a strong community formed and consequently the Jewish Board of Guardians was set up in 1859 to aid poor Jews in London. Additionally, the community ran various clubs and provided Jewish education through private schools. However, during the depressions of the 1890s and 1900s there was a growing hostility to immigrants, which was compounded by the launch of the British Brothers League in 1901. During the First World War anti-Semitism was an issue, culminating with the internment of "aliens".

However, the clergy during the First World War continued their social work and provided an important role as listeners, comforters and confidantes in a war that involved more of the civilian population than ever before. For the men at the Front the church was also important. Sir Douglas Haig "remarked to the assistant chaplain general to the British First Army 'Tell your chaplains that a good chaplain is as valuable as a good General', presuming that the value of a good general was self-evident".[19] The Anglican philosopher C. C. J. Webb "supposed that all through history hitherto, God had used war as a main instrument in the moulding of mankind".[20] Ernest Barker, the political philosopher, said that England's strength lay in her belonging to Christ's Church Militant.[21] There was no difficulty in finding priests and pastors for chaplaincy work.

---

[16] Ibid, p25

[17] Russell, C. and Lewis, H. S., *The Jew in London* (1900)

[18] See Map of Jewish East London. Reproduced by the Museum of the Jewish East End and Research Census from "The Jew in London 1901" (Guildhall Library, City of London)

[19] Robbins, Keith, *The First World War* (Oxford, 1984) p157

[20] Ibid. p157

[21] Ibid. p157

At the beginning of the war 113 served the British forces, but by armistice day there were 3,480.[22]

The Recruitment of Men

The Bishops played an important part in the recruitment of men to go to the Front. The Bishop of Stepney, the Reverend Henry Luke Paget, whose son Sam, was already at the Front, "obtained 56 recruits as the result of an appeal at the Clapton Orient football ground on Saturday for the 10th Middlesex (Hackney Battalion)".[23] But, it was Arthur Foley Winnington-Ingram, who had been Bishop of Stepney between 1897 and 1901 and by the war years was Bishop of London, who more successfully called the men to arms. There was a great need for men to recruit, he said, as:

> A regiment is like some great river – always the same but always changing, as draft after draft flows out from England to take the place of those who fall out of the ranks, having done, as the soldier put it 'their little bit for their country'.[24]

Winnington-Ingram travelled all over the country recruiting and at "one large gathering he addressed early in the war [he] was instrumental in securing 10,000 additional troops for the Front".[25]

One worry faced by the recruited men was how best to take care of the wives they were leaving behind. Winnington-Ingram was often a confidante for the men and he recalled that his "old motor was a sort of sanctuary". One man said, "What am I to do, Bishop? My wife says she will poison herself and the two children if I go".[26] Winnington-Ingram wrote to the local clergyman who managed to persuade the woman "to take a more reasonable view".[27] However, in Winnington-Ingram's authorised biography, his extraordinary persuasiveness with women is extolled. "Mothers who had been trying to induce their boys to stop at

---

[22] Ibid. p157

[23] *The Times* 11 October 1915

[24] Smith, Rev. G. Vernon, *The Bishop of London's Visit to the Front (A. F. Winnington-Ingram Bishop of London)* (1915) p60

[25] Colson, Percy, *The Life of the Bishop of London: An Authorised Biography* (1935) p172

[26] Winnington-Ingram, Arthur Foley, *Fifty Years' Work in London 1889–1939* (1940) p110

[27] Ibid. p110

home went straight back after hearing him speak to pack them off to the nearest recruiting office".[28] Winnington-Ingram told the women that their first duty was "to stir … to encourage – the perfectly noble instinct which makes your boy or your brother want to go out and stand up for his country at the great second Battle of Waterloo which is coming".[29] As an example, he referred to one mother who said: "Well, my boy, I don't want you to go, but if I were you I should go".[30] Thus, women were encouraged to say "Go, with my love and blessing".[31]

From the declaration of war on 4 August 1914, the Stepney Battalion London National Reserve was ready to receive orders. With a large number of recruits presenting themselves at Stepney Battalion headquarters, 66 Tredegar Road, Bow, it was announced in the *East End News* that recruits should go to the headquarters on Tuesday and Thursday evenings between 8.30 and 10pm.[32] As an initial incentive to potential recruits, it was reported that jobs at Messrs Pearce's Chemical Works, Bow Common, were being kept open for those who had enlisted and that they were receiving half pay during their absence. There were also "crowds clamouring to join up outside the Whitechapel recruiting station"[33] which contained several hundred young Jews, who were "more English than the English in their expression of loyalty and desire for service".[34] In September 1914, the Jewish Recruiting Committee held a meeting at Camperdown House (Aldgate headquarters of the Jewish Lads Brigade) which produced 150 enlistments.[35] The Committee was to embark on a campaign of enlistment which by December 1914 saw nearly 300 old boys of the Jews Free School enlisted and a further 107 from the Stepney Jewish Lads Club.[36] However, such a picture of patriotic harmony is misleading, according to Julia Bush, as "many thousands of East London Jews turned a deaf ear to the recruiters",[37] due to either foreign nationality or foreign inclinations and attitudes.

---

[28] Colson, op. cit. p172
[29] Winnington-Ingram, Right Rev. Arthur Foley DD, Lord Bishop of London, *A Day of God Five Addresses on the subject of the Present War* (1914) p49
[30] Ibid. p51
[31] Ibid. p51
[32] *East End News* 11 August 1914
[33] *Jewish Chronicle* 7 August 1914
[34] Ibid. 7 August 1914
[35] Ibid. 11 September 1914
[36] Bush, Julia, "East London Jews and the First World War" *London Journal 6* (1980) p149
[37] Ibid. p150

After the Mayor of Stepney, Hugh Chidgey, attended one particular recruitment meeting in September 1915, 150 men volunteered of which only 15 of them were accepted after medical inspection. This was a very poor figure when compared to the average yield of London of nearly 1,200 men per day.[38] This highlights one of the major factors in the argument of a "Lost Generation". J. M. Winter, for example, suggests that many of the men who volunteered to go to war came predominantly from a higher social status. The working-class men were generally physically unfit for combat duty and were therefore shunted into clerical and support jobs. Those recruited were placed into four categories:

> Grade I men without any disability who were 'capable of enduring physical exertion'; Grade II men with a partial disability, but who nevertheless could 'endure considerable physical exertion not involving real strain'; Grade III, 'men with marked physical disabilities' who were fit for clerical work, but not able to undergo physical exertion; and Grade IV men 'totally and permanently unfit for any military service'.[39]

Winter suggests that of all the men examined, 36 per cent were placed in Grade I, 22.5 per cent in Grade II, and 41.4 per cent in Grades III and IV.[40] In industrial areas, the proportion of recruits placed within Grades III and IV was considerably higher than in the total population.

In October 1914, with recruitment slowing down, the height restriction was lowered to men of 5 ft 4 in, in height, with a chest measurement of 34½ in and aged between 19 and 38 years, an increase of three years.[41] By, 10 November 1914, the height restriction was lowered again to 5 ft 3 in, making the qualifications to enlist the same as they had been at the outbreak of war. They had been altered because "the great rush to the colours was then more than the military authorities could cope with".[42] It was hoped that such alterations would bring brisker recruiting as more men were desperately needed but, the *East End News* remarked at the time, "if the voluntary system fails to yield that number required the Government may be driven to 'take other steps'".[43]

---

[38] *East End News* 29 September 1914
[39] Ministry of National Service 1917–19 *Report upon the Physical Examination of Men of Military Age by National Service Medical Boars from November 1 1917 – October 31 1918,* Vol. I CMD 504 (1919) XXVI
[40] Ibid. CMD 504 November 1 1917 – October 31 1918
[41] *East End News* 27 October 1914
[42] Ibid. 10 November 1914
[43] Ibid. 10 November 1914

When Winnington-Ingram visited the Front after the first winter of war he said, "the thoughts of everyone at home had been with the men in the trenches".[44] The Bishop knew that he would be welcomed at the Front "not only as a messenger of the church, but as one going out from home who would be able, as he passed along the lines, to bring a word of love and greeting from friends in England".[45] Rev G. Vernon Smith cites an example of Winnington-Ingram himself being regarded as a greeting from home:

> One young man, little more than a boy, just carried in from the trenches, shot through the shoulder, at a Clearing Hospital at the Front, held out his arms towards me with a radiant smile. I thought for the moment he was in delirium, but he was an East End lad, a communicant at an East End church, who saw the Bishop he knew so well passing his bed.[46]

In 1916 Winnington-Ingram toured the Grand Fleet. When he visited the *Iron Duke* and the other ships with her, he looked "into the faces of the Lower Deck" and said "I suppose some of you have heard of Bethnal Green, Whitechapel and Stepney", and "they all beamed back with pleasure, as many of them (as I knew) came from there".[47]

But at home the need to maintain recruitment was a constant issue. It was reported in April 1915 that "recruits have come along well during the past week".[48] As to figures relating to recruitment, in "seven days 160 were enrolled, which constitutes a record for London";[49] with Captain Stableford, a recruiting officer, being "delighted with the quality of the men coming forward"[50] and also suggesting that joining the 17th London Regiment was "... the quickest way to the Front, for the men now being trained will be in the firing line within three months of enlistment".[51] By October 1915 with volunteers unable to keep pace with the number of recruits needed, Lord Derby, Director General of Recruiting, promoted a semi-voluntary recruiting scheme in which "unenlisted men were invited to 'attest' their willingness to serve, on the understanding that single men would be called up first".[52] With the Derby scheme failing in Stepney,

---

[44] Smith, op. cit. p10

[45] Ibid. p10

[46] Ibid. p76

[47] Winnington-Ingram, *Fifty Years'* op. cit. p121

[48] *East London Observer* 24 April 1915

[49] Ibid. 24 April 1915

[50] Ibid. 24 April 1915

[51] Ibid. 24 April 1915

[52] Davis, John, *A History of Britain 1885–1939* (1999) p125

more attention was being focused upon the Jewish community, as they were being accused of "shirking" military service. This was linked to fears that aliens and their offspring were replacing British soldiers in jobs and businesses, which were in turn fuelled by the growing prosperity of the Jewish Community.[53]

It was clear, by December, that Derby's scheme was not working and 1916 saw the introduction of the Military Service Act, "under which first all single men aged 18–41 and later all single and married men in that age group were deemed to have enlisted".[54] In the Stepney area, Mr A. W. Yeo, former Mayor and current Liberal MP for Poplar, was reported to have said at a meeting at the tunnel entrance, Poplar, "the country was at stake, and no man who had any love for his country would hang back now. They were to combine whole-heartedly and thus prevent a German invasion".[55]

The 17th London Regiment (Poplar and Stepney Rifles) was mobilised and brought up to strength, through intensive training at St Albans and Hatfield, and on 9 March 1915 the 1st Battalion proceeded to France, where they fought throughout the war. A 2nd Battalion was formed on the 31 August 1914, and in June 1916 they also moved to France as part of the 180th Brigade, 60th Division. After intensive warfare the 2nd Battalion was drafted to Salonika, from where in June 1917, it was drafted to Egypt "where it gained the name 'second to none' for its great work in the Palestine campaign".[56] In June 1918, the Battalion returned to France and became part of the 30th Division. A 3rd Battalion was formed shortly after the 2nd in 1914; however, this battalion was to remain in England to help with the training and supply of men to the two other battalions. Those who were rejected by the recruiting officials as unfit or too old to join the army were encouraged to prepare themselves for Home Defence and joined the Borough Volunteer Training Corps. By March 1915, the drill times for the Home Defence were announced in the papers with: "Thursday afternoon drill for shopkeepers. Shooting practice on a miniature range is being provided".[57] Despite these improvements in recruiting there continued to be a significant number of men who would not or could not be recruited. Many of these men seemed to belong to the social group often termed as "Aliens".

---

[53] Bush, "East London Jews" op. cit. p151
[54] Winter, J. M., *The Great War and the British People* (1985) p39
[55] *East End News* 20 April 1915
[56] *East London Observer* 29 March 1924
[57] Ibid. 13 March 1915

"We just missed being blown to pieces!"

German bombers mounted their first air raid against Britain on 16 December 1914, with an attack on three east coast towns: Hartlepool, Whitby and Scarborough.[58] It was not until 31 May 1915 that London was attacked with a Zeppelin raid, killing seven and injuring 35.[59] The first London raid directly affected Stepney, as we shall discover. Between June and October 1915 nine more raids occurred, killing 127 and injuring 352.[60] The raids did "little to damage morale, but rather confirmed the popular image of Germans as ruthless killers of civilians".[61] Trevor Wilson states: "Churchill epitomised the national indignation when he dubbed the raiders 'baby-killers'",[62] an expression often used by the press.

For the purpose of identification, Air Raid Precautions issued posters depicting both British and German airships and aeroplanes. If German air craft were spotted then shelter was to be sought "… in the nearest available house".[63] German aeroplanes were characterised by wings that sloped backwards, while Zeppelins had a distinctive arrangement for their passenger cars. By 1916 British air defences had improved and the Zeppelins' weakness revealed. The Zeppelins "were slow moving, difficult to fly in high winds, and vulnerable to incendiary bullets since they were filled with highly explosive hydrogen gas".[64]

The Germans replaced in September 1917, the vulnerable Zeppelins with the new twin-engined Gotha bomber plane. This resulted in serious damage to British targets. The map below depicts the raids on London and shows the concentration of bombing in the City. For Stepney, the majority of bombs struck the west side of the area which bordered the City.

During June 1917, 20 Gothas dropped 10 tons of bombs on London in broad daylight. The Zeppelins, in contrast, usually struck at night. The worst zeppelin raid, on 13 June 1917, saw 162 people killed and 432 injured. Eighteen of those killed were school children from Poplar. Between September 1917 and May 1918, regular night raids on Britain occurred and "some 300,000 Londoners nightly took refuge in Underground stations".[65]

---

[58] Reported in the *Weekly Times* 18 December 1914
[59] Robb, op. cit. p199
[60] Ibid. p199
[61] Ibid. p199
[62] Wilson, Trevor, *The Myriad Faces of War: Britain and the Great War 1914–1918* (Cambridge, 1986) p157
[63] MEPO 2/1621 Public Warning Poster by Air Raid Precautions
[64] Robb, op. cit. p200
[65] Robb, op. cit. p200

THE **Daily Mail** MAP
OF
ZEPPELIN AND AEROPLANE BOMBS ON LONDON.

Reprinted from "The Daily Mail," January 31, 1919.

Fig. 1-2 Map of the positions where Zeppelin and aeroplane bombs landed in London (Collage collection k1237916)

In theory, Zeppelin attacks were directed against naval and military targets, but with poor weather, limited night-time visibility, and frequent navigation errors Zeppelins often dropped their bombs indiscriminately on civilian targets, a fact commented on by David Wilson, a *Punch* cartoonist.

31 May 1915 saw the first Zeppelin raid on London. The German Commander "Captain Linnartz in LZ18 found the blackout so ineffectual that he had little difficulty in spotting Commercial Road and headed for the

SOLACE.

Little Binks (who prides himself on his tact—to injured and uninsured householder, victim of a recent Zeppelin raid). "It is comforting to think, Sir, is it not, that they've never yet succeeded in striking the same spot twice?"

Fig. 1-3 Solace *Punch* 25 October 1916 p297 (Reproduced with permission of Punch Ltd)

docks".[66] Stepney took fifteen direct hits. A Stepney Superintendent described the damage:

> The first bombs on the division were apparently dropped in the immediate vicinity of the Great Eastern Railway and Bishopsgate station, thence across Spitalfields, Whitechapel, St George's and Stepney. The last bomb on this division was, I believe, dropped in Duckett Street, near the Commercial Gas Works, and while the first bombs dropped were all incendiary, those on St George's and Stepney were nearly all explosive.[67]

---

[66] Castle, H., *Fire over England* (1984) p59–60
[67] MEPO 2/1650 Zeppelin Raid on London "H" division 1 June 1915, 11am–8pm and 11am–14pm 31 May 1915. The first incendiary bomb was at Osborne Street, Whitechapel; then the churchyard of St Mary's Church, Whitechapel Road; the roof of No. 3 Adler Street, Whitechapel, a boot warehouse; the Jewish Synagogue, 45 Commercial Road; Messrs Walker's Distillery, 33 Commercial Road, where an explosive bomb fell; in Commercial Road, nearly opposite Plummer's Row two bombs were dropped; in a stable yard at the rear of No. 13 Berner Street, St

The two bombs which fell on the carriageway of Christian Street, St George's were to cause the most injury. Twelve people, all of whom were in the street at the time, were injured, one fatally: Samuel Reuben, 10 years old. There were numerous fires, which appear to have been attended to promptly by the fire brigade and one bomb dropped on the carriageway at Burslem Street, St George's which "shattered but did not explode".[68]

In a letter to Sydney Schiff, Isaac Rosenberg, a war poet, mentioned this first raid quite casually, saying "... We just missed being blown to pieces by a bomb the other night, a factory nearby was burnt to pieces and some people killed".[69] Sylvia Pankhurst noted that "... unaccustomed visitors came flocking to the East End – well-dressed people in motors, journalists, photographers, high military officials, Red Cross nurses, policewomen, travellers from all over the world"[70] showing how the East End, was often seen as a curiosity, separated from the rest of London.

During the air raid of 7 July 1917, six male residents were killed, one being only 11 years old. Two more people died of heart attacks shortly afterwards. The Commercial Gas Company noted that "the company works sustained no damage on this occasion ... a few pieces of shrapnel only falling on the company's works".[71] This incident raised the question of "whether additional steps could be taken to prevent the congregation of large numbers of people" on the streets during a raid. Hugh Chidgey, the Mayor of Stepney and commandant of the "H" division of Special Police, thought it:

> Very desirable that in the western portions of the borough, official notices should be published by the police in Yiddish advising people to remain in their own houses when warning is given rather than rushing along the streets to certain large buildings.[72]

George's; Christian Street, St George's, two explosive bombs fell; an explosive bomb, which did not explode on Burslem Street, St George's; 11 Jamaica Street, a shoe factory; No. 5 East Arbour Street, Stepney; Charles Street, Stepney; 16 Benjonson Road, Stepney; 31 Lomas Buildings, Benjonson Road, Stepney; and finally 130 Duckett Street

[68] MEPO 2/1650 Zeppelin Raid on London "H" division 1st June 1915, 11am–8pm and 11am–14pm 31st May

[69] IWM Special Miscellaneous I4: Letter from Isaac Rosenberg to Sydney Schiff 4 June 1915

[70] Pankhurst, Sylvia E., *The Homefront* 2nd Edn. (1987) p193

[71] Commercial Gas Company Minute Book 1915–18 19 July 1917

[72] Minute Book No. 25 of the Public Health Committee of the Stepney Borough Council July 1917 – November 1918

Lists of public shelters were printed and distributed throughout the borough, "announcing that such premises are available as shelters after a police warning, and that the public may at their own risk take shelter therein".[73] The use of different air raid warnings, not issued by the police, also began, with the council "taking steps to fix a light warning to every other arc lamp in the main roads of the borough".[74] In October 1918, it was reported that 140 public air raid shelters were in use in the borough and that they accommodated approximately 133,000 persons,[75] which was less than half the population.[76]

The threat of Zeppelin raids brought blackouts and in the middle of 1915 Arthur James Balfour, then first lord of the Admiralty appointed Sir Percy Scott, to create a gun defence system for the capital. H. E. Miles, a diarist of the war years commenting on the first night of the new restriction, states that people were saying "... London has not been so dark since the days of George I" and that the blackness of London is "very weird and terrifying".[77] She writes that there are "no lights on the street lamps and shopkeepers and householders are fined if they have too bright a light"; however "there's one light that cannot be dimmed, and that's the moon".[78] The streets were therefore a dangerous place for pedestrians. At the inquest of Charles Williams, 73, a verdict of accidental death was returned. He was fatally injured near the Limehouse Town Hall, Commercial Road, after being knocked down by a "motor bus". A month prior to this it was reported a woman had been injured in the same spot. The Coroner at Charles Williams' inquest stated that "crossing any road at night in these days required great circumspection and care".[79]   By December 1914 it was required that vehicles, which had dimmed headlights already, were to have in addition "a lamp which shows red light to the rear ... to protect vehicles from being run into from behind".[80]

However, there were always people who sought shelter and company during the air raids and those who simply felt safer in public buildings; the

---

[73] Metropolitan Borough of Stepney – Council Minutes Vol. XVIII 9 November 1917 – 8 November 1918 Friday, 9 November 1917

[74] Ibid. 9 November 1917 – 8 November 1918

[75] Ibid. 9 November 1917 – 8 November 1918 Wednesday, 9 October 1918

[76] Census of England and Wales 1921, shows the population of Stepney in 1911 as 298,600 *Census of England Wales 1921*

[77] Miles, H. E., *Untold tales of Wartime London* (1919) p74

[78] Devey, Ernest, "Forest Gate Under Zeppelin Raid" *Cockney Ancestor* No. 16 Autumn 1982 p18

[79] *East London Observer* 22 January 1916

[80] *The Times* 15 December 1914

crypts of churches were opened nightly. People's conduct was excellent, according to the Bishop of Stepney, Henry Luke Paget, with mutual helpfulness, smiles and gratitude. There was also praise for the patrol-men who, on a nightly basis, had two men on duty in a room placed at their disposal by the Peabody Trustees. Those who arrived at the shelters would be in various states of undress and dishevelment. The toddlers were the main sufferers, often arriving half dressed. Consequently, the danger of catching pneumonia, bronchitis and other infectious complaints was far more serious than the danger of German bombs. However, overall there was a mass improvement in health and life expectancy during the First World War. The general rule was that "the worse off a section of society was before 1914, the greater were its gains in life expectancy in wartime".[81] This was because the state was more active and needed healthy citizens.

There were vast improvements and increases in food consumption during the war, with "more milk, potatoes, bread and flour, and oatmeal" being "consumed per family in 1918 than in 1914".[82] Bacon often replaced meat, and the more nutritious brown bread replaced white. From Monday, 25 February 1918 it was stated by the Ministry of Food that a butcher "must divide what supplies he has as fairly as possible between his registered customers" that he could only sell meat on production of a registered Meat Card, and that he must detach the proper number of coupons for each sale he made.[83] Similar written orders were issued for butter and margarine, with jam being rationed to 4 oz per head by the end of 1918.

Although more food was consumed, the cost was a major issue for East End families. In 1915 it was reported that the massive increase in the price of mutton and beef, was "the highest price for 70 years" and it had "added greatly to the difficulties experienced by many East London families".[84] The Public Health Committee noted offences for overcharging of foods; for example, on 26 May 1917 "an assistant of W. Rosenberg, … sold 2 lb of potatoes for which he charged 5½d equal to ¾d per lb" and again, on 5 June 1917 "R. Birkovitch in the employment of 14 Wicker Street sold 12 lb of potatoes at 8d per lb". In another example of the inconsistencies of shopkeepers, on 6 June 1917, Mr Uphill, employed in Mr Lock's grocers "informed a Mrs Levy that he had no sugar to spare, Mrs Levy then asked

[81] Winter, op. cit. p279
[82] Ibid. p215
[83] *Ministry of Food – London & Home Counties Rationing Scheme Directions to Butchers*
[84] *East London Advertiser* 29 May 1915

for ¼ lb of tea and he served this with ½ lb of sugar".[85] Throughout the war years the average weekly cost of living rose dramatically, from 23s in 1914 to 103s by 1918, peaking in 1920 at 149s.[86] Earnings rose alongside the cost of living and "earnings easily outstripped wages in wartime, due mainly to overtime pay, piece-rate payment and the eradication of unemployment".[87] The issue of employment during the First World War will be discussed further in the next chapter.

On Wednesday, 13 June 1917, 14 Gotha aeroplanes, carrying an average load of ten bombs each, attacked London with unprecedented violence. The Zeppelin raids at night had been terrifying enough but this new daylight raid was even worse because the streets, houses and shops were bustling with people going about their daily lives. The death and mutilation of people from this raid was considerable. Liverpool Street station was hit and a train there was blown to pieces causing 13 fatalities and many injuries. It was a tragic loss of life "which could have been reduced, if not avoided altogether, had the City Police warned the station authorities of the raid and people had been advised to take cover".[88]

Also, in the raid of 13 June, there was a direct hit on Upper North Street School, Poplar. The 50 kg (110 lb) bomb "penetrated three floors, killing two pupils in the process, and then exploded in the basement among a class of infants claiming the lives of a further 16 and injuring many more".[89] The school was situated in rather dangerous proximity to East India Dock Road and the hit upon the school would appear to have been the result of a rather poor aim, directed either at the docks themselves or at the very busy thoroughfare with all its heavy morning traffic. The leader of the German raiders that day, Hauptmann Brandenburg, "thought that they had successfully attacked a railway station, the Docks and Tower Bridge".[90] It was said that the joint funeral for the victims, which Winnington-Ingram and Paget took, was one of the most impressive ever seen in the East End of London.[91] Philip Ziegler cites this particular raid as

---

[85] Minute Book No. 24 of the Public Health Committee of the Stepney Borough Council March 1916 – July 1917

[86] LCC *London Statistics* (1920)

[87] Winter, op. cit. p214

[88] Fegan, Thomas, *The "Baby Killers": German Air Raids on Britain in the First World War* (Great Britain, 2002) p91

[89] Ibid. p51

[90] Ibid. p107

[91] For Paget it was something that he never forgot. See Paget, Elma K., op. cit. p207

the reason for the doctrine of dispersal of the population, evacuation, during the Second World War.[92]

During 1917, Winnington-Ingram believed that "a great weariness of the war was creeping over the nation".[93] For Stepney, this was partly due to the devastation caused by the raid of 13 June. In response to this, Winnington-Ingram set out on his Mission of Repentance and Hope in order to attend to the Home Front. Support for his mission can be found in a letter from William Robert Robertson to Winnington-Ingram in October 1916 to wish him "complete success" in his "National Mission work".[94] He visited centres of civilian warwork in London – hospitals, munition factories, railway depots "encouraging the workers with his sympathy and optimism … when death rode triumphant and the streets were black with mourning, he was a tower of strength to the bereaved".[95] The point of his mission was "… to call for the further million men which the country now requires".[96] The National Mission was also looking towards creating a new world after the war:

> Picture … the waste of blood and treasure if we go back after the war to our old bitterness between class and class, our old misunderstanding between men and women, or even our old danger of civil war.[97]

Therefore, Winnington-Ingram's Mission sought to remind the people why they were fighting this war: in order to gain a better future, later summed up as "a fit land for heroes". Ingram did not want the work of the past 40 years to be undone.

On Monday, 28 January 1918 a *Giant* plane, one of the German's most formidable ariel machines, was escorted by several Gothas and succeeded in penetrating the Metropolitan area. In the East End the population had become peculiarly sensitive to the dangers of raids. Most evenings saw people trekking from Spitalfields and the surrounding area to the comparative safety of Bishopsgate Goods Station, which for many months

---

[92] Ziegler, Philip, *London at War 1939–1945* (Great Britain, 1995) p9. See chapter seven of this book titled: *The Second World War and the Evacuation of Schoolchildren in Stepney*

[93] Winnington-Ingram, *Fifty Years'* op. cit. p125

[94] Letter from William Robert Robertson 1st Baronet (1919) to Arthur Foley Winnington-Ingram in Winnington-Ingram Papers MS 3406 Lambeth Palace Library

[95] Colson, op. cit. p173

[96] Winnington-Ingram, Arthur F., Lord Bishop of London, *Cleansing London* (1916) Call to Arms Address p38

[97] Ibid. p41

had been thrown open nightly to the public. However, due to the damage
that the nightly visitors were causing, it had been decided by the railway
company that the gates would be locked to the station until there was an
official air-raid warning.

On the night of 28 January hundreds of people were crowding the
station gates while across the road a large queue for the Olympia Music
Hall performance had gathered. Warning rockets were heard and people
believed that a raid was imminent. Everyone, those queuing for the music
hall and those crowding at the station gates, panicked and rushed for the
locked gates, and a stampede at the side entrance ensued. In this desperate
rush for safety 14 people were killed by suffocation. There was a similar
stampede at Mile End, and minor tragedies at Jubilee Street, Florida Street,
Bethnal Green, and upon the tramlines in Commercial Road. Another
tragedy occurred at Messrs Oldham's printing works in Wilson Street, also
used as a public shelter, which resulted in 38 fatalities and nearly 100
serious injuries when the premises were hit by a bomb. On this single day
a total of 162 people were killed and 432 injured, "the highest toll of the
war for a single air raid".[98]

With the crisis worsening by Easter 1918, due to the Allies falling back
at the front, before the German counter-offensive on the Western Front,
Winnington-Ingram preached a sermon at St Paul's Cathedral on Easter
Day, entitled "They Shall Not Pass" – a slogan later used by anti-fascists
at the 1936 Battle of Cable Street. Here, one can see an early reference to
this well-known slogan. In 1918, Winnington-Ingram took the message
from young heroes' graves. "Ils ne passeront pas" (They Shall Not Pass)
was the cry of Frenchmen who settled down with their rifles; the British
soldiers repeated the cry, "with characteristic coolness", and looked as if
there was no danger near; the mourners also cried that the Germans should
not pass the Allied frontiers.[99] In 1936 at the Battle of Cable Street, the
Fascists could not pass or push aside the people of Stepney.

A vivid picture of the air raids on Stepney can be found in *Records of
the Raids* by the Right Reverend Henry Luke Paget DD, Bishop of
Stepney. *Records of the Raids* was a pamphlet issued as a "souvenir" to be
kept by children and grandchildren. At the back of the pamphlet, several
blank pages were left for "My own notes on the Raids" and "it was meant
especially for East Londoners".[100] Paget had simply asked his clergy for
reports and they were published as they came in. As a sample of the

---

[98] Fegan, op. cit. p52
[99] Winnington-Ingram DD, Arthur Foley, "They Shall Not Pass" A Sermon
preached at St Paul's Cathedral, Easter Day 1918 (1918) p15
[100] Paget, Elma K., op. cit. p201

experiences of Stepney residents during the air raids it is evocative of the work of Nina Masel in the Second World War. Masel was the "East End Unit" for Mass-Observation and carried out work on the impact of war on the people of Stepney.

The new experience of attack and invasion by air caused people great distress. As one of the clergy pointed out, "the strong men have all gone from the crowded areas, and only the overworked, the anxious, and the fragile are left behind".[101] Because the East End was one of the first places to receive such invasive attacks the Bishop of Stepney suggested that numerous people preferred to stop at home when the alarm was given and did not attempt to seek refuge.[102]

There appears to have been a very naive view of what was happening, as the following descriptions of the Zeppelins show. One woman expressed her disapproval of flying generally, and of air raids in particular, when she said "I don't think they ought to be allowed to make them things to go up there prying into the Almighty's private affairs". Another woman described them as "a handsome sight, but a wicked one".[103] Many believed flying machines to be unnatural. With hindsight one must remember that this was the beginning of aviation and that a few decades prior to this flying had been merely a dream. A riverside dweller that caught her first sight of a Zeppelin when she was out in her back yard one day, said "So I runs into me kitchen, and in a minute or two I looks out at the front door, and blast if it wasn't waiting for me there. I don't call it natural".[104]

The Internment of "Aliens"

The day after the declaration of the First World War, 5 August 1914, the House of Commons passed the Aliens Restriction Act. This allowed the government to control the activities of all aliens with regard to entry, residence and registration in Britain. The act also identified "enemy aliens" who endured more severe restrictions, for instance internment, than those not regarded as such.[105] In Stepney with a high population of foreign residents, there was, as Panikos Panayi suggests, the "… systematic

---

[101] Ibid. p203

[102] For example, one stout-hearted lady said "I'd sooner die among me own pots and pans". Paget, Henry Luke, *Records of the Raids* op. cit. p6

[103] Ibid. p7

[104] Ibid. p7

[105] Panayi, Panikos, *The Enemy in Our Midst: Germans in Britain during the First World War* (Oxford, 1991) pp46-61; Bevan, Vaughan, *The Development of British Immigration Law* (1986) pp72-3

persecution of racial and ethnic minorities".[106] The official reaction to such minorities in wartime was the implementation of internment, deportation or resettlement. In Stepney, internment of military aged men was the predominant action.

The position of the Jewish population during the First World War was complicated. Some were still aliens, in that they had not been naturalised and were therefore technically still German or Russian citizens. Others, who had been naturalised and become part of the British social fabric, were nevertheless widely known to have German or Russian origins. As previously shown in this chapter, some of the "Anglo-Jewry played ... [their] full part in the war effort". "Isaac Rosenberg, the poet, who joined in 1915, and was killed three years later on the Somme, on April Fool's Day, was not an isolated case".[107] But those alien Jews who "showed a reluctance to fight ... aroused the most serious anti-Semitism during the war",[108] which was generally directed towards the Russian-Jewish population in Leeds and East London. After the sinking of the *Lusitania* in April 1915 there was an outburst of rioting and pillaging in which "many a harmless shopkeeper who had the misfortune to have a German name had his property wrecked".[109]

The Times, at the outbreak of war, reported that:

> There are at this moment in the UK as many as 50,000 alien enemies, subjects of the German and Austrian Empires. 34,000 of these are known to be in the Metropolitan Police District and the chief problem is therefore a London one. Many of the East End Germans are known to the authorities as ex-criminals; some of them are regarded as dangerous men. This type is mostly to be found in the Whitechapel district which has the unenviable distinction of accommodating more alien enemies than any other area in London.[110]

By 23 October 1914:

> Definite instructions were given to the police in all parts of the country, including London, to arrest all unnaturalised male Germans, Austrians and Hungarians of military age; that is to say between 17 and 45 and to hand

---

[106] Panayi, Panikos, "Dominant Societies and Minorities in the Two World Wars" in Panayi, Panikos (ed.), *Minorities in Wartime* (Oxford, 1993) p3
[107] Holmes, Colin, *Anti-Semitism in British Society 1876–1939* (1979) p126
[108] Ibid. p126
[109] Peel, C. S., *How We Lived Then 1914–1918* (1929) p34–5
[110] *The Times* 25 August 1914

them over to the military authorities for internment in concentration camps.[111]

About 40,000 men in London were interned. But, with regards to the East End, it was reported that because "there is a very large colony of aliens, the police were engaged throughout the day in making arrests. It is understood that about 1,200 aliens altogether were apprehended in the Metropolitan Police area yesterday".[112]

One major problem was that:

> owing to lack of accommodation the arrests could proceed only slowly, and in the Metropolitan Police district in particular the persons liable to arrest were divided into classes, unmarried or destitute men being taken first. When, however, some 8,000 or 9,000 had been interned all further arrests were brought to an end by the want of accommodation.[113]

Another problem with mass "drives" of internment was that "several days thereafter are taken up in clearing up the many details incidental to a 'drive', such as appeals from rabbis, solicitors, doctors, etc, the aliens trying every possible excuse and subterfuge to escape being sent to manual labour".[114] It was suggested by the authorities dealing with the "clear up" from internment drives that if 10 to 12 enemy aliens were dealt with five days a week, then "their cases could be cleared up daily".[115] There were specific demands for enemy aliens by manual labour companies such as the road board, timber supply department and air board, who would require between 100 and 300 enemy aliens at short notice. This was due to the enlistment of men from such companies. For example, from road workers, 57 per cent of the July 1914 labour force had enlisted by July 1918.[116] The government realised that a National Register of the supply of men was essential in assessing the supply of men for military and industrial purposes through a reliable statistical basis.[117] One of the main drawbacks for the manual labour companies was that "75–80 per cent of

---

[111] Ibid. 23 October 1914 also see CAB 37/122/182 Internment of Enemy Aliens December 1914

[112] *The Times* 23 October 1914

[113] op. cit. CAB 37/122/182 December 1914

[114] LAB 2/633/ED17118/57/1918 Employment of Interned Male Enemy Aliens

[115] Ibid. LAB 2/633/ED17118/57/1918

[116] See Table 2 *Enlistment in the United Kingdom, 1914-1918* in Dewey, P. E., "Military Recruiting and the British Labour Force during the First World War" *The Historical Journal*, 27, 1 (1984) p204

[117] See Grieves, Keith, *The Politics of Manpower: 1914-1918* (Manchester, 1988)

the number examined state that they are physically incapable of manual labour, which means that practically every man has to undergo medical examination".[118] It was therefore decided by the examining body that only a selection of enemy aliens should be examined in smaller batches of ten per day, so as to provide a "reservoir of enemy alien workers" who were "ready for national work".[119]

Those male civilians interned ended up lodging "… onboard ships, in barracks, in some large buildings which have been taken over for the purpose and some in huts which have been constructed".[120] For those interned from Stepney, the nearest camp was "Ritchie's Works, Carpenter Road, [Stratford], a jute factory which had not been in use for several years".[121] Up to 400 civilians could be held at this camp. It was reported that "confinement on bread and water for 24 hours" was "the most severe punishment which had been given".[122] This camp was only for men of fighting age as "there were no boys under 17 and no men over 55 in this camp".[123] In total 12,400 were interned after successive operations, which still left 25,500 male aliens above 17 years of age, of which 12,300 were in London.[124] By January 1915 a curfew was being placed on aliens still living in communities. Those males above the age of 16 were to remain in their registered place of residence between the hours of 8.30pm and 6am unless they had a permit to do otherwise.[125]

By August 1916, the government was considering the internment of "all persons of enemy birth, whether male or female, naturalised or not"[126] by the council of Stepney. Paddington Borough Council had sent a communication to Stepney urging for this and had "passed a resolution urging upon HM Government the necessity for taking immediate steps"[127] in this matter. They stated that they hoped Stepney, would make similar representations. Hackney Borough Council expressed the desire that "HM Government should take immediate steps to intern all enemy aliens of

---

[118] op. cit. LAB 2/633/ED17118/57/1918
[119] Ibid. LAB 2/633/ED17118/57/1918 Letter 13 November 1918
[120] PO 383/106 No. 1564 – German POWs in English Concentration Camps – Memorandum
[121] PO 383/106 27th February 1915 Mr Jackson's report on camps in the United Kingdom
[122] Ibid. PO 383/106 27th February 1915
[123] Ibid. PO 383/106 27th February 1915
[124] CAB 37/122/182 Internment of Enemy Aliens December 1914
[125] CAB 37/123/10 Curfew for Alien Enemies 5 January 1915
[126] Metropolitan Borough of Stepney – Council Minutes Vol. XVI 9 November 1916 – 8 November 1917, Wednesday 2 August 1916
[127] Ibid. Wednesday 2 August 1916

military age, and to repatriate all such as are over military age, women as well as men".[128] Again, Hackney Council wished for Stepney to support them. In fact, Stepney Council sent communications to the Prime Minister, Home Secretary and the MPs for the borough "expressing the opinion that HM Government should take steps immediately to intern all persons, male or female, naturalised or unnaturalised of enemy birth".[129] It was most likely the lack of accommodation to be able to deal with the male internees that stopped any of this action being taken.

The problems faced by those regarded as aliens within the borough continued throughout the war. In August 1917, the Anglo-Russian Military Service Agreement concluded that Russian aliens should be placed under the provisions of the Military Service (Conventions with Allied States). This resulted in "all Russian male subjects who chose to remain in Britain" coming "within the operation of the Military Service Acts of 1916 and 1917, as if they were British subjects ordinarily resident in Great Britain".[130] Their alternative was to return to their own country for military service.

The repercussions of this were still being discussed in 1918 by the council. It was recommended to the government that "all male aliens of military age should be either called up for military service, interned or repatriated",[131] thus showing that there were still many free "aliens" within the borough. It was also felt by the council that "… no aliens should be permitted to open or acquire businesses which our own people have been compelled to relinquish owing to the national crises", and they urged the authorities "to take steps forthwith".[132] The council reported the following month that a "considerable number" of the Russian, French and Italian subjects of military age "have already been incorporated in the British Army or have returned to their own country in order to fulfil their military obligations".[133]

Even by 1921 there was still a considerable alien population in Stepney. Of a total population of 249,657, 16 per cent of Stepney residents had been born in foreign countries.[134] Of these, 71 per cent were of "alien"

---

[128] Ibid. Wednesday 2 August 1916
[129] Ibid. Wednesday 2 August 1916
[130] Holmes, op. cit. p128
[131] Metropolitan Borough of Stepney – Council Minutes Vol. XVIII 9 November 1917 – 18 November 1918, Wednesday 19 June 1918
[132] Ibid. Wednesday 19 June 1918
[133] Ibid. Wednesday 31 July 1918
[134] *Census of England & Wales 1921*

nationality, thus showing the on-going presence of a substantial foreign
population within Stepney.[135]

Conclusion

The Zeppelin raids blurred the lines between the soldier and civilian
fronts, as the raids literally brought warfare into ordinary peoples' homes.
The role of the office of Bishop of Stepney was crucial to many people of
the area, as the churches provided shelter and the clergy acted in the role
of a listener and confidante as well as being a source of encouragement.
The Bishops had an awareness of the need to keep up morale both for
those in Stepney and those away fighting at the Front. In 1917
Winnington-Ingram set out on his Mission of Repentance and Hope in
order to address the waning morale of the people at home and to
encourage a further million men to sign up. He also visited the men at the
Front on numerous occasions and thus provided a crucial link between the
men away fighting and those left behind in Stepney. In the Second World
War, as we shall discover, the Mayor, Frank Lewey, and politicians of
Stepney visited the evacuated children from the area. This meant that the
children and young mothers could have news from home, and also in the
aftermath of the visits, that the parents left behind could be assured that
their children were safe. Thus, in times of war, family ties came to the fore
and the Bishop could facilitate a two-way stream of information between
Stepney and the fighting Front.

Winnington-Ingram was also a key figure in the recruitment of men
into the forces, throughout the First World War. He was a great orator and
used this skill to carry out numerous campaigns to enlist men. Perhaps
even more crucially, he persuaded the women that it was their duty to let
their men go off and fight and to actively encourage them to do so.

Paget however, was most troubled by worries about the welfare of
those left behind in Stepney. He opened up the crypts for the people to be
able to shelter in and he was concerned that such a war, which affected
Stepney so deeply, with numerous raids and huge losses of men, should
not be forgotten by future generations. His pamphlet *Records of the Raids*
should be regarded as a very important piece of work, as it deals with the
immediate reactions of the people of Stepney to a war which was unlike
any prior war, in that the conflict was taken to people's homes.

Through this chapter, the origins for future events can be found.
Firstly, with Winninton-Ingrams Sermon entitled "They Shall Not Pass",

---

[135] Ibid. 1921

which was used against Mosleyites in 1936. But more importantly, the bombing of Upper North Street School was crucial in the argument for the dispersal of the population at the outbreak of the Second World War.

CHAPTER TWO

WAR WORK

During the First World War, with men going away to fight at the Front, a new workforce had to be found and women were "substituted" for men. In this chapter the focus will be on two particular areas of war work: munitions and clothing. Clothing was a traditional trade for East London and, with such a high demand for "khaki" uniforms, trade naturally turned in that direction. In the manufacturing of munitions, many smaller industrial businesses in Stepney adjusted themselves to this kind of production and thus aided the war effort. As Gail Braybon has written, the demand for women's labour during the war years "may suggest that at this time, if no other, views of women's position and role might [have begun to] change". This has "been the conviction of many ... social historian[s} when describing the granting of women's suffrage".[1] However, others have argued that many negative perceptions of women remained consistent, with the possibility that traditionalist views were in fact encouraged by the events of the First World War. As fighting ceased there was a desire to regain the "normality" and the "stability" of peacetime, which encouraged women to "abandon their wartime jobs and 'go home'".[2] It is important to note, according to Braybon, "that women did not escape from the classic female trades",[3] such as clothing, and that they were viewed as mere "substitutes" for the men fighting at the Front. This in turn tells us something of the "relationship of women to male workers, and demonstrates theories about a dual labour market and a segmented labour force".[4]

---

[1] Braybon, Gail, *Women Workers in the First World War* (1981) p13
[2] Ibid. p13
[3] Ibid. p14
[4] Thom, Deborah, *Nice Girls and Rude Girls: Women Workers in World War One* (1998) p7

The "substitutes"

In the first few months of the war, the main war work to be had was voluntary. Significant numbers of women in a financial position to do so spent their time knitting and sewing for the troops. Lady Jellicoe, appealed in *The Times* for warm clothes to be made for the soldiers and sailors, in particular, after a letter she received from her husband, Admiral Sir John Jellicoe.[5] Stepney responded to this appeal. In the *East London Observer* it was reported that a Mrs Hasted, from the Stepney Women's Conservative and Unionist Association, had sent a parcel of a "100 woollen knitted garments for the sailors".[6] Another parcel was also to be dispatched of a similar number of items for the soldiers at the front.

By the summer of 1915 the extensive use of women as "substitutes" for men in work was widespread. There was such a rush of women into engineering and explosives that by 1916 there was a shortage of female labour in the textile and clothing trades.[7] An example of the huge increase in the numbers employed in munitions can be seen at the Woolwich Arsenal which employed 125 women in 1914 and 25,000 in 1917.[8] In 1917, with a lack of women apprentices in dressmaking, the London dressmakers were forced to consider improvements in working conditions such as shorter and more regular hours of work for the women. Such developments support Arthur Marwick's argument that:

> … the fundamental fact remains that in participating in the non-military aspects of the war effort, hitherto under-privileged groups find themselves in a very strong market position: government, and private employers *need* them; hence improvements in wages and conditions'.[9]

One question Gail Braybon raises is the issue of who exactly were the recruits to munition factories. Barbara Drake has suggested that the majority would have been paid workers before the war and that most of them came from domestic service. Middle-class women who took up war work were in the minority. With more workers still needed, however, it was to married women that industry turned. Previously, once a woman married, she was generally expected to stay at home and raise a family. In

---

[5] *The Times* 13 October 1914
[6] *East London Observer* 12 December 1914
[7] Braybon, op. cit. p45
[8] Andrews, I. O., *The Economic Effects of the World War upon Women and Children in Great Britain* (Oxford, 1921) p77
[9] Marwick, Arthur *The Deluge* (1991) p19

1911, a mere 7,315 or 15.5 per cent of Stepney's employed women were married, whereas 28,973, 61 per cent were unmarried.[10] During the war years, however, married women were invited back to work in industry and they were to make up a large proportion of the total numbers being employed, particularly as "some firms had a definite preference for soldiers' wives as workers". It was felt that soldiers' wives "... could guarantee a sense of patriotism, as well as loyalty to the firm, and it was [considered] obvious that such women would readily relinquish their jobs to returning men".[11] Throughout the country 40 per cent of working women were married. The main effect of the war was to let women move between trades for the first time and also to allow those who had previously been excluded to return to work.

Munition Workers

By January 1915 2 million men between 17 and 45 were in the forces. They were joined by a further 1.28 million during 1915.[12] In total some 4.9 million industrial workers were to join up. Thus women had to fill the gaps with 800,000 going into engineering alone.[13] Women's employment in certain departments of the Commercial Gas Company, Stepney, was approved on 30 March 1916.[14] The Armament Output Committee commenced work in the War Office in April 1915 with the main objective to increase the production of the shells which were so urgently required. The committee also divided the country into areas and were aided by permanent business men. Such organisations were to secure "the service of all firms capable of making shells". There was a particular effort by the Armament Output Committee to enlist "firms who had previously machined shells" and specifically those had made smaller sized shells.[15] The Commercial Gas Company became a munitions foundry from 1915 to 1917. In 1915, the company was turning 18–pounder shells and gained a tender to cast 25,000, 100 gage fuses.[16] London, with its smaller workshops, was more suited to the manufacture of component parts, as

---

[10] LCC *London Statistics 1913-14* Vol XXIV (1915) pp76-77
[11] Braybon, op. cit. p49
[12] Pearce, Malcolm and Stewart, Geoffrey, *British Political History 1867–1995: Democracy and Decline* (1996) p211
[13] Ibid. p211
[14] Commercial Gas Company Minute Book 1915–18
[15] MUN 4/606 23 April 1917
[16] Commercial Gas Co. op. cit. Minute Book 1915–18

"they concentrated more ... on gauges, fuses, [and] primers".[17] Lloyd George, Minister of Munitions, stated that "he looked to London particularly to produce a surplus of fuses which would enable the ministry to fit the 'complete round' from shells made in other parts of the country".[18] The Commercial Gas Company worked under the Poplar and Stepney District[19] of the Metropolitan Munitions Committee. The committee employed over 400 firms, "none of which were on munition work before" the war. The firms ranged "over 60 different classes of manufacturers from patent food makers to large motor firms".[20] The following list gives an idea of the classes of firms with whom contracts were placed:

> Advertisement Contractors, Biscuit Works, Confectioners, Doctors, Guano Works, Leather Works, Newpapers, Perforated Music Makers, Printers, Sports Outfitters, Tobacco Works, Baby Food Manufacturers, Candle Makers, Cinematograph Manufacturers, Flour Mills, Institute of the Blind, Livery Manufacturers, Organ Manufacturers, Photographic Appliance Makers, Publishers, Stationers, Wallpaper Manufacturers.[21]

Because of the original nature of the firms the committee believed that it was necessary for them to receive "every possible assistance [and] technical advice". Along side this, the committee felt constant supervision was also necessary.[22] The list of classes of firms involved illustrates that an all-encompassing effort was made to increase the output of munitions. Overall, the Metropolitan Munitions Committee was able to deliver "over 14,000,000 stores of munitions composed of 65 different articles".[23]

---

[17] MUN 5/150/1121.27/8 10 August 1916
[18] MUN 5/150/1121.27/10 A History of its Origin and Work 1915–18
[19] MUN 5/279 The Poplar and Stepney District of the Metropolitan Munitions Committee were made up mainly of volunteers. The Mayor of Shoreditch H. B. Bird Esq. J.P. was on the Board of Management along with J. Vernon Esq. (Waterlow & Sons), and Alexander Duckham Esq. (A. Duckham & Co.); G. M. Gill Esq. was District Manager; J. H. Bowden Esq. Assistant District Manager; S. Y. Knight Esq. Munitiion Engineer; T. L. Hart Esq. Visiting Inspector along with G. M. Callender Esq., B. Heaviside, R. A. Tait Esq., V. Cruikshank Esq. and A. B. Coster Esq. all had their expenses paid; C. G. Madgett Chief Clerk £4 per week; D. Davis Typist £1.12.0 per week; W. N. Anderson Jr. Typist 15/- per week; E. Grout Office Cleaner 2/6 per week; J. C. MacDonald, W. Fisher, A. E. Williams, L. S. Tooth, and R. P. Harris were all voluntary inspectors
[20] MUN 5/150/1121.27/8 op. cit. 10 August 1916
[21] MUN 5/150/1121.27/10 op. cit. A History 1915–18
[22] Ibid. MUN 5/150/1121.27/10 A History 1915-18
[23] MUN 5/150/1121.27/8 op. cit.10 August 1916

The Clothing Industry

Stepney had a tradition of being particularly active in the clothing industry. At the census of 1911, 20,693 or 23.6 per cent of all working men in Stepney and 16,084 or 38.8 per cent of women worked in "Dress", which was the highest single classification of employment for both men and women in the area. Overall, the highest employer of men for the City of London and the metropolitan boroughs was in the "Conveyance of men, goods and messages" encompassing eighteen per cent of those employed. The "Conveyance of men, goods and messages" was the second highest employer of males in Stepney at 18,883 which accounted for 21.5 per cent of the males engaged in work. For women, the dominant employer was, predictably, "Domestic office or service" with forty per cent of all those employed in that occupation.[24] Although the domestic service sector was the second highest employer of women in Stepney, it took in only 18.7 per cent of all women employed, thus showing the dominance of the dress industry (38.8 per cent of those engaged in occupations), for female residents of the area.[25] This was due to the industry being predominantly carried out on a casual basis at home.

Jerry White argues that with the outbreak of war "the whole of the East End tailoring trade, suffered a severe setback". The tailoring trade was notoriously unstable, which for the workers meant that he or she could be laid off at any time, particularly when there was a lack of orders. The slack season, as it was called, set in early in 1914 which meant that thousands of garment workers were laid off.[26] The war contracts that were to bring unprecedented earnings to those in the garment industry, along with unprecedented profits to their employers, were still a few months away. With steeply rising food costs and higher rents, life was particularly hard. Only one area of the East End clothing trade appeared to be prospering and it was those shops making trousers. One such shop was Harry Temple's in Hunton Street, which during the early part of 1915 had War Office sub-contracts. Thus, in Temple's shop, workers were in demand:

> They were begging you to come in and work ... there were plenty of jobs
> during the war, and I went round and I saw the ads and I went in and asked
> if he wanted a machinist and he said yes, and I worked there. We all

---

[24] All figures worked out from the Census material on occupations published in the LCC *London Statistics* Vol XXIV (1916) pp72-3 & pp76-77
[25] Ibid, pp76-77
[26] White, Jerry, *Rothschild Buildings* (1980) p212

worked there; my father worked there, [my brother] worked there, we all worked there.[27]

At Harry Temple's shop they made breeches for the officers. The shop itself:

> ... wasn't bad at all. It was airy. It was a sort of a house, but it was a big room, and he had his office downstairs; if you wanted something we used to go down to the office. It wasn't bad at all as workshops go; I worked in worse ones than that ... The place that we had a strike in I worked there when it rained and you had to hold an umbrella on the machine because the rain was coming in.[28]

After a few months, the garment industry recovered from the uncertainty following the declaration of war, with military work – "the khaki" – flooding into the East End shops. "The khaki" cloth came ready cut, and was delivered by motor vans from the main contractors. Minnie Zwart was a basting hand. She described the material as:

> ... too heavy to sit with on your lap, so you sat on the table and the table took all the weight of it. Very heavy coats they were ... I used to do a bit of finishing, put the buttons on sometimes when there wasn't enough basting to do, little odd jobs, you know. Very good at the needle. [Was it hard on the fingers?] Oh yes, sore from the work. Hard work. Get good money but it was hard work.[29]

The rates of pay were indeed good, with the average woman's wages soon rising two and a half times above the pre-war level. Sarah Zissman remembers taking home weekly wages as high as £2, 5s, and when profits were even higher she would have probably taken home 7½d for each pair of trousers. Harry Temple's shop would have received 10d for each pair of trousers, from the contractor who in return received 1s, 8¼d from the War Office. With increased and continuous work, much of the pre-war seasonality of the industry was erased. The increase in work also brought longer hours. This meant a rise in living standards, as more money could be spent on food and even other small "luxuries" such as linoleum for the floor, a dressing table or other pieces of furniture, or better clothes.

---

[27] Sarah Zissman, (a pseudonym) recalling her family working for Harry Temple's Mrs G, Tape 31, transcript pages pp1-4, Bancroft Local History Library (Tower Hamlets)
[28] White, op. cit. p213
[29] Ibid. p214

However, with increases in food prices and rents, wages had to rise in order to keep pace. Wage increases generally appear only to have come after a struggle. In October 1916, for instance, there was a strike of some 500 men and women at Schneider's Whitechapel clothing factory "in protest at the management's demand that workers buy trimmings and cotton from the firm at prices higher than were charged elsewhere".[30] After a week of strike action the company gave in. In the case of munitions workers strikes, were banned due to the Munitions Act of July 1915, which outlawed "strikes and lock-outs ... for the duration of the war".[31] A general idea of wage increases for tailors during the war can be understood by consulting the following table:

Table 2-1: Shirt-making Trade Board (GB) Minimum rates of wages (as varied) for female workers. Effective as from 26 December 1913 and 22 November 1918

During 1st 6 months of Employment	14 & under 15 years per week				15 & under 16 years per week				16 & under 21 years per week				21 years & over per week				
	1913		1918		1913		1918		1913		1918			1913		1918	
	s	d	s	d	s	d	s	d	s	d	s	d		s	d	s	d
	3	0	4	9	3	8	5	6	5	2	8	0	1st 3 mths	6	9	10	0
2nd	4	6	8	0	5	2	9	0	6	9	11	9	2nd 3 mths	8	4	14	6
3rd	6	0	10	3	7	3	13	3	9	5	16	0	3rd 3 mths	10	11	18	6
4th	7	3	12	3	8	10	15	0	12	6	21	3	4th 3 mths	12	6	21	3
5th	8	4	14	6	10	11	18	6									
6th	9	5	16	0	12	6	21	3									
7th	11	5	19	9													
8th	12	6	21	3													

Table 2-1 from LAB 35/332 Shirt-making Trade Board (GB)

From these figures, it is easy to see that wages increased substantially during the war period, which inevitably caused companies, like Messrs.

---

[30] *The Woman's Dreadnought*, 24 June 1916
[31] Wrigley, Chris, "The State and the challenge of Labour in Britain 1917-1920" in Wrigley, Chris (ed.), *Challenges of Labour, Central and Western Europe 1917-1920* (1993) p272

John Cantor & Co., to increase their prices when their contracts came up for renewal.

In 1917, Messrs. John Cantor & Co. were asked by Stepney council "whether they would be prepared to undertake an extension of their contract for a period of twelve months". Due to price rises, however, Messrs. John Cantor & Co. "were unable to see their way to agree to an extension at the prices in the contract".[32] The council put the contract out for tender inviting eleven persons and firms to submit tenders and sample of prices. In reply, the council received communications from five firms "regretting their inability to submit tender". In fact, only Messrs. John Cantor & Co. submitted a tender.[33] With no other applications being received, Messrs. John Cantor & Co.'s tender was accepted. In the following year, 1918, the contract of Messrs. John Cantor & Co.'s came up for renewal once again, with the council suggesting a continuation of the contract for a further twelve months. Once again a revised price was agreed at this time.[34] However, the hardship caused by war and the council's lack of monetary resources can be seen in the words of Councillor Miles, vice-chairman, and Councillor T. J. Evans who talk of "the possibility of renovating the uniforms last issued".[35] Miles and Evans remark that:

> … as a result of their inspection of these uniforms, instructions have been given for those of the caretaker at the public health offices, the messenger in the town clerks office and the caretakers and hall porters at the public libraries to be cleaned and renovated.[36]

The rising costs in clothes manufacturing during the war can be seen in the J. Compton & Sons Ltd contracts. Based at St Katharine Dock House, Tower Hill, they made railway uniforms for Taff Vale Railway, Cardiff. The contract that saw them through the war years was entered into six months prior to the outbreak of war. By December 1915, J. Compton & Sons Ltd were writing to the Taff Vale Railway Company, asking for a 20 per cent increase in pay for the remainder of their contract due to the fact that "cloths and other material used in the manufacture of the clothing, has

---

[32] Minute Book Vol 17 of the Council of the Metropolitan Borough of Stepney 1916-1917 L/SMB/A/1/17
[33] Ibid. L/SMB/A/1/17 1916-1917
[34] Minute Book Vol 18 of the Council of the Metropolitan Borough of Stepney 1917-1918 L/SMB/A/1/18
[35] Ibid. L/SMB/A/1/18 1917-1918
[36] Ibid. L/SMB/A/1/18 1917-1918

advanced by leaps and bounds until now the cost is from 50 to 75 per cent in excess of those at the time the contract was made".[37] They note that "most of our running contracts have been increased by 25 per cent".[38] The increase they asked for was agreed "subject to the right on their [Taff Vale Railway] part to terminate or vary this arrangement in the event of a change in circumstances (such as the termination of the war)".[39] However, with the continuation of the war, prices were to rise rather than fall and by 1918 when prices were sent to Taff Vale Railway it was stated that, "materials are more than three times their original value, added to which the cost of manufacture has increased enormously". A ticket collector's serge jacket was now to cost 29s when it had been 21s, 9d. The cost of the ticket collector's vest had also risen from 6s, 3d to 8s.[40] The contracts that were entered into required that workers were highly skilled, as the company involved reserved "the right to submit the clothing supplied to such tests as they may consider desirable, and to reject all garments which in their judgement are inferior to sample".[41] Any garments rejected would have to be replaced at the expense of the contractor.

In areas such as Stepney, where workers often worked from home, the Home Office was concerned at the "possible danger of infection to the troops".[42] It was therefore decided that the Medical Officer of Health inspect the premises of outworkers "'to see that the work is not done in premises where there is infectious disease".[43]

Such material gives the historian an insight to some experiences of war work in Stepney. It also shows how rates of pay improved during the war years for employees. For the employing companies, there was an ever present need to renegotiate prices for contracts, as materials and wages were constantly rising throughout the war.

---

[37] Rail 684/345 Letter, 29 December 1915
[38] Ibid. 684/345 Letter, 29 December 1915
[39] Ibid. 684/345 Letter, 14 January 1916
[40] Ibid. 684/345 Letter, 12 February 1918
[41] Ibid. 684/345 Taff Vale Railway Contract 22 January 1914
[42] Minute Book No. 22 of the Public Health Committee of the Stepney Borough Council September 1914 – April 1915 STE/1121 Thursday 18 February 1915 "Manufacture of clothes for the army"
[43] Ibid. STE/1121 Thursday 18 February 1915 "Manufacture of clothes for the army"

Sylvia Pankhurst and the Suffrage Movement in Stepney

Barbara Winslow argues that the First World War not only brought tremendous change to the East London Federation of the Suffragettes (ELFS) but also to Sylvia Pankhurst personally. The ELFS was "from its inception a radical, militant, working-class, feminist organisation", that was not solely concerned with votes for women, although suffrage was a primary focus. It was a community organisation that would admit men, but was always led by women. "Its main purpose was to expose the exploitation and oppression of women in all aspects of life".[44] Nellie Cressall, later Poplar Borough Councillor and Mayor, says that she "could not agree that men should be the sole parent, that a mother could not even say whether her child should be vaccinated or not — or that women should receive half pay and many other things as well …".[45] Hers was a wider vision of emancipation based upon daily experiences of economic and social inequality.

Pankhurst's views could be read in her newspaper, the *Women's Dreadnought*, which dealt with "the franchise question from the working woman's point of view", and reported on "the activities of the votes for women movement in East London".[46] During the campaign for women's suffrage, one tactic in use was rent strikes. As one suffragette, Melvina Walker stated:

> Remember we working women can never help ourselves until we get the power of the vote! In this 'No Vote, No Rent' we Suffragettes want to help you. We have learned through persecution to stand by each other and you must do the same.[47]

Rent strikes were also used to urge the government to control the supply of food,[48] as this was becoming an increasing concern. However, Pankhurst was to find herself in a dilemma: "do you consistently oppose the war, or do you campaign for better wages and working conditions for workers in war production?"[49] Her conclusion was to fight for the rights

---

[44] Winslow, Barbara, *Sylvia Pankhurst* (1966) p41
[45] Councillor Mrs Cressall at the Memorial Meeting in honour of Sylvia Pankhurst, Caxton Hall, Westminster 19 January 1961, Nellie Cressall Papers, private family collection in Davis, Mary, *Sylvia Pankhurst: A Life in Radical Politics* (1999) p37
[46] *Women's Dreadnought* 8 March 1914
[47] Ibid. 15 August 1914
[48] Ibid. 8 August 1914
[49] Winslow, op. cit. p90

of the community. Thus, from April 1915, the ELFS launched a vigorous campaign on women's pay as well as against the horrors of the sweated trades. Sylvia Pankhurst stated that:

> The Stepney Public Health Committee declared army contracts were often four times sub-let, each sub-contractor making a profit at the expense of the sweated women doing the work. Soldiers' trousers were being finished at 1, ¾ d per pair'.[50]

In a communication from the War Office dated 28 October 1914, it was noted that minimum rates of pay had been fixed under the Trades Board Act 1909 and any infringements of this should be made to the Secretary of the Trades Board, with the War Office being informed of contractors against whom allegations were being made.[51] The Medical Officer of Health was instructed "to supply to the Office of Trade Boards any particulars of sweating which may come to his notice either through members of the committee or otherwise".[52] Pankhurst said that she "complained to the War Office about the rates for soldiers' shirts paid by a Stepney firm" but that all the employer did was transfer "the shirts to outworkers, and kept the indoor workers to blouse-making". Pankhurst notes that "the rates for the shirts were not increased".[53] The Public Health Committee found that "2s, 9d" was paid for making a khaki jacket and "3s, 8d" for an overcoat. Its report stated that "members assured the committee that these prices do not provide a living wage" and that "in view of the stringency of the inspections of the completed goods, only experienced persons could do the work satisfactorily".[54]

A constant campaign in the *Women's Dreadnought* was the demand for a minimum wage of 5d an hour or £1 a week "for all women employed in relief works subsidised by public funds, or employed by government contractors".[55] The paper also complained that women workers in the munitions factories were earning just 2½d an hour, whereas the men whose jobs they had taken had been receiving 6½d.[56] The ELFS was also a provider of two penny meal restaurants in the East End as well as baby

---

[50] Pankhurst, Sylvia E., *The Home Front: A Mirror to Life in England during the World War* (1932) p91
[51] Minute Book No. 22 of the Public Health Committee op. cit. September 1914 – April 1915 STE/1121
[52] Ibid. STE/1121 September 1914 – April 1915
[53] Pankhurst, op. cit. p91
[54] Minute Book No. 22 op. cit. September 1914 – April 1915 STE/1121
[55] *Women's Dreadnought* 10 October 1914
[56] Ibid. 21 August 1915

clinics and milk depots dispensing "a quart of milk a day to nursing and expectant mothers".[57] They helped set up nurseries which cost 3d a day (including food), all aiding women engaged in paid work.

The ELFS established its own factories in order to provide unemployed women with work. At the outbreak of war many women lost their jobs due to the upper classes cutting back on "luxuries". The ELFS established a boot and shoe factory and later a toy factory. There were other practical examples of groups or committees, who attempted to provide relief, not given by the government, in order to alleviate the misery caused by the war. The Central Committee of Women's Employment found it desirable to give an impetus to local committees with practical examples of how relief workrooms should be started. Consequently a number of experimental workrooms were established in Bethnal Green, Stepney, Hackney, St Pancras, Camberwell and Shoreditch. They were called the Queen Mary's Workrooms, which Pankhurst was to label as "Queen Mary's sweat shops" because the wages were very low at about 10s a week.[58] Pankhurst strove to maintain wages at £1 a week. The Stepney workroom was at the Raines School. Each room employed between 600 and 700 women. It was said, "the main work done in the committee's experimental workrooms is the making of various kinds of clothing".[59] These were distributed for free amongst the poor and needy. In addition to these workrooms, experimental Domestic Economy Training Centres were also established. Stepney had one of these centres, where women were employed for up to 40 hours a week. Of these, five hours were spent attending classes arranged by the London County Council (LCC), either on the training scheme premises or at neighbouring LCC centres. Classes were held in home cookery and laundry work, dressmaking, needlework, health and home nursing.[60]

The Women's United Services League seemed to try to support and educate women during the war in two ways: "a) by definite teaching in such subjects as mother craft, housecraft, etc," and "b) by corporate life which encourages courtesy, unselfishness, love of the beautiful, good music, good literature, good manners, self-respect".[61] In 1917 the Stepney Women's War Club had about 150 members and a subscription fee of 2d

[57] *Gertrude Tuckwell Collection* 369, ELFS *The Star* 28 September 1914

[58] Holloway, Gerry, *Women and Work in Britain Since 1840* (2005) p132

[59] IWM Women at Work Collection, Interim Report of the Central Committee on Women's Employment 1915

[60] Ibid. Interim Report 1915

[61] IWM Women at Work Collection, Booklet: The Women's United Services League Conference on the Work of the League 14 February 1917

monthly. In Stepney, nursery and infant welfare centres had been set up. Cookery classes had been tried, but a lack of accommodation had brought them to a halt. There were also regular needlework competitions, concerts, teas, summer outings, lectures and visits.[62]

In 1916 suffrage became a "living question" as it seemed likely that the government would enfranchise all the fighting men before the war was finished. Thus Pankhurst, with the Workers' Suffrage Federation (WSF), held demonstrations to demand adult suffrage and urged workers to come in crowds: "You will need the vote after the war to get back the liberties you have so freely surrendered, whether you are a man or a woman".[63] There was support for the idea that the Independent Labour Party (ILP), the Labour Party and their Members of Parliament, should exert pressure to ensure that all women as well as men should gain the vote. For example, in April 1917:

> Woolwich ILP, Richmond ILP, Leicester ILP, Stratford branch of the National Union of Railway Men, Bradford Women's Humanity League and East London BSP all met to pass a resolution that the proposals in the Speaker's Conference were unsatisfactory and were unacceptable to the working class unless they were to provide for complete adult suffrage for men and women.[64]

In 1917, the government proposed that only women over 30 should be given the vote. In the event, it was this far more limited measure, rather than full adult suffrage, which was adopted by the government in the Representation of the People Act of 1918.

By helping with the community's wartime needs, there was a marked departure "from the old suffragette tactic of organising thousands of people to force the government to pass women's suffrage legislation". This departure lost the ELFS/WSF a great deal of its earlier strength. As Emma Boyce commented in 1917: "the federation seemed more like a 'charity organisation with suffrage tacked on'".[65] However, it can be argued it was the real needs of East End women that the organisation was now addressing. The suffragists had always maintained a sense of balance between home and politics. Sandra Stanley Holton argues that "the

---

[62] Ibid. 14 February 1917
[63] *The Call* 6 April 1916
[64] Hannam, June and Hunt, Karen, *Socialist Women: Britain, 1880s to 1920s* (2002) p125
[65] Minutes of the General Meeting of the Workers' Suffrage Federation, 15 January 1917

majority of suffragists ... fitted in their political activity alongside other more everyday aspects of being a woman: work, family commitments, love and friendship".[66]

Conclusion

Through this chapter we have discovered that war work was a catalyst for change as suggested by Arthur Marwick in *The Deluge*.[67] The war brought with it a general movement in the population. The men enlisted and went to the Front, which left the women to fill the positions they left behind. This was to alter the position of women in the work-place, as married women, were encouraged back to work, and women who had worked in domestic service often found work in munition factories. Those in the business of manufacturing clothing found they were in demand and that the industry lost much of the seasonality of the work. For both the munitions and clothing industries, the need for workers brought about improvements in wages and conditions. Although women were often viewed as "substitutes" for male workers it was essential that they were drawn into the country's workforce in order for production to continue. With the end of the war, women were expected to go back to the home in order for the men to have work. However, as a reward for such selflessness shown by the population a greater number were granted the right to vote, as we shall see with the general election of 1918 and thus the all encompassing war caused a catalyst to the political environment.

---

[66] Holton, Sandra Stanley, "The Suffragist and the 'Average Woman'" *Women's History Review* Vol 1 1992 p11
[67] Marwick, Arthur, *The Deluge* (1991)

CHAPTER THREE

POLITICAL DEVELOPMENT AND THE 1918 ELECTION

This chapter charts a key change in the outlook and attitude of Stepney's citizens, from being passive bystanders to being politically active. Through the formation of the Stepney Labour Party, the population would have improved representation as it brought better political cooperation between the Irish and Jewish populace. As the book progresses through the 1920s and 1930s, a significant number of political events will be explored. It was due to the Representation of the People Act 1918, which greatly increased the numbers qualifying to vote, that Stepney began on such a political journey. The Act was also the product of the First World War due to the widely perceived need to reward participation in the war effort. In the case of Stepney, in 1914 the electorate had numbered 24,151.[1] By 1918 this figure had more than tripled to 74,772.[2] Therefore the end of the war can be regarded as a "watershed" in political history, especially regarding the franchise, but also due to the changes in party political structure.

With the end of the fighting came a "desire to repair the disruptions of war, to reward participation in the war effort, and to acknowledge the widespread sense that so cataclysmic a war must be succeeded by a better world".[3] With the Representation of the People Act:

---

[1] At this point Stepney was within the Borough of Tower Hamlets, so the figures for Limehouse, Mile End, St Georges, Stepney and Whitechapel have been totalled in order to obtain the above figure. LCC *London Statistics 1913-1914* Vol. XXIV (1915) p21

[2] Stepney was a parliamentary district by this time with three divisions: Limehouse, Mile End and Whitechapel & St Georges. Again a total has been obtained for the three divisions for the above figure. LCC *London Statistics 1915-20* Vol. XXVI (1921) p15

[3] Marwick, Arthur, *The Deluge* (1991) p32

Women were allowed to qualify in 1918 if they were local government voters or the wives of local government workers, provided they had attained the age of thirty.[4]

The exclusion of women between twenty-one and thirty years of age ensured that women only had a limited parliamentary franchise and were a minority electorate. Stepney was made up of three constituencies: Mile End, Limehouse, and Whitechapel & St George's. Women, in Stepney, for example made up 30,075 or 40 per cent, of the electorate, whereas 44,697, 60 per cent, were men.[5] For men:

> ... in order to be qualified to be registered as a parliamentary elector, [they] must be of full age (except, under certain conditions, naval and military voters ...), and not subject to any legal incapacity.[6]

In Stepney, the number of men who gained a naval or military vote was 16,669 or 37 per cent[7] of the male population, making them a significant proportion of the male electorate.

The general election of 1918 was a "watershed in twentieth century politics"[8] as it meant that 21 million citizens now had the right to vote. The election had three main political consequences. Firstly, it was to mark the beginning of a twenty year era of Conservative dominance. Secondly, it dealt a blow to the Liberals from which they never fully recovered. This stemmed from the party's split during the First World War, due to dissatisfaction with Asquith's leadership of the coalition government. Lloyd George formed the new coalition in 1916. At the 1918 election Lloyd George and his Liberals allied with the Conservatives against Asquith's independent Liberals and Labour. The division of the party was to continue into the post-war years, with the Liberals fighting as rival sections. Thirdly, it gave Labour a chance to emerge as the leading opposition party for the first time. In all three constituencies of Stepney, Labour was the leading opposition party in the 1918 General Election. The Labour party officially became the opposition party after the 1922 general election, when its representation more than doubled to 142, while the combined Liberal representation fell to 115.

---

[4] Pugh, Martin, *The Evolution of the British Electoral System 1832-1987* (1994) p9
[5] LCC *London Statistics 1915-1920* op. cit. p15
[6] Ibid. p13
[7] Ibid. p15
[8] Pugh, Martin, *The Making of Modern British Politics 1867-1945* (Oxford, 2002) p161

The "Coupon" and the New Voters

With the end of the war came the General Election of 1918. There were two distinguishing factors of the 1918 General Election. One was the "coupon" and the second was the new voters.[9] Candidates who supported the coalition received a joint letter of endorsement from Lloyd George for the Liberals and Bonar Law for the Conservatives. This letter was dubbed the "coupon" by those who refused it, namely Asquithian Liberals, Labour candidates and some Conservatives. Of the many new voters on the register "women in particular with their particular inexperience were thought to add to the air of quiet puzzlement".[10] Also, many voters were still abroad in the armed forces. Of the 2.7 million service men sent ballot papers, only 0.9 million voted.[11] It must also be noted that this election was a long time in coming and that:

> The main arrangements had been made in contemplation of an election to be held while the fighting was still going on, and whose real issue would be whether to fight the war to a finish or to attempt to conclude a negotiated peace with Germany.[12]

Even at the point of less than eight weeks till the Armistice, the Lloyd George Liberals "were as far as ever from any definite conclusion about the timing or the theme of a general election".[13] It was also still being "assumed that the election would take place while the war was still being fought"[14] and thus one of the themes of the election would be "the prosecution of the war itself". It appears that no one positively argued for the election to be postponed until after the war.[15]

---

[9] Morgan, Kenneth O., *Consensus and Disunity: The Lloyd George Coalition Government 1918–1922* (Oxford, 1979) p152
[10] *The Nation* 4 January 1919
[11] Pugh, *The Making of Modern British Politics* op. cit. p162
[12] Douglas, Roy, "The background to the 'Coupon' election arrangements" *The English History Review* Vol. April 1971 p318
[13] Ibid. p318
[14] Ibid. p318
[15] Ibid. p328

Table 3-1 The Parliamentary Electorate 1914:

Parliamentary divisions	Population 1911 (Census)	Number of electors 1914	Percentage of electorate to population in 1914 (a)
Limehouse	52,329	6,488	12.7
Mile End	47,880	5,821	12.2
St Georges	48,666	3,180	6.7
Stepney	63,194	4,601	7.3
Whitechapel	67,526	4,061	6.4

Table 3-2 The Parliamentary Electorate 1918:

Parliamentary divisions 1918	Area in acres	Population Census 1911	Parliamentary electors, autumn, 1918				Percentage of electorate to population
			Men	Women	Total	Naval and military voters (b)	
Limehouse	566	73,627	17,231	12,044	29,275	6,132	39.8
Mile End	526	93,658	13,342	8,789	22,131	5,235	23.6
Whitechapel & St George's	674	112,519	14,124	9,242	23,366	5,302	20.8

(a) Calculated upon an estimated population at the middle of 1914
(b) Included in Total column
Table 3-1 & 3-2 are made from LCC *London Statistics* 1913-14 & 1915-20

Using the above figures to calculate the percentage of electorate to population in 1914 the figure stands at 10.2 per cent. As a result of the Representation of the People's Act 1918, this figure can be seen to increase dramatically to 26.7 per cent, thus aiding Martin Pugh's suggestion that the end of the war marks a "water shed" in politics.[16] As one can see from the above tables, the lowest number of voters is in the Whitechapel and St George's area, which would have contained a large concentration of foreign nationals. The 1899 Jewish East London Map vividly shows the disproportionately high percentage of Jewish residents in the Whitechapel and St George's area.[17] At the time of the 1911 census

---

[16] Pugh, *The Making of Modern British Politics* op. cit. p161
[17] Jewish East London Map showing by colour the proportion of the Jewish population to other residents of East London, street by street in 1899. Reproduced

the largest concentration of foreign nationals in Stepney came from Russia, which included Asiatic Russia.[18] By the 1921 census, the numbers for "Russia" now incorporating Poland were 40,624 or 86.5 per cent of foreign residents in Stepney.[19] Of this total 24,946, or 71.1 per cent, still had alien nationality status that year. Overall, the total number of people with alien nationality status in Stepney was 28,581 persons or 70.3 per cent of all foreign residents.[20] The concentration of foreign nationals in the Whitechapel and St George's area therefore accounts for the variations in the percentage of electorate to population within the three districts of Stepney in 1918.

Amongst the minority of Jewish people who had the vote, conflicting pressures were felt. Those who had supported the war probably shared the general mood of loyalty to the coalition government. However, for the thousands who had opposed the war, there was "little reason to support a government which had so harassed the immigrant community over the military service question".[21] Lloyd George had begun his campaign speaking about a "sane peace settlement and social reconstruction, but he found his audiences excitedly demanding vengeance".[22] With an election held in the immediate post-war period, wartime emotions ran high. In Stepney the issue of the alien population was part of the campaign.

Mr C. H. Rodwell, National Party candidate, hoped that "… no aliens would be allowed to trade in open shops, as formerly, and even at present, thus depriving Britishers from gaining a livelihood";[23] he wanted aliens to be deprived of being granted license to trade. The National Party was formed in August 1917 by Brigadier-General Henry Page-Croft and consisted of 7 MP's and 17 members of the House of Lords.[24] The aim of the party was to promote national unity,[25] with the ultimate desire of

---

by the Museum of the Jewish East End and Research Census from "The Jew in London 1901" by kind permission of the Guildhall Library, City of London

[18] 28,681 persons came from Russia (including Asiatic Russia) see Census figures in LCC *London Statistics 1913-14* (1915)

[19] *Census of England & Wales 1921* (1922)

[20] Ibid. 1921

[21] Bush, Julia, "East London Jews and the First World War" *London Journal* 6 1980 p151

[22] Pugh, *The Making of Modern British Politics* op. cit. p161 & see DeGroot, Gerard J., *Blighty: British Society in the Era of the Great War* (1996) p314

[23] *East End News* 22 November 1918

[24] Wrigley, Chris (ed), *Warfare, Diplomacy and Politics – Essays in Honour of AJP Taylor* (1986) pp93-4

[25] Rubinstein, William D., "Henry Page Croft and the National Party 1917-22" *Journal of Contemporary History* 9 1 1974 p139

becoming "... the only party in an ideal single party state".[26] According to William D. Rubinstein, the failure of the party may be due to the limited class appeal. The party's leaders were drawn almost exclusively from the upper and upper-middle classes. The only person who could be described as working-class was Rodwell who was the clerk of a coal company in Limehouse. With the party's anti-"alien" stance it is not surprising that Rodwell gained so few votes at the General election.

Another crucial campaign during the 1918 election was the creation of "A fit land for heroes",[27] and one of the first tasks of the Coalition Government was to try to attain this aim. During the war, slum clearance and housing had fallen sadly into arrears and it was widely felt that these were schemes "upon which the well-being of the nation so largely depends".[28] For Stepney a programme of slum clearance was crucial as so many dwellings were in a poor state. The Labour Party demanded that a substantial and permanent improvement to the housing of all the people should be achieved. They proposed that "at least a million new houses must be built at once at the State's expense, and let at fair rents, and [that] these houses must be fit for men and women to live in".[29] The Labour Party also stood for "complete adult suffrage, in industry for equal pay and the organisation of men and women workers in one trade union movement".[30] However, there was also the introduction in 1918 of a new constitution for the Labour Party. This made possible the formation of Labour parties in every parliamentary constituency, which would be joined by individual Labour supporters who could not, or would not, join an affiliated organisation – for instance a trade union.[31] In Stepney the Labour parties were established primarily in Mile End and Limehouse. These separate Stepney Labour parties were to amalgamate in order to gain local and parliamentary votes – since as a united party they would be far more successful than as separate parties.

---

[26] Sykes, Alan, *The Radical Right in Britain* (Hampshire, 2005) p40

[27] Taken from David Lloyd George's election speech in which he said: "What is our task? To make Britain a fit country for heroes to live in ... Slums are not fit homes for the men who have won this war or for their children. They are not fit nurseries for the children who are to make an imperial race" published in *The Times* 25 November 1918

[28] Craig, F. W. S., *British General Election Manifestos 1918–1966* (Chichester, 1970) p3

[29] Ibid. p6

[30] Ibid. p6

[31] Harris, Kenneth, *Attlee* (1995) p42

The formation of the Stepney Labour Party

In 1918, the Mile End, Whitechapel and Limehouse branches of the Labour Party formed an alliance in Stepney, known as the Stepney Central Labour Party. This brought with it the political unification of much of the Irish and Jewish populace, due principally to Oscar Tobin and a few others including Matt Aylward and Tom Williams. Aylward was a Limehouse radical Irishman. It has been suggested that the Irish grouping "had been a front for Sinn Fein, the Irish republican movement" which "was 'handed over' after the granting of Irish independence to Catholic Action, a group dedicated to fostering close ties between the Irish and their church".[32] Bertha Sokoloff, later a Communist borough councillor, also observed that "the Catholic clergy took an active interest in local politics, which were Labour politics".[33] In 1918 Alyward founded the Limehouse Labour Party, a few weeks prior to Tobin establishing the Mile End Labour Party. Aylward led the Limehouse Irish into the Stepney Borough Labour Party and under Tobin's leadership "made them a unique power in Stepney politics".[34]

Tobin was a Romanian Jew by birth. He had come to Britain at 18 to escape the Bucharest persecutions. He was a socialist whose ambition was to:

> ... fuse trade union members and the Independent Labour Party (ILP) with Labour Party supporters in a broad-based socialist movement which could get control of the Stepney borough councils, and win its three parliamentary seats: Limehouse, Mile End and Whitechapel.[35]

He had begun his association with the Labour Party early on when he helped and worked with John Burns, Ben Tillett, and other pioneers "who laid the foundations of the edifice on which today is built the hopes of 'the bottom dog'".[36] Tobin moved to Poplar where he joined the Poplar Labour League and ardently supported Will Crooks. Later he moved to Limehouse, and it was here that he managed to win the lodgers' vote and

---

[32] Interviews, Tom Rampling, Banbry, Oxfordshire, 20 January 1979, Montagu Einhorn, London, 10 December 1978 Srebrnik, Henry Felix, *London Jews and British Communism, 1935–1945* (Essex, 1995) p69
[33] Sokoloff, Bertha, *Edith and Stepney* (1987) p69
[34] Harris, op. cit. p42
[35] Ibid. p42
[36] *East London Observer* 12 February 1920

"was elected to the Old Vestry for the North Ward".[37] In 1900, Tobin, along with Tom Williams and a few others, unsuccessfully founded the Limehouse Labour Party. With the onset of war he "promoted recruiting, afterwards serving on the Stepney Military Tribunal, the Jewish Tribunal, the War Savings Committee and in 1917, was co-opted on the Stepney Borough Council".[38] Tobin was also chairman of the General Purposes Committee and served on the LCC Main Drainage and Old Age Pensions Committee in 1920.[39] He was later the organiser of the National Union of Shop Assistants,[40] thus an influential figure of Stepney.

Interestingly, twenty-four hours after being demobilised, Clement Attlee, was back in Stepney. He had been introduced to Stepney when he joined his brother Laurence on a visit to the Haileybury Club, in October 1905. Within two years of this visit, Attlee had become manager of the Haileybury Club, and Stepney was his home. The first person he saw on his return from military service was Oscar Tobin, the "East End of London's most influential political 'boss'".[41] Tobin led Attlee through his chemist shop to the back and upstairs to the first floor, where the politically ambitious chemist held his meetings. With pride, Tobin described the new composition of Stepney Labour and the prospect of power in the East End. A majority on the borough council was in sight. Tobin suggested that Attlee stood for one of the two Mile End seats at the next London County Council election. As we shall discover, Attlee, on reflection, instead took Aylward's advice and stood for Limehouse, where he had lived for several years and had a strong local reputation.

After the alliance of the various branches of the Labour Party in Stepney, considerable electoral success was achieved throughout the inter-war years, as we shall discover in the next chapter. The East London Labour parties worked hard for the votes they received in the 1918 General election. They were, as Julia Bush comments, "united by their broad commitment to make the voices of East London workers heard and to redress the balance of power and wealth in their favour".[42] Thus, the war had "helped to convince East Londoners that change was possible, and the Labour Party was ready to take advantage of the fact".[43] The war's

---

[37] Ibid. 12 February 1920
[38] Ibid. 12 February 1920
[39] Ibid. 12 February 1920
[40] *East London Advertiser* 28 January 1922
[41] Harris, op. cit. p42
[42] Bush, Julia Frances, *Labour Politics and Society in East London During the First World War* PhD (1978) p15
[43] Ibid. p15

impact on the home front and the battlefront had made workers more aware and less tolerant of social divisions, creating high expectations for post-war reconstruction. It was to be the Labour Party who embodied such expectations in its policies, which the government failed to fulfil. In the 1918 election, the East London workers voted in the "simple belief that the Labour Party stood for their interest, whereas the coalition government represented the opposing interest of the employers and profiteers".[44]

The Election

It was not until Tuesday, 5 November 1918 that the *East End News* published a list of probable candidates for the general election.[45] This only left a short period in which to canvass the electorate, with the election taking place on 14 December. Mr Rodwell opened his campaign as the National Party candidate for Limehouse on Friday, 22 November 1918 "by addressing a meeting of supporters at his committee's centre in Commercial Road on Thursday night".[46] He said that it should be the "first consideration of the Government to make full provision in the form of pension, and allowances for the men who had gained such a glorious victory for the homeland".[47] He believed that the men needed "a just reward for [their] heroism";[48] this would be shown through better housing and the establishment of industries for their support. He believed that "Germany must be made to pay every pound and every penny that the war has cost"; also that "every interned German must be sent back and a law passed preventing them returning".[49] Mr Rodwell advocated that his party consisted "of *Conservatives and Liberals* who have broken away from the old 'SYSTEM' because it left them no freedom to criticise or condemn things they knew were rotten to the core".[50]

The official candidates for the Coalition Party in Stepney were: Sir W. Pearce – Limehouse; Mr Walter Preston – Mile End; Mr G. Cohen – Whitechapel and St George's. Mr Pearce acknowledged that the new

---

[44] Ibid. p361
[45] Mile End: W. Daveney (Labour); Walter Preston (Unionist). Limehouse: Sir W. Pearce (Liberal); Sir P. Rose-Innes (Unionist); C. H. Rodwell (National); D. Sheehan (Labour). Whitechapel & St George's: Dr Ambrose (Labour); Wedgwood Benn (Liberal); J. D. Kiley (Liberal) See *East End News* 5 November 1918
[46] *East End News* 22 November 1918
[47] Ibid. 22 November 1918
[48] Ibid. 22 November 1918
[49] Ibid. 6 December 1918
[50] Ibid. 6 December 1918

Suffrage Act had enlarged the parliamentary boundaries of Limehouse, and that as a result the number of electors had trebled. In 1914 it was estimated that the electorate numbered 6,488 or 12.7 per cent. By 1918, the changed parliamentary boundaries had increased this to 29,275, or 39.8 per cent of the population.[51] Pearce believed that standing for office was "an honour and a responsibility which I have highly valued and endeavoured to deserve". He appealed to the electorate "once more for support and confidence", stating that the "duty of the new parliament was to lay the foundation of [a] better and happier time for the nation as a whole".[52] Walter Preston appealed to the electorate for the restrictions on food, which have been borne throughout the war, to be removed as speedily as possible. He called for improved housing and a better, freer, brighter and happier Britain for the returning soldiers. A minimum wage that would ensure a decent standard of living for everyone was to be a top priority. Mr Preston asserted that "Great Britain has had a great past – she has an infinitely greater future".[53] Mr Cohen insisted that it was the Coalition Government who had won the war and that it was now essential that they "should decide the terms of Peace".[54]

The day before the election, the newspapers were teeming with polling day fever, the suggestion being that every voter (man or woman) should go and vote. In honour of the election a universal half-day holiday was declared, in order to give the electorate ample time to get to their respective polling stations and also to ensure that there would be absolutely no excuse for "those unseemly crowds and rushes that have been witnessed outside the polling places immediately before closing time at many previous elections".[55] However, the electoral turnout was poor, with Stepney's three constituencies seeing an overall turnout of 27,971 which was only 36.3 per cent of the electorate.[56]

The newspapers, reporting on Election Day, told of the "deterrent influence of the downpour of rain upon the attendance at the polling places, especially during the earlier portion of the day".[57] A great number of the men sacrificed their vote in order to stay dry "rather than incur the

---

[51] For 1914 figures see LCC *London Statistics 1913-14* op. cit. p21 & 1918 figures, see LCC *London Statistics 1915-20* op. cit. p15
[52] *East End News* 3 December 1918
[53] *East London Observer* 7 December 1918
[54] Ibid. 14 December 1918
[55] *East End News* 13 December 1918
[56] The turnout for each constituency was: Limehouse – 33.4 per cent, Mile End – 43.1 per cent and Whitechapel & St George's – 37.0 per cent. Craig, op. cit. 49-51
[57] *East End News* 17 December 1918

certainty of a saturated coat".[58] The women however, had a much better
turn-out during the first half of the day, outnumbering the "men by ten to
one".[59] However, this was not the case in East London; it was reported that
in South Poplar, Bow and Bromley, and Mile End "the proportion of men
to women voters was comparatively negligible until the afternoon".[60] The
vote for women was still seen as a little dubious as it was reported that
"one woman voter refused to go to the poll, stating as her reason that 'she
was a respectable woman'".[61] H. E. Miles, a diarist of the time, appeared
excited at the prospect of the vote, commenting "... fancy us women
having won the vote through the war".[62] The women appear to have taken
their right to vote very seriously and had a kind of "that's that" attitude
once they had dropped their slip in the ballot box. Many husbands and
wives went and voted together but whether they "kissed" the same
candidate is of course a matter for speculation. Lloyd George "... claimed
that it was the women's vote which was the basis of the Coalition's
success".[63] Overall, the number of voters was low and the *East End News*
put this down to the fact that "many refused to risk a soaking for the sake
of casting their votes, regardless of the great issues that were at stake".[64]
The results for Stepney were:

---

[58] Ibid. 17 December 1918
[59] Ibid. 17 December 1918
[60] Ibid. 17 December 1918
[61] Ibid. 17 December 1918
[62] Miles, H. E., *Untold tales of War-time London* (1919) p163
[63] Morgan, op. cit. p152
[64] *East End News* 17 December 1918

Table 3-3 Parliamentary Election Results

Electoral District	Electors	Turn-out	Candidates	Party	Votes	Percentages
Limehouse	29,275	33.4	Sir W. Pearce	Co. L	5,860	59.9
			D. D. Sheehan	Lab	2,470	25.1
			C. H. Rodwell	Nat. P	1,455	14,9
			Coalition Majority		3,390	34.7
Mile End	22,131	43.1	W. R. Preston	Co. C	6,025	63.2
			W. Devenay	Lab	2,392	25.1
			C. J. O. Sanders	L	1,119	11.7
			Coalition Majority		3,633	38.1
Whitechapel & St Georges	23,366	37.0	J. D. Kiley	L	3,025	34.9
			D. R. Ambrose	Lab	2,522	29.2
			G. A. Cohen	Co. C	2,489	28.8
			J. R. Raphael	Ind.	614	7.1
			Liberal Majority		503	5.7

Table 3-3 drawn from results published in Craig, F. W. S. *British Parliamentary Election Results 1918-49* 49-51

It can be seen from these results that: Limehouse was represented by a Coalition Liberal, Mile End by a Coalition Conservative, and Whitechapel by a Liberal. Interestingly, Mr Rodwell campaigned for the three main post-war policies of punishing the Kaiser, making Germany pay the full payment of the war and the expulsion from Britain of all Enemy Aliens. This did not gain him votes, as he attained less than 15 per cent of the vote in Limehouse. However, the weakness of his party would also have dissuaded people from voting for him. Mr Ambrose was commended for an "extraordinary good show", as "he captured the Catholic vote en bloc".[65] This shows the Catholics interest in Labour politics and validates Bertha Sokoloff's comments on the Catholic clergy taking an interest in

---

[65] *East London Observer* 4 January 1919

local politics.[66] Mr Kiley, the winning candidate for Whitechapel ascribed his victory "to his personality, to that remarkable number of friends who helped him", and to "the efficiency of the organisation for which Mr Sumper, with the experienced assistance of Mr C. T. Legg, was responsible".[67] Whitechapel was the only East London constituency in which a Coalition candidate, General Cohen, fared badly. Overall Stepney voted in the Coalition Government, which nationally was "returned with a vast and unreal majority", as it had 526 supporters in the new House, including 473 possessors of the "coupon", of which 127 were Liberals, 13 Labour and NDP, and 333 Unionists.[68]

The Labour party in Stepney during this election campaign had proved itself to be a serious contender. Throughout the Stepney constituencies Labour provided the leading opposition candidates and received 26.4 per cent of the vote.[69] Whitechapel & St George's had the greatest quantity of the electorate voting Labour, at 29.2 per cent.[70] The Coalition candidates received 51.4 per cent of the overall votes in Stepney, while Mile End gained 63.2 per cent of the vote for W. R. Preston, a Coalition Conservative candidate.[71] This shows the influence of the "coupon" with the coalition candidates and the general belief that as it was the Coalition Government who had won the war, it was now essential that they "should decide the terms of Peace".[72] However, the Coalition Government's failure in the immediate post-war years was to strengthen the Labour Party in Stepney and to turn the area into a Labour Heartland. Locally, the Labour Party was strengthened by unification, which by the local elections of 1919 saw Labour explode onto the political scene. As Julia Bush asserts:

> ... despite the lack of election success and the comparative weakness of working class organisations in the area, the Labour Party was making progress through socialist societies, trade councils and trade unions and was therefore busy laying foundations of future labour success.[73]

In the years to come, Labour candidates stood in increasing number at local elections in Stepney and thus Labour's postwar achievements were

---

[66] Sokoloff, op. cit. p69
[67] *East London Observer* 4 January 1919
[68] Morgan, op. cit. p42
[69] Craig, op. cit. 49-51
[70] Please see the above table on Parliamentary election results
[71] Craig op. cit. 49-51
[72] *East London Observer* 14 December 1918
[73] Bush, *Labour Politics and Society* Phd op. cit. p9

the "result of continuous growth rather than cataclysmic influence of war on party politics".[74] What the war had done was to focus attention on class divisions which underlay party politics and in doing so altered political attitudes. According to Bush the war had created more determined propagandists and more receptive audiences than Stepney and the East End had ever seen before.[75] The result was that with the end of the war, "East London refused to return to the fatalistic acceptance of poverty and helplessness which had characterized the area in 1914".[76]

Conclusion

The Representation of the People Act greatly enhanced the electorate, although on the day of the election many did not take their opportunity to vote due to the weather. For Stepney, this meant that over 25 per cent of the population could register their political views, whereas before the war only 10.2 per cent of the population had had the vote. The figure was particularly low because of the area's vast immigrant population – many of whom still had alien nationality status. However, with a second generation growing up as British citizens, one can begin to see the integration of immigrants into local political life, and thus the expansion of the electorate. The 1918 General Election was to mark the beginning of a new era for Stepney which saw the working classes taking a much greater interest in politics.

---

[74] Ibid. p9
[75] Bush, Julia, *Behind the Lines – East London Labour 1914-1919* (1984) pxxii
[76] Bush, *Labour Politics and Society* Phd op. cit. p361-2

CHAPTER FOUR

STEPNEY IN THE 1920S:
SOCIAL AND POLITICAL ISSUES

In this chapter the development of the Stepney Labour Party will be charted through focusing on local concerns: housing, employment and the Aliens Restriction Bill. Stepney also became a Labour heartland during this period. In 1919, the Labour Party made its first serious gains in Stepney. There had been no Labour councillors in 1912. In 1919 there were 42.[1] Nationally, it was estimated that Labour had gained over 900 council seats, of which just over 500 were in London,[2] thus indicating a potential stronghold for Labour in London. This success was regarded by Herbert Morrison, Secretary of the London Labour Party, as a consequence of "the general progress of political Labour organisations in London" and "the assistance of a far larger number of active workers in the fight than in any previous electoral contest". He also noted that through the columns of the *Daily Herald* the party was able "to record the progress of the fight".[3] The party's proposals with respect to housing, health and the sources of municipal revenue established the victory of the Labour party at borough level in Stepney. After 1920, however, the Labour Party had a competitor, on the left, the newly established Communist Party. Both vied for the same section of the electorate, but it was Labour who dominated the elections. However, as we shall see, the Communist Party in Stepney was to be a crucial campaigner for specific causes such as housing and employment throughout the inter-war years.

Local government, according to James Gillespie, "was used as a means to mobilise opposition to the politics of the central government".[4] This use of the labour movement can be viewed as the high point of postwar

---

[1] *Daily Herald* 4 November 1919
[2] Ibid. 5 November 1919 The number of Labour councilors had increased from 48 to 573 *Daily Herald* 7 November 1919
[3] Ibid. 7 November 1919
[4] Gillespie, James, *Economic and Political change in the East End of London during the 1920s* (Cambridge, 1983/4) Phd Abstract

London radicalism, since the "radical movement [was] apparently capable of transcending the barriers of ethnic, occupational and gender conflicts which had long served to stultify the London socialist movement".[5] In her article "Class, ethnicity and politics in the Jewish East End, 1918-1939", Elaine Smith attempts "... to disengage myth from reality and to show that the Jewish political experience in the inter-war East End was the product of a complex relation between class and ethnic factors".[6] In the inter-war years constituency level Labour parties endeavoured to transform themselves "from small groups of men, usually trade unionists, supervising electoral work at particular times, to larger and more continuous organisations of men and women with an array of campaigning, political social functions".[7] With people's leisure time increasing, Labour Party activists held social events to attract new members and to reaffirm the commitment of those already in the party; events such as "bazaars, raffles, jumble sales, sweepstakes and dances became standard and often profitable points of party activity".[8] Thus "political and social activity began to coalesce" and "social gathering doubled as fund-raising schemes that also included political speeches and propaganda".[9]

Support for the Labour party "provided the political conditions in which trade unions could be consolidated for the first time".[10] As one can see from the *Stepney Trades Council and Central Labour Party* report of 1919-20, 42 trade union branches and socialist organisations were affiliated to the Labour party, which represented a membership of over 12,000.[11] Also in 1919, Stepney had its first Labour Mayor, Clement Attlee. The Labour party commented that:

> ... Stepney Borough Council is now in the hands of the workers ... the Labour movement of Stepney was united and determined to win ... every seat was contested, and a uniform fight and a uniform programme was decided upon.[12]

---

[5] Gillespie, James, "Poplarism and proletarianism: Unemployment and Labour Politics in London 1918-1934" in Feldmen, David and Jones, Gareth Stedman, (ed.), *Metropolis London – Histories and representations since 1800* (1989) p163
[6] Smith, Elaine R., "Class, ethnicity and politics in the Jewish East End, 1918-1939" *Jewish Historical Studies* Vol XXXII 1990-1992 p355
[7] Worley, Matthew, "Building the Party: Labour Party Activism in five British Counties between the Wars" *Labour History Review* Vol. 70 No. 1 April 2005 p90
[8] Ibid. p86
[9] Ibid. p86
[10] Gillespie, James, *Economic and Political change in the East End* Phd op. cit. px
[11] Stepney Trades Council & Central Labour Party *Annual Report 1919-1920* p3
[12] Ibid. p3

With such a plan the result was a remarkable victory. 42 seats were won and six Labour Aldermen appointed.[13] Of those candidates voted onto the Borough Council, were Oscar Tobin as Chairman of the Public Health & Maternity & Child Welfare Committee, and Matt Aylward, as Chairman of the Works Committee, both of whom were founders of the Stepney Labour Party in 1918. Labour's Attlee held the position of Chairman of the Valuation Committee, in addition to his mayoral duties.

According to Geoffrey Alderman, the Jewish population, along with the Jewish trade unions, "played a crucial role in the establishment of the Stepney Central Labour Party in June 1918".[14] In the postwar period, young East End Jews "... threw themselves wholeheartedly into the local British political scene".[15] They did not regard this as "a denial of their Jewishness but as an outward expression of their Jewish identity in East End society".[16] Although the East End Jews constituted a separate ethnic group, they went "out of their way to emphasize that the political causes which they pursued were not in any sense parochial, but had a wider relevance for the whole of society".[17] It was this understanding of local issues which would gain them votes in future.

By the LCC elections of 1919, "Jewish Labour candidates were commonplace".[18] The Stepney Labour Party, for example, put up Isaac Sharp, a Jewish union activist who was local secretary to the Bakers Union and the Boot and Shoe Co-operative for the March LCC elections of 1922. He was, in the end, unsuccessful, and the election developed into a straight fight between two Labour men (C. Norman and J. Scurr) and two Municipal Reformers (G. Leigh and O. Wakeman).[19] By November the Stepney Borough Council elections had seen 10 Jewish candidates nominated by Labour, including Alfred Valentine, a former Progressive borough councillor and president of the Whitechapel and Spitalfields Costermongers Union.[20] He stood and won a seat for Labour in the constituency of Whitechapel Middle.[21]

---

[13] Ibid. p3
[14] Alderman, Geoffrey, *London Jewry and London Politics 1889-1986* (1989) p77
[15] Smith, Elaine R., op. cit. p359
[16] Ibid. p359
[17] Ibid. p366
[18] Alderman, op. cit. p78
[19] The Municipal Reformers gained the two seats with 54.6 per cent of the vote see Willis, Alan and Woollard, John, *Twentieth Century Local Election Results* Vol. 1 (2000) p22
[20] *East London Advertiser* 1 April 1922
[21] Willis & Woollard, op. cit. p250

In the 1919 Borough elections, the Union of Stepney Ratepayers (USR) put up candidates for election. The USR's president was Major Earl Winterton MP, a Conservative, who during the 1920s held office as parliamentary under-secretary for India.[22] The USR advocated amongst other matters:

> Such a reform of the present inequitable system of Equalisation of Rates as will give greater relief to the borough of Stepney and safeguard the autonomy and independence of the borough council; particularly the equalisation of rates of the various parishes comprising the borough of Stepney.[23]

The USR won seats in Mile End New Town, Whitechapel East and Whitechapel Middle. The programme for the Municipal Reformers was:

> To oppose the Labour Socialist attempts to secure control of the borough councils with the intent to use them as a means of establishing extreme socialism, and to resist any form of nationalising or municipalising British industries which will add to the burdens of the people and the cost of living.[24]

Again there was support for the equalisation of rates which, as we will discover, was to come to fruition two years later when it became Labour Party policy. The Labour Party stated their support for the "payment of [a] Trade Union rate of Wages". They insisted that, in the case of all contracts the contractor should observe "these conditions as well as the hours decided on by Trade Unions".[25]

Overall, there were 157 candidates for the 60 seats in the Stepney Borough Council election of which it was said:

> 34 USR candidates will take the field in the forthcoming Stepney Borough Council election, 21 candidates are contesting 6 seats in the St George's East North Ward, 12 licensed victuallers, 6 ministers of religion, 3 medical practioners and 1 barrister are numbered amongst the persons nominated for election as councillors of the borough of Stepney.[26]

---

[22] Rose, Kenneth, "Turnour, Edward, sixth Earl Winterton" (1883-1962) *Oxford Dictionary of National Biography* Oxford, 2004; online edn, January 2008

[23] *East End News* 3 October 1919

[24] *East London Observer* 25 October 1919

[25] Ibid. 25 October 1919

[26] Ibid. 25 October 1919

Of the Labour candidates standing, Mr Ware was a discharged and disabled soldier contesting the seat in Mile End Old Town (Centre Ward) on a Labour ticket, for which he won 51.1 per cent of the votes.[27] Prior to his election it was reported in the press that "canvassers for the Labour Party are knocking vigorously and withdrawing confidently. So says their official report which must be very encouraging if seriously considered".[28] This gives an idea of the growing air of confidence within the Labour Party at the time. In the Stepney Central Ward of Mile End Old Town the USR was also convinced they could win. It was reported that W. Hasted, T. Evans and W. Myers "are receiving strong support and an easy victory is predicted by those canvassing on their behalf".[29] However, their confidence turned out to be misplaced as none of them were elected. Labour took the majority share of the vote with 51.1 per cent. The USR received only 25.6 per cent.[30]

Oscar Tobin, secretary of the Stepney Trades Council and Labour candidate for Mile End Old Town (West Ward), said in October 1919 he was "confident in his belief that Stepney will have a "Labour" mayor next month".[31] His hunch was proved correct when Clement Attlee became mayor. He had not stood as a candidate in the borough elections, as Matt Aylward had vetoed a move by Tobin to make him a candidate, "on the grounds that his duty was to nurse the parliamentary constituency".[32] Instead Attlee managed Labour's campaign. The party campaign, according to David Howell, "emphasised the dire state of much East End housing and milked working-class disenchantment with the post-war record of the Lloyd George Coalition".[33] In Limehouse, Attlee's own territory, the Labour Party won all fifteen seats, something which "was noticed everywhere in the Labour Party".[34] Following these victories the next objective in London Labour circles became the establishment of "a strong force of socialist MPs in the national Parliament". As Kenneth Harris remarks:

---

[27] Ibid. 25 October 1919 and Willis & Woollard, op. cit. p220
[28] Ibid. 25 October 1919
[29] Ibid. 25 October 1919
[30] Willis & Woollard, op. cit. p220
[31] *East London Observer* 25 October 1919
[32] Harris, Kenneth, *Attlee* (1982) p45
[33] Howell, David, *Attlee* (2006) p16
[34] Harris, op. cit. p45

Attlee was seen as one of the prototypes of the desirable candidate: well-to-do middle-class intellectual, committed socialist, but neither Marxist nor pacifist, involved but disinterested, sober, respectable, trusted.[35]

The Labour leaders in each of the three divisions of Stepney all had equal claims to influence the choice of mayor. Whitechapel, the largest division, with thirty seats out of sixty on the council, had its Labour contingent divided between "immigrant Irish Catholics, working in various trades, members of a variety of unions, dominating about two-thirds of the seats; and Protestant members of the Transport and General Workers' Union, mainly dockers and drivers, who dominated the remainder".[36] The Jewish garment workers had the power of Tobin's citadel in Mile End and in Limehouse. As Harris says, "the ILP minority had now established an excellent working relationship with the Irish".[37] With such cohesion the Limehouse division was consequently the strongest and could therefore usually get its own way. As Attlee had served the borough well during the recent election, the Limehouse contingent pushed for his claim with Alyward, adding that "besides his other qualifications, Attlee would stand a better chance of getting the Tory minority on his side".[38] Attlee became the first Labour mayor for Stepney at the age of thirty-six and was also to be the prospective Labour candidate for Limehouse at the next parliamentary election.

In focusing upon local issues the Labour party managed to turn the East End's response to politics on its head. In contrast, as James Gillespie asserts, "before the First World War the response of East London's working class to all forms of party politics, Tory, Liberal, and Labour, was notorious for its crushing apathy".[39] He adds that the party also "developed their strength out of novel political answers to the specific problems of their local economy".[40]

---

[35] Ibid. p45
[36] Ibid. p46
[37] Ibid. p46
[38] Ibid. p46
[39] Gillespie, James, "Poplarism and proletarianism: Unemployment and Labour politics" op. cit. p164
[40] Gillespie, James, *Economic and Political change in the East End* Phd op. cit. px

Aliens Restriction Bill

Through the controversy surrounding the Aliens Restriction Bill, much about the activities of the Labour party are revealed. In October 1919, the *Aliens Restriction Bill* asserted that:

> ... no person, firm, or company ... should be entitled to employ, without the licence of the Secretary of State to be granted for special reasons, any aliens to a greater number than 25 per cent of the total number of the persons employed.[41]

Mr Kiley, Labour councillor for Whitechapel, opposed the amendment stating that "aliens were not voters", but instead asserted that "they were citizens who had played an important part in the commercial development of the country".[42] They were, he said, important for bringing skilled knowledge to Whitechapel and had been responsible for changing the area "from a place of poverty to a place of substantial prosperity, giving employment to our own people, and doing a large export trade as well".[43] This was particularly true of those working in cigarette and clothes making. Kiley also cited the war work of the "aliens" who produced some ten million sterling works of khaki uniforms, which the government would have otherwise had to go abroad for. Such a restriction, he argued, would have a negative effect, as "aliens" from both allied and enemy countries would be hoping for the League of Nations to produce a "larger degree of international friendship".[44]

Another clause of the Act which the Stepney Labour Party opposed was one for the deportation of certain Jews in the aftermath of the First World War. Jewish Labour councillors such as Alfred Kershaw and Oscar Tobin, by now Mayor of Stepney (1921–22), fought against the practice of deporting Jews without a judicial tribunal. Following the Aliens' Restriction Act of 1919, it became possible for the Home Office to deport Jews without trial. Prior to this a successful case made to the Appeal Court could reverse the decision of the Lower Court and thereby quash the recommendation for deportation.[45] The Home Office dealt with deportation cases by considering written statements, which would have provided many problems within Stepney's Jewish community as Yiddish was their mother

---

[41] *Jewish Chronicle* 24 October 1919
[42] Ibid. 24 October 1919
[43] Ibid. 24 October 1919
[44] Ibid. 24 October 1919
[45] HO 45/24765 Deputation from the Jewish Board of Deputies 18 June 1928

tongue rather than English. It was also argued that if the aliens had been British citizens the method of dealing with them would have been judicial. The fear of deportation was to hang over all aliens. With the passing of the 1919 amendment, former enemy aliens could be immediately deported unless "within two months after the passing of this Act [the 1919 amendment]" they made "an application to the Secretary of State in the prescribed form to be allowed to remain in the United Kingdom".[46] Stepney councillors Alberts and Kershaw strongly protested against the deportation of aliens without trial,[47] and in a letter they stated that:

> ... a serious situation had been created by the wholesale deportation of inoffensive alien Jews. In no case, it was declared, were reasons given for these deportations, which were effected in the most brutal and callous manner.[48]

Many of these aliens had been incarcerated in Brixton prison prior to their deportation. As one prison officer stated, that "he saw a lot of so-called Bolsheviks ... men who had lived ... in Stepney for years ... who were there through the despicable action of the Government".[49] The alien issue was a very contentious one, which could arouse much indignation in the East End. To take one example, an interview with Mr Booth, the magistrate at Thames Police Court, published in the *Evening Standard* of 21 April, stated that he "described the East End Aliens as contemptible, 'a race of liars' and as having evaded service by every means in their power".[50] During this period, condemnation of Jews featured in the House of Commons, as when Horatio Bottomley, local MP for Hackney, and an infamous scoundrel with a trail of disastrous get-rich-quick schemes to his name, asked the Home Secretary if his attention had been called to the observations of the Thames Police Court Magistrate regarding:

> The character of the aliens who had migrated into his district, possessing no loyalty to the flag under which they enjoyed comforts and liberties not known in their own countries, and who habitually lied and suborned to perjury in court, whilst at the same time following occupations which

---

[46] Ibid. HO 45/24765 18 June 1928
[47] Minute Book Vol 20 of the Council of the Metropolitan Borough of Stepney 1919–1920 20 April 1920 p4357 Alien Jews – Deportation of L/SMB/A/1/20
[48] *Jewish Chronicle* 30 April 1920
[49] Ibid. 30 April 1920
[50] Ibid. 30 April 1920

would be better filled by British subjects, and occupying houses solely needed by British workers; and what action, if any, he proposed to take.[51]

The magistrate's words show the contempt felt by some for the "aliens", views that could be applied just as much today towards the Bangladeshi community living in what was formerly Stepney. The Jews were overall, a community who had escaped persecution in their own country to come to Britain in order to start a new life. The Jews formed themselves into unofficial ghettos, speaking Yiddish and continuing traditional customs, such as marking the Sabbath on Saturday. It was not until a second generation emerged that a break with these traditions occurred. There was a partial abandonment of their Jewish heritage which was replaced with an interest in politics, as a way of making an impact upon the new community. Many younger Jews of this era refused to converse with their parents in Yiddish. Willy Goldman for instance, recalls how he made his parents "muster what English they could when desiring verbal communication".[52] Elaine Smith suggests that the rejection of the Yiddish language was due to its "negative associations with the poverty and persecution of East European ghetto life".[53] In rejecting one culture they cultivated another, which was "based around a network of informal social and political meeting places".[54] In doing so, they initiated the rise of a politically active group, one which became increasingly diversified.

Many Jews supported the Labour Party but those with extreme radical views joined the Communist party. Communist party members believed it stood for a pure form of socialism. Although this second generation of Jews were often alienated from both their parents and their peers, they managed to forge a new way of life centred on radical politics. It was through their political involvement in the struggle for better housing and employment that their integration into the community began.

---

[51] Ibid. 30 April 1920

[52] Goldman, Willy, *East End My Cradle: Portrait of an Environment* (1988) p12 Cesarani suggests that young British born Jews were cut off from the culture of their parents and yet they did not feel that they were fully accepted into British society. Thus the vacuum of culture and political leadership was filled by ideology and activism of the left. Cesarani, David, "The East London of Simon Blumenfeld's Jew Boy" *London Journal* 13 (1987) p51

[53] Smith, Elaine, op. cit. p357

[54] Ibid. p357

The Housing issue

Lloyd George's 1918-22 coalition government promised to build half a million houses which were worthy of the "heroes" who had won the war. This was because the Cabinet believed that without such physical reconstruction, the nation would follow in the footsteps of Russia and Germany into a Bolshevik revolution.[55] The slogan "fit homes for heroes" was adopted. The Housing Act of 1919 was to make local authorities the major suppliers of housing for the first time. The housing programme, according to Kenneth and Jane Morgan "… was a radical new departure in subsidised welfare" because the government "for the first time, recognised housing as a national responsibility and a vital component of public welfare policies".[56] Bentley Gilbert suggests that for many people, housing was reconstruction in the post war era.[57] There was therefore a vital need to get houses built. For Stepney, the clearance of large areas of slums followed by redevelopment was crucial.

The Housing Committee of Stepney estimated that the "total number of inhabited houses is 36,217 occupied by 56,949 families or separate occupiers, giving an average of persons per house 7.7".[58] Since the war overcrowding had intensified. In 1914 it was said, there were "a 1,000 new houses in the borough [and that] it is not likely that even that number would meet the demand for houses at the present time".[59] In Stepney, there were additional considerations to be made for the "definite communities bound by ties of race, religion and friendship, who would be very unwilling to be separated from these connections".[60] The lack of housing provision in Stepney was exacerbated during the war, as the building trade halted domestically. In the post-war era it was stated that the "whole area of Stepney needs to be demolished and reconstructed".[61] As was noted at the time by Stepney Borough Council this need was strengthened by "the lack of building laws and sanitary regulations". These conditions, the council felt, should no longer be tolerated.[62] Houses were overcrowded

---

[55] Senarton, Mark, *Homes fit for Heroes* (1981) p189
[56] Morgan, Kenneth & Jane, *Portrait of a Progressive: The Political Career of Christopher, Viscount Addison* (Oxford, 1980) p278
[57] Gilbert, Bentley B., *British Social Policy 1914-1939* (1970) p142
[58] Minute Book No. 2 of the Housing Committee of the Stepney Borough Council Mar 1920-Mar 1922 L/SMB/A
[59] Ibid. L/SMB/A Mar 1920-Mar 1922
[60] Ibid. L/SMB/A Mar 1920-Mar 1922
[61] Ibid. L/SMB/A Mar 1920-Mar 1922
[62] Ibid. L/SMB/A Mar 1920-Mar 1922

and cottages, which were originally built for one family, now housed two or three families. Baths were rare. The provision for proper cooking facilities was lacking and the lack of space within houses meant families often had to do without larders for storing food or even lacked a place for keeping coal.[63] A local council member commenting at the time on the lack of sinks, noted that:

> [the] difficulty of obtaining water at all is aggravated by the difficulty of getting it hot, coppers are placed in the kitchen-wash-house living room, and washing day is thus one of much upset and discomfort – seems superfluous to mention the need of food cupboards (larders is too grand a word) and of baths in the face of these elementary necessities.[64]

The Housing Committee of Stepney considered the conditions of the west side of the borough, which included parts of Spitalfields and Whitechapel, as the worst in the area. Official representations regarding two deprived districts within these parishes were made to the LCC in 1919. The first was the Bell Lane area, between Commercial Street and Wentworth Street. It was noted by the committee that, "Bell Lane and Butler Street is about 4½ acres in extent and comprises 286 houses and tenements and [that] the number of persons in occupation at the time of making the representation was 1,267".[65] This would have meant there were 218.6 persons per acre, which was more than 50 per cent higher than the borough average of 141 persons per acre at the time of the 1921 census.[66]

The district singled out by the committee for scrutiny was the Ellen Street area of the back of Church Lane, which was about 1¼ acres in size and included some 112 run-down houses for a population of 560. The number of persons per acre was 448, more than three times the census average of 141 persons per acre. This shows that there were pockets of extreme overcrowding within the borough of Stepney. In one five roomed cottage situated in an alley the Housing Committee were told that "two rooms were let by the tenant; in the remainder he, his wife, and eight children (eldest 15) together with a lad of seventeen – his wife's brother – lived".[67] The Whitechapel area would have been predominantly occupied by members of the Jewish community, as can be seen from the 1899

---

[63] Ibid. L/SMB/A Mar 1920-Mar 1922
[64] Ibid. L/SMB/A Mar 1920-Mar 1922
[65] Ibid. L/SMB/A Mar 1920-Mar 1922
[66] *Census of England & Wales 1921* (1922)
[67] Minute Book No. 2 op. cit. Mar 1920-Mar 1922

Jewish East London map.[68] The postwar problems also tell us something of the lack of planning in the pre-war years which allowed parts of Stepney to develop "a network of courts and by-ways with the consequent crushing in of houses and absorption of original air space".[69] An example of this was in Pell Street, St George's:

> ... where a street 620 ft long, covering not quite two acres has no less than 11 by-ways and courts. The combined road and pathways are nowhere more than 20 ft wide.[70]

The harsh reality of a land not fit for heroes can be appreciated if we consider the following scene, which took place at a funeral of one of *H M S Brokes* heroes who had come from a street known as Wapping Alley. The alley-way, the Borough's Housing Committee noted, was so narrow there was not:

> ... much opportunity to sight-seers. The home of this brave lad ... is one of the smallest in London – there are many as small – So small is it that it is impossible to get the coffin out of the front door, and the blue-jackets who came today and reverently covered it with a Union Jack had to bring it out by the window, which had been bodily removed for the purpose.[71]

The full description of the alley continues:

> ... it consists mainly of a row of houses built as an afterthought on part of what should be the back gardens of others and covering so small a space that a substitute for a backyard has been found across the alley in front. There they have their wash-houses and sanitary conveniences, and as if this might be too great a luxury for the provision of each, here and there a bit of the yard is cut off and a tiny cottage (4 in all) planted opposite the regular row. It was in one of these cottages that the naval hero had lived.[72]

---

[68] Jewish East London Map showing by colour the proportion of the Jewish population amongst residents of East London, on a street by street basis in 1899 reproduced by the Museum of the Jewish East End and Research Census from "The Jew in London 1901" by kind permission of the Guildhall Library, City of London

[68] 28,681 persons came from Russia (including Asiatic Russia) see *Census of England and Wales 1921*

[69] Minute Book No. 2 op. cit. L/SMB/A Mar 1920-Mar 1922

[70] Ibid. L/SMB/A Mar 1920-Mar 1922

[71] Report from an article in *The Star Newspaper* in Minute Book No. 2 op. cit. Mar 1920-Mar 1922

[72] Ibid. L/SMB/A Mar 1920-Mar 1922

The poor living conditions that people endured were remarkable. In another example, preserved in the committee's minutes "a family lodger was found sleeping in what was really a landing cupboard, without a window or fireplace".[73] It was reported by the Housing Committee that many cottages were extensively restored in the postwar period, and that their original conditions warranted the need for such constructive measures. In a certain row of four houses, two storeys high, the committee noted that they had "a 9ft wall in front and a 12ft wall behind" and "only one ha[d] an upper back window".[74] Commenting on the establishment of large buildings for mass dwelling, the Housing Committee remarked on the tendency of modern design "to get over economic difficulties by building these remunerative blocks".[75]

The Labour Party in Stepney was to strengthen its position by its association with slum clearance and new housing. The Housing and Town Planning Act, 1919, "was designed with a view to dealing with the shortage of housing accommodation which had arisen as a result of the war".[76] This was crucial for Stepney, with its shortage of housing for the people. It was proposed in the housing act that local authorities should adopt a scheme of "renovation" – whereby a local authority, instead of clearing a whole slum area should, "pull down houses here and there in order to better the ventilation or to give more open space, and improve the individual houses".[77] Stepney was the first borough to take advantage of the powers conferred by the Housing and Town Planning Act, which allowed them to conduct systematic sanitary inspections. The result was that an enormous number of insanitary dwellings were condemned as uninhabitable. Conditions in some cases were called "deplorable" thanks "to parts of the premises being demolished in compliance with dangerous structure notices served by the District Surveyors".[78] Tenants still remained in occupation of these premises, however, since there was a shortage of accommodation elsewhere.

Following the Housing and Town Planning Act, the borough was mapped out and houses were systematically inspected. Any necessary work was then carried out by the borough at the expense of landlords wherever necessary. This, it was noted in the *Stepney Trades Council and*

---

[73] Ibid. L/SMB/A Mar 1920-Mar 1922
[74] Ibid. L/SMB/A Mar 1920-Mar 1922
[75] Ibid. L/SMB/A Mar 1920-Mar 1922
[76] LCC 1922 *London Statistics* Vol XXVII 1920-21 (1922) p101
[77] HLG 52/934 Unhealthy Area – parts I and II of the Housing Act of 1890
[78] Minute Book Vol. 21 of the Council of the Metropolitan Borough of Stepney 1923–24 L/SMB/A/1/24 Monday 17 December 1923 p746

Central Labour Party Annual Report 1919-20, "struck terror in the hearts of the landlords and their agents".[79] Initially, it was reported that there were a large number of prosecutions but these dwindled quickly, and thus from a sanitary perspective the situation must have improved greatly. However, in 1921 Oscar Tobin stated his belief that the housing question still aroused considerable anxiety and that there was a good deal of overcrowding in the borough, in spite of the restriction of immigration. "This was due to two main causes" he said: "the suspension of building operations during the war and the growing industrialisation of certain portions of the borough".[80]

A problem encountered by the Housing Committee, while waiting for new accommodation to be built, was that suitable temporary accommodation was also in short supply. In November 1919, the committee began negotiations with the Guardians of the Parish of St George's-in-the-East. The committee desired the council to take over part of the house known as the "Able-bodied Men's Quarters". This was to "assist in accommodating persons displaced by reason of the council's building operation".[81] It was suggested that the council take on an agreement of three years, and that they should adapt the building at their expense, but that upon the termination of the tenancy, they should return the building back to a "condition answerable to the present state".[82] However, by March 1920 the council had received a communication from the clerk to the Guardians of the Hamlet of Mile End Old Town. Dated 23rd February, 1920, it referred to the conference a question regarding:

> ... one or more of the workhouses being given up for the purpose of relieving the shortage of housing accommodation; and mentioning that the Guardians do not, in view of the heavy cost that would be incurred in adapting the premises and the few families that could be accommodated, consider the proposal advisable.[83]

It was resolved by the Council that the communication should be received with deep regret.

The housing crisis also caused a major political fracas between Councillors Miriam Moses and Dan Frankel. Moses suggested that the

---

[79] Stepney Trades Council and Central Labour Party op. cit. p15
[80] *Jewish Chronicle* 25 November 1921
[81] Minute Book Vol 20 of the Council of the Metropolitan Borough of Stepney 1919–1920 L/SMB/A/1/20 Wednesday, 19 November 1919 p3984
[82] Ibid. L/SMB/A/1/20 Wednesday 19 November 1919 p3984
[83] Minute Book No. 2 op. cit. L/SMB/A Mar 1920-Mar 1922 L/SMB/A p11

council faced a difficulty in accommodating residents whose homes had been pulled down. She wanted to use her influence as a person of Jewish origins to ask the "wealthy people of the Jewish race to interest themselves in building houses in Stepney for the working classes".[84] This proposal was met with opposition by Councillor Dan Frankel, also Jewish, who argued that it would bring a racial element into the housing problem. Issy Vogler, another councillor, argued that "only a properly financed local authority could solve the problem".[85] The re-housing of residents was to become an ongoing issue as many residents had a strong desire to stay within the community surroundings that they knew. Housing continued to dominate local politics well into the post-Second World War period when many former residents of Stepney and its neighbouring boroughs were re-housed in new satellite towns, such as Dagenham and Harlow.

On 22 January 1924, the first Labour government took office, after the election and the defeat of Baldwin's Conservative Government in the House of Commons. Labour won all three constituencies of Stepney with Clement Attlee and Harry Gosling (elected in a 1923 by-election)[86] holding onto their seats in Limehouse and Whitechapel. In Mile End, John Scurr was elected with a majority of 1,478 votes. Some, like Richard Lyman, have argued that Labour's greatest weakness was the inexperience of its members. He makes the case that the first Labour government "marked a stage in the process of converting a band of missionary zealots into a responsible political party, bidding for the difficult and compromising job of governing the country".[87] John Shepherd and Keith Laybourn support this and point out that "most of the new Labour MPs, even those with local government experience, had only entered the Commons in 1922".[88] For Stepney, Attlee had entered the Commons in 1922, and was a junior minister in the 1924 Labour government. After just nine months in power the electorate were called to cast their votes once more and the Labour government was defeated. In Stepney, however, all three Labour candidates were returned. Nationally, the Conservatives gained 155 seats

---

[84] *East London Advertiser* 4 March 1933
[85] *Jewish Chronicle* 27 January 1933
[86] He took the place of Charles Mathew, who had died suddenly on 15 January 1923. Harry Gosling commented that "those election days in the East End were some of the saddest in my life" and that if he had "not known how wholeheartedly he would have urged me to carry on I should never have had the courage to go through with the fight". Gosing, Harry, *Up and Down Stream* (1927) p230
[87] Lyman, Richard W., *The First Labour Government 1924* (1958) p281
[88] Shepherd, John and Laybourn, Keith, *Britain's First Labour Government* (Hampsire, 2006) p48

and therefore returned to power. Labour lost 40 seats which were largely from marginal areas, where gains had been made the previous year. For example in Greater London representation fell from fifteen to seven. However, Wheatley's Housing Act of 1924 was "seen to be Labour's most striking success"[89] as it allocated subsidies to local authorities in order to build houses for rent. Also, measures were introduced to protect tenants from eviction, which would have a far-reaching impact upon Labour's working-class constituents as it enabled local councils to improve living standards. For Gosling, as Minister of Transport, there was the passing of the London Traffic Act, which *Punch* commented:

THE TRAFFIC PERIL.

ANCIENT ROMAN GEESE (*to* MINISTER OF TRANSPORT). "WE SAVED OUR CAPITOL, MR. GOSLING.
WE TRUST YOU WILL BE WORTHY OF YOUR NAME AND SAVE YOUR METROPOLIS."

Fig. 4-1 The Traffic Peril *Punch* 28 May 1924 (Reproduced with permission of Punch Ltd)

---

[89] Worley, Matthew, *Labour, Inside the Gate* (2005) p79

On evaluating the work of the Stepney Labour Council in the post-war
years, many felt that they had done their fair share to improve housing
matters. There were a number of large housing schemes completed in the
1920s. One of the most ambitious was that of Riverside Mansions in
which "894 persons were rehoused in a 2.07 acre area of 163 flats in six
blocks a project which was completed in 1928".[90] There were many
distinguishing features to this scheme: lock-up shops, an infant welfare
centre, a clubroom, gymnasium and drying room, and an electric passenger
lift, all of which were thought to substantially improve living conditions.
Also completed in 1928 was the Brunton Wharf Scheme covering 1.2
acres with 86 flats in three blocks: Brunton House, Hardie House and
Regent House, capable of accommodating 427 persons with ten lock-up
shops. The largest scheme undertaken was the Limehouse Fields Scheme,
which began after the First World War. This scheme was not completed,
however, until the 1960s.[91] Such building schemes show the Stepney
Labour Council's long-term commitment to the issue of housing.

Another reason for the quantity of properties built under Labour was
the great fire which occurred in 1926. The *East London Advertiser*,
reporting in January 1927, commented that the disaster:

> ... broke out during the biggest winter gale known for half a century.
> Before the Brigade could get to work, the fried fish shop where it began
> was blazing like a torch and a big slice of St George's was in flames within
> half an hour.[92]

The mayor, John Sullivan, said that it was the "biggest slum clearance
since the fire of London",[93] as it had cleared practically all the slum
properties between Tower Square and Limehouse church. Therefore, one
could argue that the catastrophe brought improvements, some of which
had been striven for over many years. "[O]ut of disaster good has come"
commented the Town Clerk. The mayor joked that "people don't want to
go to Ilford or Leytonstone to live now – nor even to Hampstead". "Our
workmen's flats which have been put up alongside the Stepney river
promenade are as good as any in London".[94] Almost a decade after the end

---

[90] Stepney Borough Council *The Metropolitan Borough of Stepney – Official
Guide 10th Edition* (1962) p101
[91] Ibid. p101
[92] *East London Advertiser* 15 January 1927
[93] John Sullivan was mayor from 1926 to 1927. Ibid. 15 January 1927
[94] Ibid. 15 January 1927

of the First World War, an ex-serviceman commented that "Homes for heroes" had "at last" been built.[95]

Employment and unemployment

In Stepney during the inter-war years poverty increased. Tailoring and cabinet-making, industries which employed many Jews were severely affected by the depression. One Stepney resident Solly Kaye, for example, had left school and entered the family trade of cabinet-making. However, work soon dried up leaving him unemployed. Kaye was fortunate to find alternative work as a furrier.[96] Overall though, the "unemployment rate at the end of December 1936 was at 10.3 per cent compared to 6.7 per cent for London as a whole".[97] The mayors of Labour borough councils felt that the government had yet to turn its attention to the rising numbers of unemployed persons in their area.

Demonstration at 10 Downing Street

On 18 October 1920 a group of demonstrators made their case to the Government on behalf of the unemployed of London. Fifteen mayors of London boroughs including Clement Attlee, Mayor of Stepney, had been granted an interview with Lloyd George, the Prime Minister. The fifteen mayors were all Labour Mayors who, under Herbert Morrison, the young Hackney Labour Leader, had "formed an association ... for the purpose of meeting together and co-ordinating policy".[98] Attlee was appointed as their chairman. The mayors were to be accompanied as far as the Embankment by orderly columns of demonstrating unemployed people, each mayor marching with the contingent from his borough. Attlee recalled leading "... the Stepney contingent – a big one – from Mile End Waste".[99] Attlee led the mayors into 10 Downing Street and the columns of unemployed demonstrators waited patiently on the Embankment. However, as the mayors emerged from 10 Downing Street, "the excitement grew amongst the unorganised crowd" and:

---

[95] Ibid. 15 January 1927

[96] IWM Sound Archives ID 9479 Solly Kaye

[97] Srebrnik, Henry Felix, *London Jews and British Communism, 1935–1945* (Essex, 1995) p28

[98] Attlee, C. R., *As It Happened* (1954) p49

[99] Ibid. p50

... men retaliated against the police with stone throwing. The mounted
police drew their batons and charged straight at the dense mass of
demonstrators, orderly marchers and disorderly crowd together. Battle
raged and casualties were heavy until Whitehall was cleared.[100]

Attlee, upon emerging from Downing Street:

... went round by George Street and found the Stepney contingent
marching down Bridge Street in perfect order with a police sergeant at its
head, about to be led into the scrimmage. I ordered the column to halt and
turn about and led them back to Stepney, thus saving some broken
heads.[101]

The following morning the London County Council (LCC) met and the
unemployed were in the gallery in full force, as they had heard of Lloyd
George's response to the London mayors' requests:

He had admitted that the Government had made promises to ex-soldiers,
which had to be kept, and [that] now he would request the LCC to start
work on the scheme for arterial roads with a 50 per cent Government
grant.[102]

The men in the gallery repeatedly chanted "We want grub, grub, grub".[103]
Harry Gosling, leader of the transport workers declared:

It is clear that the proceedings in Whitehall have lent the Government
wings. It is an awful feeling to know you are going home without any food
for the kiddies. You can't argue like well-fed people. The unemployed are
not going to stand still this winter and starve.[104]

This was followed by a shout from the gallery, "No, by God we are not".[105]
    The origins of this demonstration can be found in the Stepney Council
Minute books, which describe earlier meetings called to organise the
demonstration which took place at Deptford Council. In *As It Happened,*
Attlee recalls that he called the Conference on Unemployment on behalf of
the London Mayors, which was held in Shoreditch Town Hall.[106] Stepney

---

[100] Kingsford, Peter, *The Hunger Marches in Britain 1920-1939* (1982) p14
[101] Attlee, op. cit. p50
[102] Kingsford, op. cit. p14
[103] Ibid. p15
[104] Ibid. p15
[105] *Daily Herald* 20 October 1920
[106] Attlee, op. cit. p49

received a communication from the Town Clerk of Deptford on 29 July 1920:

> ... intimating that a Conference would be held in the matter of unemployment among ex-Servicemen and others on Friday 17 September 1920, and inviting the Council to appoint four delegates to represent them thereat; and in this connection, the Council being in vacation, Alderman Tobin, and Councillor Aylward, Lyons and O'Brien were requested by the Mayor to represent the Council.[107]

The Conference of Local Authorities of London carefully considered the means by which employment could be found for ex-Servicemen in some useful industry. It was decided that private enterprise would be "incapable of adequately coping with the problem of finding such employment at a reasonable standard of living".[108] The only course of action was to look to Government to take immediate:

> steps to provide employment by manufacture of the means of transport, reclamation of foreshores, a forestation, repaving of roads, development of agriculture on suitable land, improvement of canals, waterways etc, for the purpose of absorbing in some useful function not only ex-Servicemen but the whole of the unemployed.[109]

The second resolution of the Conference was:

> That a Committee consisting of the Mayor of each of the Metropolitan Borough Councils, or his nominee, and one representative of each of the Comrades of the Great War, the National Union of ex-Servicemen the National Federation of Discharged and Demobilised Sailors and Soldiers, and the London Trades Council, be appointed to organise a demonstration to Downing Street to convey the above resolution to the Prime Minister.[110]

At the Conference the date for the demonstration was fixed for Wednesday, 13 October, should it be convenient for the Prime Minister. Obviously the date was inconvenient, as the demonstration took place on 18 October. Stepney Council agreed with the resolutions passed at the Conference and the Mayor, Attlee, "expressed his willingness to represent

---

[107] Metropolitan Borough of Stepney Council Minutes Vol. 20 9th November 1919 to 8th November 1920 Monday 4th October 1920
[108] Ibid. 4th October 1920
[109] Ibid. 4th October 1920
[110] Ibid. 4th October 1920

the Council".[111] Interestingly, in the aftermath of the demonstration and
the LCC meeting, the Honourable Clerk of the Metropolitan Borough's
Standing Joint Committee, wrote to Stepney Borough Council to tell them
that he was "convinced that the scheme for the construction of arterial
roads would not provide a sufficient remedy". He stated that it was the
Joint Committee's judgement that "the solution was more likely to be
found in the provision locally of work of a useful character".[112] Kenneth
Harris suggests that Attlee considered these "some mild measures' to deal
with the unemployment problem – his concern, like that of the Conservative
and Liberal mayors, being less in creating work than in reducing the
burden of relief measures on rates".[113]

What the violent conflict of 18 October had achieved was to make the
men think about organising themselves. Also the resentment it produced
"gave rise to the first steps towards a national organisation of the
unemployed".[114] The ex-servicemen had found that the promised "fit land
for heroes" was not materialising and local committees springing up
spontaneously, joined together as the National Union of Ex-Servicemen.
During the same period the political commitment of the National Shop
Stewards' and Workers' Committee Movement (NSS & WCM) increased,
while its industrial influence shrank. Peter Kingsford cites a parallel link
with the formation of the Communist Party of Great Britain in 1920:

> Wartime experience in the Workers' Committees had led the shop
> stewards' leaders to believe that because those bodies were essentially
> rank-and-file ones, independent and powerful, they had a revolutionary
> potential far greater than the pre-war ideas of syndicalism and industrial
> unionism.[115]

The Russian Revolution of 1917 had persuaded the Workers'
Committees to see themselves as "soviets" who could overthrow capitalism,
as they had in Russia. Since the Communist Party had guided the soviets
to power, it was thought that a Communist Party was required in Britain.
In 1918, the British Socialist Party resolved that the time had arrived "for
the cooperation of all Socialist forces". This commitment culminated in
the Unity Conference of 1920 and the formation of the Communist Party

---

[111] Ibid. 4th October 1920
[112] Ibid. 1 November 1920
[113] Harris, op. cit. p47
[114] Kingsford, op. cit. p15
[115] Ibid. p15

of Great Britain (CPGB).[116] The Conference, as well as the formation of the CPGB was supported by the NSS & WCM of the eight members of the body's National Administrative Council, elected in 1917, six joined the Communist Party in January 1921.[117]

Three days after the "Battle of Downing Street" the newly formed Communist Party mobilised its members to circulate a call to give maximum support to the unemployed. As unemployment continued to rise, the struggle of the unemployed for fair treatment became more vigorous. There was the adoption of the slogan "Go to the Guardians", in reference to the marches made by many of the unemployed to the poor law offices. As Peter Kingsford notes in his book, *The Hunger Marches in Britain, 1920-39*, these men and women demanded unconditional relief and there were cases of people occupying the guardians' board room "until it was granted or until they were expelled by the police".[118]

By November 1920, the movement was claiming success for its agitation and organisation. As Kingsford notes, the government had by then "raised the rate of unemployment benefit to 15 shillings for men and twelve shillings for women".[119] However, after only three months unemployment benefits were reduced to their 1920 level, which served to fuel the movement's anger. Encouraged by the circulation figures of *Out of Work* and the *Communist,* after two further years of struggle the movement decided to organise the first national march which took place in September 1922. John Shepherd cites June 1921 as the date when planning for the NUWM's pioneer hunger march from London to Brighton began. George Lansbury addressed the NUWM marchers on Brighton beach. At the 1921 annual Labour party conference, held at Brighton Dome, Lansbury persuaded members to allow the young Communist Wal Hannington, and his associates to address the crowd.[120]

In 1921 Oscar Tobin was preoccupied with the problem of unemployment. 20,000 were unemployed in Stepney at the time. By 1931 the percentage of those claiming unemployment benefits had risen to a total of 77 per cent. The *New Survey of London Life and Labour* made the case that this showed the "rising tide of unemployment in submerging

---

[116] Ibid. p15
[117] Kendall, W., *Revolutionary Movements in Britain 1920-21* (1969) in Kingsford, op. cit. p15
[118] Kingsford, op. cit. p20
[119] Ibid. p21
[120] Shepherd, John, *George Lansbury* (Oxford, 2002) pp216-7

competent and steady workers".[121] Looking at monthly reports of the National Amalgamated Furnishing Trades Association (NAFTA) it can be seen that the situation was critical by January 1937. Out of the total of 1,254 members who made up the two East End branches, No. 15, East End United and No. 141, East London Organising 180 were unemployed.[122] This put rates of unemployment for branch No. 15 at 13 per cent, for branch No. 141 it was 18 per cent. For those people employed by the council, a minimum fixed wage of £4 was introduced, which was "perhaps the best work accomplished"[123] by the Labour council. Previously, council employees had been sweated and underpaid – a situation that was now rectified. In addition to this employees were to be granted a fortnight's holiday per year with pay, and all employees were allowed to be members of a trade union.[124]

Once John Scurr had been elected as a Member of Parliament for Stepney's Mile End constituency, he took up the question of unemployment in the House of Commons. Scurr asked the Minister of Labour, Sir A. Steel-Maitland, "how many men and women, respectively, were on the Employment Exchange register for the Metropolitan Borough of Stepney for the years 1922, 1923 and 1924".[125] The Minister of Labour circulated the following answer:

---

[121] Smith, Hubert Llewellyn, *The New Survey of London Life & Labour: Volume III Survey of Social Conditions Eastern Area* (1932) p14

[122] National Amalgamated Furnishing Trades Association (NAFTA) Monthly Report Vol 36 No. 1 January 1937

[123] Stepney Trades Council and Central Labour Party op. cit. p15

[124] Ibid. p15

[125] House of Commons, *Parliamentary Debates: Official Report 1924–5 Vol 181 2 March – 20 March 1925* (1925) p1308

Table 4-1 The Number recorded on the register of The Stepney Employment Exchange

Date (end of the month)		Number recorded on the register of The Stepney Employment Exchange	
		Men	Women
1922	March	6,601	1,868
	June	5,449	854
	September	5,677	802
	December	6,259	1,462
1923	March	6,498	1,555
	June	7,070	1,236
	September	5,980	1,175
	December	6,771	1,617
1924	March	6.153	1,176
	June	6,476	981
	September	6,547	1,037
	December	6,592	1,677

Figures from House of Commons *Parliamentary Debates: Official Report 1924–5 Vol 181 2 March – 20 March 1925*

As can be seen by looking at these figures, the approximate amounts of unemployment benefit paid in the area in the years 1922, 1923 and 1924 were £268,000, £270,000 and £288,000 respectively.[126] Because of the equalisation of rates, Stepney was able to pay out high levels of benefit. This was something John Scurr had been a campaigning for since the First World War when he had been chairman of the Stepney Board of Guardians. The first time he stood for Stepney Mile End in 1922 he lost to the Conservative candidate Sir W. R. Preston, but this result was reversed in 1923 and in the two subsequent elections of 1924 and 1929. Scurr's election agent was Israel Shafran, "a charismatic figure who was responsible for making the Mile End party the largest and most effectively organised

---

[126] Ibid. p1308

branch of the Labour Party".[127] Shafran brought a new professionalism to the Mile End Labour Party through his organisational skills. This resulted not only in the success of both Scurr and Dan Frankel, but also in the record membership numbers of just over 2,000 in 1930.[128] Also in this year, the Mile End Labour Club established in the Jewish neighbourhood of Stepney Green was "praised as the finest Labour Club in East London".[129]

According to *The Times,* the most important elections for London were the Poor Law Guardian elections. An article, dated March 1928, noted that "these bodies will be charged with the administration of poor relief during the next three years".[130] The Labour-Socialist policy, according to the London Municipal Society, for poor law was that:

> … an able-bodied man should, if unemployed, receive out of the rates and taxes as much as he could earn if engaged in his trade at trade union rates of wages.[131]

With so many people in the East End feeling the brunt of the depression, councils struggled to raise enough in rates to assist those unemployed and make necessary housing improvements. There was, it was acknowledged, an "accumulation of public works neglected during the war"[132] that needed immediate attention. The Labour controlled Stepney Council argued that less than a third of the amount of rates raised went to the council itself. They made their belief known that "there is no way out of the difficulty except the complete abolition of the rating system" and that, in the meantime, the equalisation of rates was adequate. In 1921, "Poplarism", the favouring of outdoor relief policies and rate equalisation, came to the fore. In the Poplar Rates Rebellion, John Scurr, along with 29 other council members, including his wife, were imprisoned for six weeks for refusing to collect the rates. Poplar and Stepney had recently had the largest increases in Poor Law relief. In 1920–21 Poplar had an expenditure of £64,237. This increased in the 1927–28 period to £564,778. Relief levels for Stepney rose from £112,094 in 1920-21 to £366,301 in 1927-

---

[127] Smith, Elaine R., "Jews and Politics in the East End of London 1918-1939" in Cesarani, David, *Making of Modern Anglo Jewry* (Oxford, 1990) p152
[128] *East London Observer* 18 January 1930 and *Stepney Citizen* February 1930
[129] *Stepney Citizen* January 1930
[130] *The Times* 28 March 1928
[131] Ibid. 28 March 1928
[132] Stepney Trades Council and Central Labour Party op. cit. p19

8.[133] However, circumstances by this time had also altered. The *East London Advertiser* commented that there was a "spreading of the burden of unemployment over the whole of London and the promise of an equalisation rate for London".[134] Stepney Council, although not totally satisfied with the outcome, reserved the right to take further action if necessary. Alderman Attlee seconded Alderman Tobin in the motion that the Labour Party was to continue campaigning to force the government to deal with the question of unemployment.

The formation of the Communist Party

Communism has been described by Ed Glinert as "an international phenomenon, a monster whose heart was in Paris, whose head veered from Moscow to St Petersburg, and whose hands could often be found in London".[135] In 1920 the "Hands off Russia" campaign had "wide-ranging support in the Labour movement".[136] The leaders of the Labour Party and the Trades Union Congress (TUC) set up a Council of Action. The council pledged to use "the whole industrial power of the organised workers"[137] to prevent Britain from being involved in war with Russia over Poland.[138] Dockers at the East India docks managed to prevent a ship, the *Jolly George*, from sailing by refusing to load its cargo of "munition intended by the government to assist counter-revolutionary forces in Russia".[139] Such action caused many people, both left and right wing, to anticipate the spread of revolution to Britain. However, due to British Communists complete lack of resources, Special Branch intelligence wrote that the chances of any group "launching a revolution in Britain were negligible".[140] The small, quarrelsome organisations of the far left, according to Martin Pugh, were "receiving subsidies from 'the eye of Moscow' and other

---

[133] *The Times* 28 March 1928

[134] This included the wealthier boroughs in West London, e.g. Westminster *East London Advertiser* 29 October 1921

[135] Glinert, Ed, *East End Chronicles* (2005) p188

[136] Wrigley, Chris, "The State and the challenge of Labour in Britain 1917-1920" in Wrigley, Chris (ed.), *Challenges of Labour, Central and Western Europe 1917-1920* (1993) p271

[137] Labour Party Conference Report 1921 p11

[138] Harry Gosling, later MP for Whitechapel and St George's, was on the membership list for the Council of Action under the TUC. Also see Macfarlane, L. J., "Hands Off Russia in 1920" *Past and Present* Vol. 38 No. 1 1967 pp126-152

[139] Pugh, Martin, *"Hurrah for the Blackshirts!"* (2005) p27

[140] Ibid. p27

exotically named sources".[141] Soviet agents tried to persuade the factions to join forces and eventually a Unity Convention, held in July 1920 led to the formation of the Communist Party of Great Britain.

The party was to the extreme of left-wing political thinking and was founded "in the aftermath of the 1917 October Revolution in Russia by a small group of British workers and intellectuals who considered themselves the advance guard of the proletarian revolution".[142] The aim of the party was to affiliate with the Labour Party – something which Labour refused to consider. In fact "after 1924 dual membership of the two parties was banned by the Labour Party".[143] However, the party's efforts to infiltrate larger organisations gave some grounds to the exaggerated right-wing fears about Bolshevik influence in the Labour Party, the trade union movement and the nationalist movements in Ireland and India.[144]

One of the founder members of the British Communist Party in 1920 was Palme Dutt who had served for two years on the Labour Party's advisory committee on international questions. He joined the Communists via the National Guilds League, one of the smallest groups fusing to form the new organisation, along with the British Socialist Party (BSP), the Social Liberal Party (SLP), and the Unity Committee.[145] However, by the summer of 1920 there were two British Communist Parties in existence. Sylvia Pankhurst changed the name of her Workers' Socialist Federation, an East London Federation which fought for full social, political and economic emancipation, into the "Communist Party (British Section of the Third International)".[146] "Parliament is a decaying institution", proclaimed Sylvia Pankhurst, "it will pass away with the capitalist system".[147] London was a central core of British Communist Party activity.

In order to appreciate the workings of the Communist party in Stepney, one must look ahead to the 1930s for examples. The East End was becoming a "political parade ground"[148] according to Joe Jacobs, Secretary to the Stepney Branch of the Communist Party. With its open-air meetings continuing almost nightly, he recalls how he:

---

[141] Ibid. p27
[142] Thane, Pat, *Cassell's Companion to Twentieth Century Britain* (2001) p108
[143] Ibid. p108
[144] Pugh, op. cit. p27
[145] British Socialist Party and Socialist Labour Party along with the Unity Committee. Pelling, Henry, *The British Communist Party – A Historical Profile* (1958) p11
[146] Ibid. p6
[147] *The Women's Dreadnought* 15 September 1923
[148] Glinert, op. cit. p211

... had become a 'full-blown' public speaker by now and found myself addressing street corner meetings, attending internal meetings and doing one or two other jobs all during the course of one evening, after a hard day's work in the workshops.[149]

There were also "small groups of Blackshirts, communists and Jews dotted around the streets, particularly those near Victoria Park, looking for action".[150] With such a political atmosphere on the streets, some members of the East London Communist Party raised their voices against Jacobs and others like him frequenting street corner meetings saying that "too much attention" was being paid to such meetings and demonstrations, "and not enough work in the trade unions".[151]

In Stepney this developed, over a long period, according to Jacobs, into a "bitter struggle ... between those who advocated what we loosely called, Trade Union activity and those who favoured street work".[152] The real basis for such division, as Jacobs saw it, was the fact that the "Trade Union people saw the organised Labour movement as the most likely place from which to develop the Communist Party and so hasten the revolution".[153] However, many of those who favoured "street work" saw "the future in terms of organisation of the unorganised, who were the overwhelming majority of the working class".[154] In theory a combination of both the development of the trade unions into an organised movement and the organisation of the "unorganised" working classes was agreed upon. In practice it was a division within the party.

Although the trade unions were predominately associated with the Labour party, increasingly some of them became receptive to Communism. After the United Ladies Tailors' Trade Union, the last independent Jewish union joined the National Union of Tailors and Garment Workers (NUTGW) in 1939, the NUTGW became pro-Communist. In the National Amalgamated Furnishing Trades Association (NAFTA) there were two main East End sections: No. 15 the East End United and No. 141, the East London Organising. Increasingly the Jewish community regarded the Communist party as their "only form of self-defence".[155] It is unsurprising, perhaps, that section 15 of NAFTA, a Jewish section, became dominated

---

[149] Jacobs, Joe, *Out of the Ghetto* (1978) p113
[150] Glinert, op. cit. p211
[151] Jacobs, op. cit. p118
[152] Ibid. p129
[153] Ibid. p129
[154] Ibid. p129
[155] *Jewish Chronicle* 15 January 1937

by Communist leaders including Sid Fineman, Julius Jacobs, and his father Morris – all of whom urged anti-fascist action.[156] Even though Communist Party leadership was infiltrating trade unions, when it came to local elections the Communist sections were still advocating Labour candidates.

It was Sid Fineman who accepted Sam Clarke, a young East End Cabinet-maker, as a member of the East United Branch No. 15 of NAFTA. By then Fineman was the district organiser, and branch No. 15 was "well known for its left-wing views".[157] The Union also had a social function. It hired a room in the Netherlands Club in Bell Lane, where it held dances and where as the East End cabinet-maker Sam commented "Beer was served and people were eating pickled cucumbers and onions".[158] Once he had become a member of the Union, Sam was advised to go to Maples where they required cabinet-makers in their factory at Highgate. Sam was taken on at Maples at the Union rate of 1s, 7d per hour, "I was proud to earn a family man's wage, he recalls".[159]

The Stepney Branch of the Communist Party had smaller group meetings within the area, known as cells. Joe Jacobs's cell met at the Michaelsons' place, which was a top floor flat at the corner of Nelson Street and Turner Street. Other members of this cell were, Nat Cohen, Manny Slazberg, Hetty Stern, Harold Cohen and Joe Jacobs, from the International Labour Defence (ILD) Party faction. Also, included in the Jubilee Street cell, were Sam Berks, Leon Grill, "Mad Mick" and Alex Sheller. Other members from the ILD were Sam Master, "Tubby" Goldman and Sam Waldman.[160]

As previously shown, the Communist party was an active force in the unemployed workers movement during the interwar years. They also had considerable influence within certain trade unions, such as the National Amalgamated Furnishing Trades Association (NAFTA) and the National Union of Tailors and Garment Workers (NUTGW). The party's opposition to Franco in the Spanish Civil War and their broad anti-fascist stance attracted many members. As we shall discover in chapter six, the anti-fascist movement and the formation and activity of the Stepney Tenants Defence League made the Communist Party a strong political force within the area. Intelligence reports at the time suggested that the General Strike was "financed partly by the transfer of funds from the Soviet Union

---

[156] Srebrnik, Henry, *London Jews and British Communism* op. cit. p22
[157] Laurie, Kendrun (ed.), *Sam: An East End Cabinet-maker* (1983) p21
[158] Ibid. p21
[159] Ibid. p21
[160] Jacobs, op. cit. p118

amounting to £380,000".[161] However, the Conservative government rejected claims that money on this scale could have been contributed by Russian trade unions and their members. Subsequent investigation revealed that between 1920 and 1922 the Communist Party had received £61,500 from Russia, followed by substantial sums by the Communist International during 1925, 1927 and 1928. Such funds were transferred via the Narodny Bank, where several clerks held the money in special accounts before it was passed to the British Communist Party,[162] thus showing the potential influence of Russia on the General Strike.

It was also in the aftermath of the General Strike that female membership reached its height of 21 per cent at the end of 1926. Again, most of these new recruits did not stay.[163] By the mid-1930s membership was on the increase once more due to the rise of fascism, as we shall discover in chapter six. It would appear that the Stepney Labour Party had an advantage over its Communist rivals. The Stepney Labour Party had been founded in 1918, whereas the Communists had not formed until 1920. Labour had another advantage due to the Communist Party's lack of candidates at elections. This forced the Communist Party to pledge its support for the Labour Party when there was no Communist candidate. By the 1937 LCC election the Communist Party used the slogan "No Victory without Unity!" stating that "without the help of all working class forces, especially the Communists, Labour cannot win".[164] Although the number of party members was small overall, they took an active role in the party. For example, as we have seen, Joe Jacobs work for the Communist party took up all his free time. The Stepney Communist Party "attracted only a small number of East End Jews and they were mainly the hard core of ideologically committed individuals who had staffed the various revolutionary groups in the East End before 1918".[165] Louis Kenton also emphasises this by stating that the Stepney Communist Party was "amongst the most active branches in the country".[166] However, Kenton blurs the line between Labour and Communist party membership in the

---

[161] "General Strike: Russian Gold" Baldwins Papers 12 in Pugh, Martin, *"Hurrah for the Blackshirts!"* (2005) p94
[162] Ibid. Memorandum 1928 Baldwin Paper 12 p94
[163] Hunt, Karen and Worley, Matthew, "Rethinking British Communist Party Women in the 1920s" *Twentieth Century British History* Vol 15 Nov 1 2004
[164] Jacobs, Julie, *The LCC Elections* Discussion No. 12 (London, Communist Party) Feb 1937 p4
[165] Smith, Elaine R., "Class, ethnicity and politics in the Jewish East End" op. cit. p363
[166] IWM Sound Archives ID 9341 Louis Kenton

East End saying that he joined the Communists because a few other lads he knew were in it, but that this was no sharp decision. He could have easily been joining the Labour party.[167] The blurring of lines between Communist and Labour members can be seen in this comment made by Geoffrey Alderman in *London Jewry and London Politics 1889-1986* that in 1918 "it was possible to believe in Socialism by revolution – if all else failed – and yet be a member of the Labour Party".[168]

Conclusion

The major issues for Stepney during this period were housing, employment and the Aliens Restrictions Bill. The Labour party in Stepney, as we have discovered, was a key group in campaigning on all of these issues, through the work of various councillors who championed individual causes. For example, Oscar Tobin and Alfred Kershaw, both Jewish Labour councillors, fought against the practice of deporting Jews without a judicial tribunal. The Labour mayors of London were led into 10 Downing Street by Stepney's mayor Clement Attlee, on behalf of the unemployed of London. Once Labour candidates in Stepney became Members of Parliament, they could then take Stepney's problems and issues into the House of Commons. An example of this in practice is the case of John Scurr taking up the question of Stepney's unemployed. Such events clearly showed the determination of Stepney's Labour councillors to improve the conditions within the borough.

In the case of housing, Stepney was the first borough to take advantage of the powers, conferred by the Housing and Town Planning Act of 1919, to conduct systematic sanitary inspections, resulting in an enormous number of dwellings being declared uninhabitable. It was not until after the Second World War, with the almost total redevelopment of the area, that Stepney finally overcame its problem of overcrowding. In post First World War Stepney, there were pockets of chronic overcrowding, as in the case of the Ellen Street area where there were 448 persons per acre. When this is considered in comparison to the average for Stepney of 141 per acre at the time of the 1921 census, it is virtually impossible to imagine how many of Stepney's residents could have coped in such cramped and poor conditions. In such an area houses were eventually pulled down "here and there in order to better the ventilation or to give more open space, and

---

[167] Ibid. 9341 Louis Kenton
[168] Alderman, Geoffrey, *London Jewry and London Politics* op. cit. p77

improve the individual houses".[169] There were also many new housing projects undertaken in these postwar years. One of the largest was that of Riverside Mansions which was completed in 1928 and accommodated 894 persons in 163 flats divided into six blocks of an area of 2.07 acres.[170] There really was an attempt by Stepney borough council to make the 1918 election campaign slogan "a fit land for heroes" a reality.

Throughout the post-First World War period, the Labour Party had to contend with the Communist Party. For the first four years of its existence the Communist Party was desperate to affiliate with the Labour Party, but after 1924 Labour banned dual membership of the two parties. In Stepney, although the Communist Party membership was small in number, those who did belong to the party were loyal and committed to the cause, as we have discovered by looking at the memoirs of Joe Jacobs who was secretary to the Stepney Branch of the Communist Party. In 1920, the Communist Party was active in the unemployed workers' movement. It was during the 1930s, however, that the Stepney Branch came into its own with the formation of the Stepney Tenants Defence League and the party's fight against fascism. It can therefore be argued that the 1920s in Stepney belonged primarily to the Labour Party, which established itself as a party that stood for the working classes.

---

[169] HLG 52/934 Unhealthy Area – parts I and II of the Housing Act of 1890
[170] Stepney Borough Council *The Metropolitan Borough of Stepney* op. cit. p101

CHAPTER FIVE

THE GENERAL STRIKE OF 1926 –
A PROFILE OF STEPNEY:
HOW THE STRIKE WAS ORGANISED LOCALLY

This chapter will assess the impact of the General Strike on Stepney including its impact on the docks, and by examining the role Clement Attlee took locally in negotiating a supply of electricity to the London Hospital. The General Strike was called by the Trade Union Congress (TUC) in an unsuccessful attempt to force the government to act to prevent wage reductions and worsening conditions for the coal miners. In Stepney, the dockers striking in support of the miners caused many problems. With no dockers to unload the ships, strike-breakers, in the form of the army and students, were called in. However, these temporary replacements for the dockers were much slower at unloading. Also, when transporting the goods from the docks to Hyde Park for distribution, the strikers delayed the lorries and therefore hindered the supply of goods to the rest of London.

The General Strike has been traditionally seen as "...the logical, although rather delayed, culmination of an epoch of strikes and class antagonism, which began before the First World War and was renewed with even greater vigour after the war ended".[1] In the years prior to the First World War, the people of Stepney developed a network of practical mutual aid. In the case of 1889, the Jewish tailors' strike, which began on 26 August, followed in the wake of the dock strike earlier the same month. An example of solidarity amongst the Anglo-Irish and Jewish communities is illustrated by an incident that took place on 26 September 1889 at the tailors' strike headquarters, in the White Hart Public House, Greenfield Street. On this occasion the Dock Strike Committee, handed over £100 to the treasurer of the Jewish Tailors' Relief Fund. This was exactly twelve days after the dockers had made a favourable settlement with the

---

[1] Morris, Margaret, *The British General Strike 1926* (Pamphlet – General Strike Series No. 82) (Great Britain, 1973) p12

employers after their own strike, and, as Anne Kershen argues, this militancy and "mutual sympathy proved catalysts for a future common accord between East End Jewish and Irish workers".[2]

However, the concentrated and growing visibility of foreigners on the streets of East London gave rise to heightened anti-alienism. In 1903, the government appointed an Aliens Commission to investigate the impact of the alien presence. This was in response to demands from trade unionists and politicians such as Major William Eden Evans Gordon, a Conservative MP for Stepney and founder of the British Brothers League in 1901, for an end to pauper alien immigration. The Aliens Act passed in 1914 and 1919[3] meant that from 1914 onwards, those wishing to enter Britain, had to conform to the requirements set out in the acts.[4] For those who had previously entered Britain, and were living in Stepney, mutual sympathy between Jewish and Irish workers ensued.

During the 1912 labour disputes, for instance, the Jewish tailors and Anglo-Irish dockers raised money to support each other and fought side by side. An example of support shown by Jewish people to their Irish neighbours can be seen during the dock strike when Milly Rocker went to the dock area with one or two other women to give help to the dockers children. Rudolf Rocker (her husband) recalls that the children were "terribly undernourished ... barefoot, [and] in rags". In all, over 300 dockers' children were placed in East End Jewish Homes. Local shopkeepers donated shoes and clothes. Such work according to Ruldolf Rocker "did a great deal to strengthen the friendship between Jewish and non-Jewish workers".[5] Rudolf Rocker records that "joint strike meetings were held, and the same speakers spoke at huge joint demonstrations on Tower Hill and on Mile End Waste".[6] Under the leadership of the anarchist Ruldolf Rocker a third great strike by the Jewish tailors ended in triumph, as it brought "... the death-blow to the sweatshop system".[7] Action such as this

---

[2] Fishman, William J., "Allies in the Promised Land: Reflections on the Irish and the Jewish in the East End" in Kershen, Anne J., (ed.), *London: The Promised Land? The Migrant experience in a Capital City* (1997) p47
[3] The first Aliens Act was passed in 1905
[4] Kershen, Anne J., "Immigrants, Sojourners and Refugees: Minority Groups in Britain, 1900-1939" in Wrigley, Chris (ed.), *A Companion to Early Twentieth-Century Britain* (Oxford, 2003) pp142-3
[5] Rocker, Rudolf, *The London Years* (California, 2005) p131
[6] Ibid. p129
[7] Ibid. p131

was, as Kershen remarks, "in accord with Rocker's aim of uniting Jewish and Gentile workers in their struggles for better conditions globally".[8]

Not everyone agreed with Rocker's open and peaceful propaganda. Tchishikoff, a fellow anarchist, was contemptuous of his stance, believing that "expropriations" or armed raids on banks or commercial institutions which had occurred in Russia to obtain funds for revolutionary activities were far more productive. That way, he said, the Tsar would be paying for the revolution. Therefore the power-struggle between Bolsheviks and Mensheviks, which was tearing Russia apart, was brought to the East End. As William Fishman argues, the "young expatriates from the Russian underground were the most active and the most dangerous", as they "could not adjust to a freer life in London".[9] For example, in 1910-11 the Houndsditch murders and the subsequent siege of Sidney Street occurred. These two incidents drew the nation's attention to the level of anarchism that was occurring in the area, as *The Times* chronicled both events.[10] Fortunately, terrorists were generally the exception rather than the rule. Thus with Rocker at the foreground, with his continual argument that "terrorism was criminally counter-productive",[11] the likes of the Jubilee Street Club were able to carry on.

Fishman argues that by the end of 1910 "the *meschuggena* (crazy) Anarchists were almost accepted as part of the East End landscape, until the Houndsditch murders projected them onto the national scene".[12] Then the newspapers began to launch attacks on these people. For example, in the *Jewish Chronicle* of 6 January 1911 it was asserted that, "A piece of Russia has been transplanted to London – and the English authorities have, alas, felt themselves compelled to use methods gravely resembling Russian procedure to cope with it".[13] The problem was that the anarchists were now dividing, into those who followed the *meschuggena* Anarchists and others who supported Ruldolf Rocker and his followers of peaceful activism. This, of course, would prove to be very counterproductive as a divided force can never be as strong as a united one. Therefore, such conflict and activity marked the beginning of the downfall of the anarchist

---

[8] Kershen, *London: The Promised Land?* op. cit. p47
[9] Fishman, William J., *East End Jewish Radicals 1875-1914* (1975) p269
[10] See *The Times* 1910-1911. For a full explanation of these two events see Rumbelow, Donald, *The Houndsditch murders and the siege of Sidney Street* (1988)
[11] Fishman, *East End Jewish Radicals* op. cit. p271
[12] Ibid. p287
[13] *Jewish Chronicle* 6 January 1911, p5

movement, which later saw the youngsters of the 1930s turning their backs on traditional Jewish life.

Fishman asserts that in the two years between the 1912 Dockers' Strike and the outbreak of World War One, "the peak period of Anarchist activity..." was registered, and that "... Rocker reached the zenith of his influence".[14] Also during this period, trade union membership expanded dramatically. Thus, with such great popularity and influence the anarchists had almost achieved respectability. But, as Rocker was to muse, "who could have foreseen the collapse which followed the beginning of the Great War?"[15] In 1914 the Anarchists were the most dynamic element of the East End's political life, but by the 1920s they had already become an anachronism, and were "shadowy ghosts of another era".[16] Events during the First World War had aided the demise of the great anarchist movement. When Britain declared war on Germany, on 4 August 1914, this was to be the death of anarchism in the East End. On 2 December 1914 Rocker was arrested in his flat at St Dunstan Houses. This marked the beginning of a four year internment from which he would never return to the East End. He was repatriated to Germany via Holland in 1918. His exit resulted in the end of his group and of the strong London Jewish anarchist presence.

The Great War had a paradoxical effect as it "brought to a sudden end a period of widespread industrial strife which appeared likely to produce a general strike organized by the Triple Alliance".[17] The Miners' Federation of Great Britain (MFGB), National Union of Railwaymen (NUR) and the National Transport Workers Federation (NTWF) formed the Triple Alliance. Originally the idea behind the alliance was for each union to draw up a programme of demands "which would be simultaneously submitted to the respective employers".[18] The Triple Alliance never actually functioned in this way, "but the threat of joint action remained a real one until 1926".[19] According to Philip Bagwell "the failure of the Alliance to embrace all organised workers in the three major groups of coal mining, railways and transport undoubtedly reduced its appeal to the rank and file".[20] Harry Gosling, representative of the transport workers and

---

[14] Fishman, *East End Jewish Radicals* op. cit. p300
[15] Ibid. p301
[16] Ibid. p302
[17] Mason, Anthony, *The General Strike in the North East* (Hull, 1970) p1
[18] Ibid. p1
[19] Ibid. p1
[20] Bagwell, P. S., "The Triple Industrial Alliance, 1913-1922" in Briggs, Asa and Saville, John (ed.), *Essays in Labour History 1886-1923* (1971) p124

MP for Whitechapel & St George's (1924-9), reiterated this when he
wrote: "the alliance was not a compact body and never acted as such".[21]
With the end of the war, the immense psychological impact on the
men who had taken part now convinced them "that they were entitled to
fair treatment and were prepared to act to get it".[22] As we have seen, all
men over 21 years of age were rewarded with the vote. During the 1918
election campaign they were promised a "fit land for heroes" but in the
postwar years this promise was not fulfilled. Instead there was widespread
unemployment and a lack of housing improvements. The people of
Stepney and fifteen other London boroughs were called by the mayors of
these Labour boroughs to demonstrate at 10 Downing Street at the
beginning of the hunger marches in 1920. This was not a simultaneous
national demonstration, although there were demonstrations across the
country. The General Strike in contrast, was an all encompassing event:

> No other event between the two World Wars stirred so many people into
> activity. No other event had such an effect on the daily routines of the
> whole community. Nor was there any other occasion when the population
> was so sharply divided along class lines. The vast majority of manual
> workers supported the strike but most of the middle and upper classes
> wanted to see it defeated and many of them were eager to act as strike
> breakers.[23]

Margaret Morris argues that "the General Strike ... was a political
strike, and needed to be pursued as such if it was to make any progress".[24]
But the strike failed to help the miners and "left behind a mood of
frustration within the ranks of the labour movement".[25] The origins of the
General Strike are found in the summer of 1925 when the miners refused
to consider wage reductions or longer working hours and the owners
refused to consider anything else.[26] The General Council of the Trade
Union Congress (TUC) proposed that a "co-ordinated action" be taken,
which was put to the Trade Union on 30 April and adopted 1 May.[27]
On 1 May 1926 more than 800 delegates gathered in London at a
Special Conference of Trade Union Executives, and "voted overwhelmingly

---

[21] Gosling, H., *Up and Down Stream* (1927) p176
[22] Morris, op. cit. p14
[23] Morris, Margaret, *The General Strike* (England, 1976) p11
[24] Morris, *British General Strike 1926* (Pamphlet) op. cit. p33
[25] Ibid. p34
[26] Mason, op. cit. p6
[27] TUC General Council *The Mining Crisis and the National Strike* (London, TUC, June 1926 p32 A)

by 3,653,529 to 49,911 to empower the TUC to call a national shut-down if the coal owners' lock-out did not end within two days".[28] The General Strike began at a minute to midnight on 3 May 1926.

The East End was crucial to the success or failure of the General Strike due to the docks being one of the largest pawns for the government in the industrial unrest. Therefore, the government's plan was to make an example of the docks and portray the East End as a battleground, hoping that if it was conquered then the rest of the nation would crumble and fall. The nation's attention focused upon Stepney and the dockers who held up the food convoys at the London Docks. This resulted in army support being called in, in order that food could reach Hyde Park and be distributed. The first convoy that arrived at the docks to collect food consisted of troops from the 1st Battalion of the Grenadier Guards along with 20 armoured cars and 100 lorries manned by public schoolboys and students. The convoy managed to move a mere 150 tons of meat compared with the thousands that were generally moved out of the docks. The food convoys travelled past booing crowds along Victoria Dock Road, Barking Road, and Canning Town. As Sean Berrett and Tony Matthews commented "the police moved in with truncheons and for several days there were running clashes".[29] There were numerous arrests. Amongst those arrested by police were Albert Edward Thary, 28, and Harold George Cooper, 24, who were charged at West Ham Police Court, "under the Emergency Powers Act with attempting to commit an act calculated to delay the means of transporting food supplies".[30] The crowd had stopped a lorry, laden with food supplies, from going eastward. The bonnet was lifted and a man began to interfere with the mechanics, but when Constable Dooley had attempted to seize the man the crowds intervened enabling him to escape.

The East End strove to be well organised during the General Strike. Locally, unofficial strike bulletins, such as *The Poplar Strike Bulletin, The Live Rail* and *The Lansbury Bulletin* were distributed amongst the workers in order to keep them informed of the situation. Such bulletins were necessary due to the lack of plans made for the running of the strike by the General Council of the Trades Union Congress who left the responsibility of the day-to-day organisation of the strike to local trade union officials, branch officers and strike committees. Workers were also encouraged to

---

[28] Shepherd, John, *George Lansbury: At the Heart of Old Labour* (Oxford, 2002) p225
[29] Berrett, Sean and Matthews, Tony, *The Express* Week ending 7 May 1976 – 50th anniversary piece to the General Strike
[30] *East London Advertiser* 15 May 1926

wear their war medals to make the troops understand the position they had
been driven to. There was also support for the General Strike on a global
level. Australia's railway men sent a cable to Great Britain offering their
assistance to the strikers. Supporters in South Africa particularly Rand
miners, also pledged support. The International Transport Workers'
Federations of Norway, Sweden, Denmark and Finland "telegraphed their
readiness to refuse to unload British trawlers in Holland". They had, they
said, "forbidden Dutch trawlers to proceed to Great Britain".[31] Also, *Strike
News* reported, the "All-Indian TUC has cabled, expressing the Indian
Workers sympathy and wishes for the success of the strike and offering
co-operation in this great fight for the maintenance of life". The Palestine
Federation of Labour, too, cabled "£100 in support of the Miners".[32]

For some people, the General Strike was an opportunity to take
advantage of "get rich quick" schemes. People "brought out old lorries,
mostly of one ton size and tried to use them as buses. 'Manor Park stop
anywhere' ran the legend upon one of them, and trade was brisk".[33] When
the make-shift buses got as far as Mile End Road, however, "large groups
of men jumped upon the footboard and back of the cars and forced them to
stop and refused to allow them to proceed until their passengers had
alighted".[34] This was to stop workers breaking the strike.

The Labour councils of Stepney, Poplar, West Ham, Walthamstow and
elsewhere showed their backing for the strike by cutting off the electric
power to factories and public buildings. For Clement Attlee this caused a
dilemma. As a Labour Member of Parliament he wondered whether he
should support the strike. In parliament during the nine day long strike
Attlee did not take part in any parliamentary debates.[35] Locally he was
involved in the strike because he was chairman of the Stepney Borough
Electricity Committee. Within the borough was the London Hospital,
which was also threatened with the cutting off of electrical power. With all
members of the Electrical Trades Union being given orders to finish work
at 12 o'clock on the night of 3 May 1926, it was essential to negotiate the
continuation of power to the hospital. The Electrical Power Engineers'
Association resolved that "essential public services in connection with the

---

[31] *Workers Bulletin* No. 3 10 May 1926
[32] *Strike News* Stepney Council of Action, St George's Town Hall, No. 8 Monday
12 May 1926
[33] *East London Advertiser* 8 May 1926
[34] Ibid. 8 May 1926
[35] There is no reference to Clement Attlee in the *Parliamentary Debates: House of
Commons* Vol 195 Monday 3 May to Friday 14 May 1926

supply of electrical energy should be maintained".[36] The Committee desired the avoidance of the electricity generating station being taken over by volunteer workers, as this might result in irreparable injury to the plant and equipment. The volunteers were mainly students and army personnel. After meetings with the union and committee it was agreed that electrical supply would remain on until six o'clock the following morning.

By Thursday, 6 May, Attlee called the attention of the committee to "… the unremitting efforts made by him to ensure a supply of electrical energy to the London and other hospitals. He also drew their attention to the "agreement arrived at for the giving of such supply to the London Hospital".[37] Complaints about electricity supply being withdrawn were met by Attlee's reply:

> … my committee would remind you that the first obligation of the council is to preserve order and peace and ensure the public safety … The action of the electricity committee has been actuated by a desire to carry out this primary obligation of civic government, and in their opinion their action has been of the greatest value to the people of Stepney.[38]

The London Hospital it was "announced over the wireless was unable to keep open its outpatient department".[39] In a report from Stepney on 6 May it was stated that "the assertions made in the *British Gazette*, that the outpatient Department has been closed down owing to lack of electric light is untrue".[40] The *British Gazette* was a government backed paper under the direction of Winston Churchill. However, the *East London Advertiser* reported that the out-patient annexe had had to close down as there was "no power or light, no X-ray or light for the sun-ray or for the ear, throat and nose".[41] The paper had asked "What about the operating theatre?" and the response from the spokesman at the hospital was: "If it was a big operation, it would have to wait until 8 o'clock at night",[42] as this was the time when power was returned. The Borough Electrical Engineer Mr W. C. P. Tapper explained the difficulty his Council was in: "We are supplying current at present from 8pm to 6am and are making strenuous efforts to get a day supply as well", he said. "The Council is not responsible

---

[36] Metropolitan Borough of Stepney: Electricity Supply Committee Minute Book No. 15 STE/927 3 May 1926
[37] Ibid. STE/927 6 May 1926
[38] Ibid. STE/927 6 May 1926
[39] *East London Advertiser* 8 May 1926
[40] *Stepney General Report to the TUC* London Hospital 6 May 1926
[41] *East London Advertiser* 8 May 1926
[42] Ibid. 8 May 1926

for this. It is the result of Union action".[43] In *Lansbury's Bulletin* it was reported that the London Hospital "... stoppage of electrical power was the outcome of the Hospital's decision to close the Out-Patients' Department and the power was restored when the Hospital reversed their decision".[44] By 12 May, it was reported in *Strike News* that "we are pleased to state that we have received a letter from the London Hospital agreeing to reopen the Out-Patients' Department today".[45] One thing is evident: power supplies were a highly contentious issue during the strike.

The General Strike ended in confusion, partly because both the TUC and the Government claimed success although workers' confidence in organised labour dropped to an all-time low. By the time of the borough elections of November 1928 it was feared that, due to the General Strike, the Labour Party in Stepney would suffer losses. Trade Union membership fell to under five million for the first time since 1916 and "funds were depleted by the drain of strike pay".[46] This could be seen in the National Amalgamated Furnishing Trades Association's (NAFTA) East London branches. For example, in May 1926, branch No. 15 East End United received £200 from the NAFTA and branch No. 141 East London Organising received £130. However, the amounts received from members for NAFTA was £100 from branch No. 15 only.[47] Overall, over £9,000 was paid out in May 1926 in order to fund the General Strike but less than £2,000 was received from members.[48]

In the aftermath of the General Strike many workers tore up their union cards in disgust. Men were also not always able to return to their former employment, as many companies carried out their own victimisation of strikers. With the termination of the General Strike the general expectation the following day was "that work would be resumed forthwith. To the great disappointment of the nation this did not begin".[49] Those men who returned to work "were told they must accept fresh conditions and lower

---

[43] Ibid. 8 May 1926

[44] *Lansbury's Bulletin No. 4* 10 May 1926

[45] *Strike News* op. cit. No. 8 Monday, 12 May 1926

[46] Burke, Barry, *Rebels with a Cause – The History of Hackney Trades Council 1900–1975* (1975) p32

[47] National Amalgamated Furnishing Trades Association (NAFTA) Monthly Report Vol. 25 No. 6 June 1926

[48] This was a massive payment to the branches. In the previous month, no money had been given to the branches and £141 pounds, was received by branches 15 and 141, NAFTA op. cit. Monthly Report Vol. 25 No. 5 May 1926 and Ibid. Monthly Report Vol. 25 No. 6 June 1926

[49] *British Worker* 14 May 1926

wages. Upon instructions from their Unions they refused to do this, and were thereupon told their employers did not want them".[50] In the East End, the Port of London "claimed strikers had forfeited their right to work".[51] The terms of settlement for the London docks, affected 50,000 men, who were committed to a seven-point agreement. Employers only had to take back men when work was available. The men were not to present themselves at their usual places of engagement until 7.15am on Monday, 17 May 1926,[52] according to the right-wing paper *Morning Post*. The unions had to agree to undertake:

> a. Not in future to instruct their members to strike either nationally, sectionally or locally for any reason without exhausting the conciliation machinery of the National Agreement.
> b. Not to support or encourage any of their members who take individual action contrary to the preceding clause 5a.
> c. To instruct their members in any future dispute to refrain from any attempt to influence certain supervisory grades (to be specified later) to take strike action.[53]

For the coal miners, their lockout was no nearer a settlement as a result of the General Strike and was to continue until November 1926. They endured almost seven months of heroic struggle before they were forced to capitulate. The East End United Branch held a concert to raise funds for the Miners' Federation and raised the sum of £30 8s,[54] but this kind of fundraising was not enough. The miners and their families were starved into submission as they were supported only by minimal contributions of a levy from the TUC affiliated Trade Unions along with some financial support from the Soviet Union. With the lack of work in the aftermath of the strike, many sought relief. However, the Stepney Guardians stated in the *East London Advertiser* that at the meeting of the Board, on 6 May "… it was made clear that however much the Guardians, as a body, desire to ease matters for the strikers, they intended to keep within the four corners of the law".[55]

The General Strike resulted in certain cases being heard at Thames Police Court. Interestingly, among those attending court "were Alderman J. Scurr MP for Mile End, and several members of the Stepney Borough

---

[50] Ibid. 14 May 1926
[51] Berrett, Sean and Matthews, Tony, *The Express* op. cit. 7 May 1976
[52] *Morning Post* 17 May 1926
[53] Ibid. 17 May 1926
[54] NAFTA op. cit. Monthly Report Vol 25 No. 8 August 1926
[55] *East London Advertiser* 15 May 1926

Council and the Stepney Board of Guardians together with local agents of the political parties in East London".[56] Borough Councillor Dan Frankel, for instance, was fined £25 and ordered to pay five guineas costs for:

> Unlawfully causing an act calculated to injure or to prevent the proper use or working of the shop and bakery of Israel Kossoff and the works or plant used and adapted for the production and supply of bread belonging thereto, by threatening to cause the electric power to be withdrawn, contrary to Emergency Regulations 1926, section 20.[57]

Frankel had sent a letter to Kossoff from the "Stepney Council of Action":

> … stating that their attention had been drawn to the trade dispute which had occurred between the plaintiff and his workmen, and suggesting an immediate settlement also stating that unless the council hear from him they would be compelled to consider the recommendation of a withdrawal of electric light and power so far as his premises were concerned.[58]

At the time of the General Strike Frankel had been chairman of the Stepney Trades Council and Borough Labour Party. In his defence he claimed that he was unaware at the time the letter was written that the current supplies from the Borough Council's electricity works had already been cut off. Also, he argued the "object of the letter … was to prevent trouble arising in view of the General Strike".[59] In Parliament MP's reacted to the industrial crisis brought by the cut in electric power. A Mr P. Gates, Conservative MP for North Kensington,[60] by private notice, asked the Minister of Transport:

> Whether he is aware that manufacturers and business houses in Stepney are still without electric power during the daytime, and whether he will make arrangements that will enable such manufacturers and business houses to continue their business and avoid throwing their employees out of work?[61]

---

[56] Ibid. 29 May 1926
[57] Ibid. 29 May 1926
[58] Ibid. 29 May 1926
[59] Ibid. 29 May 1926
[60] Stenton, Michael, and Lees, Stephen (eds.), *Who's Who of British Members of Parliament Volume III 1919-1945* (Sussex, 1979) p124
[61] *Parliamentary Debates* op. cit. 11 May 1926

The First Lord of the Treasury, Stanley Baldwin (also Prime Minister) replied that the Minister of Transport was making inquiries[62]. The role of the Communist Party was also discussed in parliament. Mr Shapurji Saklatvala, Communist MP for North Battersea,[63] stated that:

> ... as far as the Communist Party is concerned, our policy has been from the first in this miners' issue to back up the miners, to work along with the miners' organisations, and to help them in every possible way in order that they may be able to realise what they demand.[64]

It was feared that the Communist Party would put forward its own demands or attempt a revolution to overthrow the capitalist system or to introduce nationalisation - something Saklatvalva denied, stating that the party had "... merely acted behind the workers' movement in order to safeguard the fall in their wages which the masters are seeking to get".[65] However, Saklatvalva described the methods of the strikers as "revolutionary" when compared with previous strikes. This current strike was he said,"... quite an innovation and of a drastically different kind".[66]

By 1928, Labour controlled 27 municipalities across the country. In London, Battersea, Bermondsey, Deptford, Finsbury, Poplar, Shoreditch, Stepney and Woolwich were all Labour-controlled. Prior to the election *The Times* had predicted that in Stepney the "blunders" of the General Strike would lower the prestige of socialism.[67] However, the votes cast in the local elections did not bear out this theory. Part of the problem for those standing as anti-socialists was that their groups went under a variety of names. The majority stood as Union of Stepney Ratepayers, but in Whitechapel and St George's 21 were "People's candidates" and a further nine were "Independent". In Mile End there were 12 Municipal Reform candidates, and three anti-Socialist candidates; and in Limehouse all 15 were "anti-Socialist".[68] Thus the division among the anti-Socialists meant that they could not decisively win the majority from Labour.

A year later, in 1929, Britain saw the election of the second Labour government, which was another, even heavier, blow for the anti-socialists. Attlee, Scurr and Gosling all claimed landslide victories for their

[62] Ibid. 11 May 1926
[63] Inwood, Stephen, *A History of London* (1998) p757
[64] *Parliamentary Debates* op. cit. 3 May 1926
[65] Ibid. 3 May 1926
[66] Ibid. 3 May 1926
[67] *The Times* 23 October 1928
[68] Ibid. 23 October 1928

constituencies in Stepney.[69] This election also saw the first Communist candidate for Stepney, W. Tapsell in the Limehouse constituency, but he only gained 245 votes which was a mere 1 per cent of the vote.[70] Although he associated himself with the votes of thanks from the candidates, he used the opportunity to object "to the deposit system, which militated against the working class putting up a representative".[71] Attlee, it should be noted, came from a privileged middle-class background, and, although he deeply wanted to change the conditions of the people of his community, he had not been raised himself in such conditions. However, the people's votes showed their continuing support for him. They were to provide an important "gateway to Attlee's rise in the party in the 1930s",[72] as we shall discover in the next chapter.

Conclusion

Prior to the First World War, Stepney was rife with unrest. The dockers and the tailors both held strikes in order to improve conditions. Through Ruldolf Rocker's actions the dockers and tailors were to come to each others aide during strike action, in order for their families to survive the deprivation and starvation they faced during such times. However, such strikes were not on a national level. Stepney was alive with political anarchism due to such figures as Rocker. However there were also the *meschuggena* or crazy anarchists who propelled the East End onto the national scene with the Houndsditch murders in 1910. With such an undercurrent of anarchy within the working classes, in Stepney, it would have been impossible for the working classes to present a united front, as was seen with the General Strike. It was in the post-First World War era, with a national feeling of unrest that the General Strike was able to occur.

The General Strike in Stepney was especially significant, due to the involvement of the dockers. They held the key in the supply chain. With

---

[69] Major Attlee had 13,872 or 55.9 per cent of the votes giving Labour a majority of 7,288 or 29.4 per cent John Scurr had 11,489 or 47.1 per cent of the votes, a Labour majority of 4,088 or 16.8 per cent. Harry Gosling had 13,701 or 63.2 per cent of the votes, and a Labour majority of 9,180 or 42.4 per cent. *East End News* 4 June 1929

[70] Craig, F. W. S., *British General Election Manifestos 1918-1966* (Chichester, 1970) 49

[71] *East End News* 4 June 1929

[72] Whiting, C. R., "Attlee, Clement Richard, First Earl Attlee" (1883-1967) *Oxford Dictionary of National Biography,* Oxford, September 2004; online edn, January 2008

no dockers to unload the ships and transport the provisions to the city, London was captive. Although, strike breakers and the army were brought in to get goods off the ships and transported, they were unused to the work and dockers protested. So, far fewer supplies got through. Therefore, Stepney was integral to the supply of food, and its support of the General Strike was to have an impact on a much larger area, London.

For Attlee, the General Strike was a training ground for his negotiating skills. He led the discussions with the Electrical Trades Union and made sure that power was available to the London Hospital. This episode, according to David Howell, "demonstrated Attlee's pragmatism as a negotiator".[73] Such activities at a local level kept Attlee away from the House of Commons for the duration of the strike, since he is not mentioned in the parliamentary debates. This demonstrates Attlee's commitment to Stepney's welfare. More generally, on the General Strike, Attlee's assessment was typical of most Labour politicians in the 1920s. Attlee welcomed the discrediting of the belief that industrial struggle might offer a shortcut to radical change. Instead, the parliamentary road was unavoidable, whatever the frustration. However, with the dawning of a new decade came a new challenge for Stepney in the form of Fascism. Once again, the people of Stepney would take matters onto the streets.

---

[73] Howell, David, *Attlee* (2006) p25

CHAPTER SIX

COMMUNISM AND FASCISM IN THE 1930S

This chapter will assess the rise of the Communist Party in Stepney through the involvement of the party in three key issues: the Battle of Cable Street, the Spanish Civil War and the Stepney Tenants' Defence League. As we shall see, Fascism had a stronghold in neighbouring Bethnal Green rather than Stepney. However, in 1934 the Fascists planned to march through the most heavily Jewish populated area of Stepney, a move which led to the Battle of Cable Street. Support for Fascism was increasing during the 1930s throughout Europe, though, in the aftermath of the Battle of Cable Street, many people in Stepney were drawn to Communism and sympathised with the plight of the Republicans in Spain. Within the borough the Communist Party formed the Stepney Tenants' Defence League (STDL) in order to protect the rights of tenants. Housing was an on-going issue, with Stepney's battle against slum conditions continuing. The 1930s saw the STDL trying to make improvements in housing conditions, through the campaign for fairer rents, and getting basic repairs carried out by landlords. As a movement the STDL was wholly successful. With the outbreak of the Second World War, it was to alter its objectives to address the new issues facing Stepney – issues which will be covered in chapter 8, "The Bombing of Stepney: the local response and the work of Mass-Observation".

The 1930s witnessed the steady gain in strength of the Communist Party in Britain with its membership increasing from 3,000 to 17,000 members. In *The Failure of Political Extremism in inter-war Britain* Richard Thurlow writes that one of the areas in which the party was most successful was the East End of London.[1] Thurlow attributes the cause of this rise to "… grassroot political activism in tenant associations and other organisations, and recruitment for the International Brigade and support for the Republicans in Spain" rather than reaction to Mosley and the Battle of Cable Street in 1936. These two were, he says "only minor factors in

---

[1] Thurlow, Richard, "The Failure of British Fascism 1932-40" in Thorpe, Andrew, (ed.), *The Failure of Political Extremism in inter-war Britain* (Exeter, 1989) p77

the recovery of the Communist party in the 1930s".[2] Elaine Smith argues
that:

> It was not until the 1930s, when the Stepney Communist Party showed its
> mettle by providing local political leadership on all the major issues
> affecting the lives of working-class Jews in the East End, that the party
> enhanced its prestige and attracted to its ranks many Jews who would not
> normally support a Marxist party.[3]

However, Smith disagrees with Thurlow about Mosley and the Battle
of Cable Street, claiming that "it was the Communist Party's militant stand
against domestic Fascism in the 1930s which, more than anything else,
attracted many young East End Jews to the party".[4] In Stepney there was a
relatively low Communist Party membership which "disguised the fact
that there were many East End Jews who supported the party's stand
against Fascism without becoming party members".[5] The Communists'
establishment of the STDL, which campaigned against high rents and the
slum-housing conditions in Stepney, won them the most support. The
STDL evolved during the Second World War and campaigned for the use
of deep shelters, which became a prominent local war issue. Also, it was
the Communist Party, according to Smith, that "provided East End Jews
with a means of expressing their Jewish identity within the framework of a
secular political culture".[6] For example, Sam Clarke, an East End cabinet
maker, went to a dance at the Netherlands Club where Young Jewish
people danced, drank beer and ate pickled cucumbers and onions.[7] At the
dance he met many other Jewish people who, he learnt, mainly originated
from Holland. Clarke noted that "they were merry and jovial, quite
different from Russian and Polish Jews who were more serious and more
religious".[8] From such social gatherings Clarke developed his political
outlook and became a member of East End branch No. 15 of the National
Union of Furniture Trade Operatives.

---

[2] Ibid. p77
[3] Smith, Elaine R., "Class, ethnicity and politics in the Jewish East End, 1918-
1939" *Jewish Historical Studies* Vol XXXII 1990-1992 p363
[4] Ibid. p363
[5] Ibid. p363
[6] Ibid. p365
[7] Laurie, Kendrun (ed.), *Sam: An East End Cabinet-maker* (1983) p21
[8] Ibid. p21

Party Politics and the elections of the 1930s

According to Thomas Linehan the Jewish-Irish coalition, generally "remained an uneasy political formation"[9] in the Stepney Labour Party during the inter-war years. Despite the presence of influential Stepney Jewish Labourites, a largely right-wing Irish-Catholic caucus, with its power-base in the Whitechapel & St George's Labour Party, remained ascendant throughout the period.[10] Influential Jewish Labourites included Dan Frankel, MP for the Mile End division from 1935 to 1945 and Morris H. Davis, who was Labour Leader of the Stepney Borough Council between 1935 and 1944. For the Irish-Catholics there were "such local personalities as 'Jack' Sullivan, and 'Jerry' Long",[11] but during the 1930's "disillusionment with the moderate political disposition of Stepney's Irish dominated Labour machine began to surface amongst the more militant sections of local Jewry".[12] Many were "particularly agitated by the Stepney Labour Party's often muted response to the advance of continental and British fascism" and so "many were to seek redress in the Stepney Communist Party".[13] Linehan states that:

> the Limehouse Branch, aware of the significance of Catholic voting potential in Stepney, targeted much of its electoral propaganda at dissident Catholic Labourites during the LCC and borough council election in Stepney in 1937.[14]

Many Labour MPs had any political credit they had accumulated in the 1920s swept away in the electoral debacle of October 1931. "Attlee was one of the lucky ones, and narrowly clung on to Limehouse by 551 votes",[15] a majority of 2.4 per cent. Overall, he gained 50.5 per cent of the vote. Barnett Janner, a Liberal, for Whitechapel & St George's, won by a majority of 1,149 votes or 4.9 per cent. He gained 46.5 per cent of the vote

---

[9] Linehan, Thomas P., *East London for Mosley: The British Union of Fascists in East London & South-West Essex 1933-40* (1996) p81

[10] Ibid. p81

[11] Ibid. p81

[12] Ibid. p81

[13] Srebrnik, H., *The Jewish Communist Movement in Stepney: Ideological Mobilisation and Political Victories in an East London Borough, 1935-45* (Birmingham, 1984) PhD

[14] Linehan, op. cit. p83

[15] Whiting, C. R., "Attlee, Clement Richard, first Earl Attlee (1883–1967)" *Oxford Dictionary of National Biography,* Oxford University Press 2004; online edn, January 2008

overall. This was due partly to Janner and his wife "nursing the constituency" as "they have undoubtedly made themselves respected and popular".[16] Whitechapel & St George's was a constituency with a large concentration of Jewish voters. Janner appealed to them as a Jewish candidate. He was devoted to Whitechapel, which was evident in a number of ways: he would visit all the synagogues in the district every year on the eve of the Day of Atonement and whilst he was MP for Whitechapel he would take groups of children round Parliament and then give them tea across the road at Lyon's Tea Shop.[17] He was to become "best-known as a leader of the Jewish community".[18]

Dr W. J. O'Donovan the National Conservative candidate for Mile End division gained a majority of 2,661 votes, a majority of 12.0 per cent in a straight contest with Labour candidate John Scurr who received only 44.0 per cent of the vote.[19] Harry Pollitt, a Communist candidate, also stood for Whitechapel & St George's but only received 2,658 votes, 11.2 per cent. In campaigning, Pollit and Janner had a meeting "in the open air on the corner of Cannon Street Road and there must have been two thousand people present".[20] Pollitt was the first Communist candidate to stand for Whitechapel & St George's. There were two minor party candidates in the campaign: Pollitt and E. Lewis the Fascist Mosleyite candidates. Ted (Kid) Lewis was Jewish and a former boxer, whose campaign slogan was "Rome wasn't built in a day".[21] Although Lewis was a famous figure on the boxing circuit he was not an orator and he only gained 154 votes,[22] or 0.7 per cent of the vote. This was blamed on the party's youth. Again in the 1935 elections the same excuse was used and by the General Election in November of that year the British Union of Fascists (BUF) was discredited by its failure to fight any constituency. Although his was a national organisation with some 472 branches, Mosley's explanation was that the movement was a mere three years old. He preferred to wait for "Fascism next time", he said. This would become the BUF's election slogan.[23]

---

[16] Janner, Elsie, *Barnett Janner: A Personal Portrait* (1984) p37

[17] Ibid. p47

[18] Wasserstein, Bernard, "Janner, Barnett, Baron Janner (1892–1982)" *Oxford Dictionary of National Biography,* Oxford University Press 2004; online edn January 2008

[19] Craig, F. W. S., *British Parliamentary Election Results 1918-49* (Chichester, 1983) 50

[20] Janner, op. cit. p37

[21] Ibid. p37

[22] *East End News* 31 October 1931

[23] *The Times* 7 November 1935 and Craig, op. cit. 49-51

The fact that Whitechapel & St George's had candidates from the Liberal, Labour, Communist and Fascist Parties, indicates the level of political diversity in the area. Limehouse also had a Communist candidate: H. L. Hodge, who gained 1.4 per cent of the vote. The 1931 election saw Attlee returned with the smallest majority he ever received as MP for Limehouse, but this was far more to do with the Labour government's failings than Attlee's. Attlee in his vote of thanks at the 1931 election said that he "was very pleased that in the flood-tide that was sweeping over the land Limehouse should remain above the flood".[24] Nationally the vote was with the Conservatives and their "national" allies. Only 46 MPs were returned for Labour, of which 32 were trade union sponsored.

At the 1935 general election, Attlee increased his majority to 7,245 votes, or 33.0 per cent, making his a landslide victory. Mile End and Whitechapel & St George's also had comfortable victories for Labour: Dan Frankel gained a majority of 3,318, or 14.4 per cent, for Mile End, and James Hall gained a majority of 2,281, or 5.1 per cent, for Whitechapel & St George's.[25] Overall the constituencies showed an increase of just over 2 per cent in the numbers of people voting in comparison with the previous general election.[26] These gains signified a significant shift towards Labour once more.

In the Labour Party leadership contest which followed the election it was expected by other party members that Attlee's position as leader was only a temporary one, and that Herbert Morrison would become the new leader. However, after the first ballot Morrison was placed second to Attlee. Once the votes of the third-place candidate, Arthur Greenwood, were redistributed, Attlee won the party leadership contest comfortably. Therefore, at both local and national level Attlee was triumphant. The next challenge for him was his key role in the government of 1940-5, which was an important step on the way to his becoming Prime Minister in the post-Second World War era.

During the 1930s Attlee was a popular and reliable Labour leader both inside and outside of parliament. He was consistently re-elected throughout the 1930s for Limehouse. Although he lost his majority in the 1931 election, he was able to achieve similar levels of support to the 1929 election, once more in 1935, when he won by a majority of 33.0 per cent, 66.5 per cent of the total votes. If one looks at the election results in the

---

[24] *East End News* 31 October 1931
[25] Ibid. 19 November 1935
[26] Limehouse 59.4 per cent against 58.1 in 1931, Mile End, 63.7 per cent against 60.3, Whitechapel 63.6 against 62.1 per cent, an average of 62.2 per cent against 60.16. *East End News* 19 November 1935

appendix for this book, one can see the extent that the people of Stepney voted for Labour candidates to represent the area at a government and local level.

Despite the strong roots of the Labour party within Stepney, many Jews in the inter-war period tried to remain faithful to the Liberal Party. The Liberal Party had had a tradition of strong support in Stepney and particularly in the Whitechapel & St George's division where "their main support came from the tradesmen's section and from a large proportion of the Jewish community".[27] During the 1930s one man, Barnett Janner, was successful as a Liberal candidate for Whitechapel & St George's. He had moved from Cardiff to London in 1929 to pursue his political ambitions. The family came to Whitechapel & St George's and in December 1930 a by-election was held and Janner contested the seat for the Liberals. He narrowly lost to James Hall.[28] Ten months later in the General Election, he won the Whitechapel & St George's seat. Locally, Janner was best known as a leader of the Stepney Jewish community. However, in Parliament he was most associated with a wider issue, that of the rights of tenants. In his maiden speech in the House of Commons, he questioned the fairness of rent increases.[29] In the 1935 election, however, he was unable to resist the electoral tide that swept away most of the remaining Liberal MPs and was defeated by J. Hall. Janner had become an MP for Whitechapel & St George's due to the area's Liberal tendency and the locals' lack of confidence in the Labour Party after the demise of the second Labour government.

Another Liberal of interest was Miriam Moses, who followed her father into a life in the public arena and Jewish communal service. She was a member of the Whitechapel and Stepney Board of Guardians and in 1922 was to become the first woman Justice of the Peace in Whitechapel. Moses and Elsie Cohen, later to marry Barnett Janner, established the Brady Girl's Club at Buxton Street School in 1925, which Moses was involved in for most of her life. In recognition of her community service she became the first woman Mayor of Stepney in 1931. Miriam Moses was also vice-president of the Stepney Liberal Association and was profoundly interested in its progress. With the Liberals having been cast out, many Jews felt politically powerless. The Tories were not considered a viable alternative, and so many Jews turned to the Stepney Labour Party.

---

[27] Srebrnik, Henry Felix, *London Jews and British Communism, 1935–1945* (Essex, 1995) p30

[28] J. Hall received 8,544 votes, B. Janner 7,455 votes, L. Guiness 3,735 and H. Pollitt 2,106. Janner, op. cit. p36

[29] *Parliamentary Debates: Official Report* (1932) 23 November 1931 pp147–9

However, some of those Jews who joined the Labour Party often felt closer in many ways to the Communists, as we shall discover throughout this chapter.

The 1930s borough elections in Stepney were very closely contested. The demand for a re-counting of votes was a central feature of the 1931 election. In Mile End Centre Ward, four re-counts were proceeded with "and at its close a demand for another was refused".[30] In Mile End Centre Ward "five votes alone stood between the Socialists and the Municipal Reform candidates", and with Councillor Frankel the highest unelected candidate he demanded a re-count.[31] After the re-count Frankel was elected to the council. The narrowness of margins between the candidates was a problem also in the Whitechapel South Ward as there were nine votes between the elected L. Don for the Ratepayers Association (RA) and Labour's J. Lang. Spitalfields West saw G. Newton for the RA and Labour's J. Lewis also demanding recounts over the question of nine votes. In Mile End – Old Town South, A. Roberts demanded re-counts with regards to a six vote's margin. Ratcliffe ward provided the closest contest of all though, with a margin of just four votes between M. Blair for the RA and M. Smith for Labour.[32] The defeat of the Labour Mayor, for St George's-in-the-East – North West district, Mr M. H. Davis, caused a sensation. He received a mere 461 votes, or 38.4 per cent of the vote – a crushing blow for Labour.[33] Such a result displayed the voters' discontentment arising from the failed second Labour government. Overall, Labour held on to 26 out of the 60 council seats available in Stepney. Councillor I. Vogler, Labour, commented that "Stepney remained as solid a Labour borough as any in the country".[34] This was, at this point, not a particularly strong comparison, though. A mere 32.73 per cent of the borough had cast a vote during this election – a decrease of 0.76 per cent when compared to the previous 1928 election.[35]

By the 1934 local elections Stepney was a solid Labour borough with all 60 seats being held by the party. Nationally, 56 boroughs had a Labour

---

[30] *East London Advertiser* 7 November 1931
[31] D. Frankel (Lab) 1065 votes and unelected A. Kershal (Lab) received 1060. *East London Advertiser* 7 November 1931
[32] For a full breakdown of the election results, see appendix: "Election Results". Also, see Willis, Alan and Woollard, John, *Twentieth Century Local Election Results* (2000) and *East London Advertiser* 7 November 1931
[33] *East London Advertiser* 7 November 1931
[34] Ibid. 7 November 1931
[35] Ibid. 7 November 1931

majority, 15 of these were in London.[36] It was reported in the *Daily Herald:* "In London, Labour is now in control of a majority of the borough councils, and, with the Labour majority on the LCC, occupies a position of commanding ascendancy in the Metropolitan area".[37] From April 1934, with Herbert Morrison's victory, Labour gained control of the LCC. But for Stepney, Labour's dominance began in 1931. The London County Council elections in 1931 saw a Conservative victory, thus emphasising Labour's hold over Stepney. This hold had first become apparent even earlier, in 1925, with Stepney Labour's landslide victory in the LCC election. Labour's progress was interrupted due to the blunders of the General Strike in the 1928 election, but the party had fully recovered by 1931 as can be seen in the "Election Results" table in the appendix. In London, Labour appeared to be strengthening in the municipal elections, with gains of two more seats at the election of 1937. They achieved another three seats at national level. In Stepney, however, "Communists gained a seat in Stepney at the expense of Labour",[38] when in 1937 Phil Piratin was elected for the Communists.

John Gollan, Communist Youth representative, wrote in the Manifesto of the London District Congress, in preparation for the November Borough Council Elections in 1937 that Communists should continue "… our propaganda work on all social issues, adapting our Labour policy to each Borough".[39] Communist propaganda stated that "the stronger the Communist Party, the stronger the Labour Movement".[40] Unity was the key to Labour's success according to the Communists. There could be "No Victory without Unity!" they argued, because "without the help of all working-class forces, especially the Communists, Labour cannot win".[41] However, even with the Communists supporting the Labour Party, 1937 still saw the election of Stepney Borough's only Communist candidate. Phil Piratin was elected in Stepney's Spitalfields East ward with 616 votes or 38.5 per cent of the vote.[42] Piratin's electoral success was most likely

---

[36] *Daily Herald* 3 November 1934
[37] Ibid. 3 November 1934
[38] Ibid. 3 November 1937
[39] Gollan, John, *To the People of London! – For Social & Industrial Advance for Unity to Drive Fascism out of London. Manifesto of London District Congress Communist Party of Great Britain April 1937* (London, London District Committee) p6
[40] Ibid. p10
[41] Jacobs, Julie, *Discussion No. 12 The LCC Elections. Women in Co-ops. My First Six Months in the Communist Party* (London, Communist Party) February 1937 p4
[42] Willis, & Woollard, op. cit.

due to his involvement in the Battle of Cable Street and the fact that his home had become "the hub of organisation" for the Battle.[43] Piratin also said that he thought that his work amongst the tenants was the most fruitful politically,[44] as he defended tenants' rights through the STDL.

The Fascists also strove for electoral success. During 1934 the BUF deliberately pushed the Jewish issues to the centre of its propaganda efforts in an attempt to win votes and on 18 July 1936 Mosley announced that the BUF would fight seats in the municipal elections the following March. "East London will be asked to choose between us and the parties of Jewry", he said.[45] This statement marked a break with the BUF's earlier claims that fighting local elections was a waste of energy, which others had often viewed as a refusal to test its claims of massive support. The BUF's campaign was thus to be specifically anti-Semitic. Mosley attacked Labour's housing record and "tried to woo the Catholic vote by emphasising such things as the corporate state concept and his own pro-Irish past".[46]

The Fascists were unsuccessful due to their inexperience in campaigning and to the election organisers misleading Mosley as to how well they were doing. The BUF speakers addressed their first open-air meeting in the Whitechapel & St George's division on 4 June 1936. It was "a large and disorderly event – at the corner of Dellow Street in the Shadwell ward".[47] In July 1936 they opened their first official District Headquarters in Stepney "in large converted stables at 29 Essian Street, at the junction of Essian Street and Dongola Road in the Mile End division".[48] After the move to their new headquarters "BUF speakers addressed a large, orderly, and appreciative audience in Duckett Street, a locality which ... would henceforth become their major centre of operations in Stepney".[49]

During February and March 1937 Anne Brock-Griggs and Charles Wegg Prosser, both Limehouse Fascist candidates for the LCC elections,

---

[43] IWM Sound Archive ID No. 10210 Phillip Sherwood Piratin

[44] Ibid. 10210 Phillip Sherwood Piratin

[45] Dorril, Stephen, *Black Shirt: Sir Oswald Mosley & British Fascism* (England, 2007) p380

[46] Mandle, W. F., *Anti-Semitism and the British Union of Fascists* (Great Britain, 1968) p50

[47] *East London Observer* 6 June 1936

[48] Arthur Mason. Information supplied in response to questionnaire in Linehan, Thomas P., *East London for Mosley: The British Union of Fascists in East London & South-West Essex 1933-40* (1996) p63

[49] HO 144/21378/262-3 Stepney Communist Party

held about 150 election meetings, with an average attendance of 1,400.[50] The BUF regarded women as "the salespersons and soft-sellers of fascism in Britain, and the movement exploited female participation for maximum publicity in the rough street politics of the East End".[51] The choice of Anne Brock-Griggs as a candidate could be interpreted as a very tactical move on the part of the BUF and it led to women being mobilised by the BUF to march, speak, canvass, organise meetings and bazaars in East London. On polling day itself, foul play and intimidation ensued with such stunts as broadcasting the close of the poll at 8.30pm when it was still open for half an hour more. In the end these tactics did not draw any more votes; the two candidates in each districts polled 23 per cent in Bethnal Green, 16 per cent in Limehouse and 14 per cent in Shoreditch.[52]

Although people were obviously concerned and interested in what the BUF candidates had to say, when it came to voting they were far more interested in a candidate who stood a likely chance of becoming a representative of the area and who could then actually implement change. The Labour Party candidates fulfilled these criteria far more successfully than the Fascists or the Communists. At this time the Jewish community was becoming far more integrated and Stepney citizens needed to work together for improvements. With the greater integration of Jews came the strengthening of the anti-fascist movement. The Houndsditch Branch of the Shop Assistants' Union formed an anti-fascist section, which called upon all other branches "to spread the truth about Fascism and its perils to all who are still ignorant of the calamities it will inflict upon the nation and its workers if we do not organise".[53] The problem for the Fascists was that their campaign was seen as "... a last desperate throw of the dice of a declining movement which was deliberately trying to imitate Nazi success".[54] For Stepney the most noticeable illustration of the Fascist challenge was the Battle of Cable Street.

---

[50] Pugh, Martin, *"Hurrah for the Blackshirts!" Fascists and Fascism in Britain between the Wars* (2006) p228
[51] Linehan, Thomas P., "Fascist Perceptions of Cable Street" in Kushner, Tony and Valman, Nadia, (ed.), *Remembering Cable Street: Fascism and Anti-Fascism in British Society* (2000) p41
[52] A. Brock-Griggs & C. Prosser, both stood for the Limehouse ward and gained 16.2 per cent of the vote. See figures in LCC *Twentieth Century Election Results.* 82 Special Branch Report 12 March 1937 PRO HO 144/21063; Special Branch Report 11 March 1937 PRO KV 2/245/282
[53] *The Shop Assistant* 5 January 1935 TUC
[54] Thorpe, "The Failure of Fascism 1932-40" in Thorpe, op. cit. p74

The Rise of Fascism

Mosley launched the British Union of Fascists (BUF) on 1 October 1932. He "envisaged ... a progressive, modernising [movement] capable of attracting working men and ex-Socialists by its social programme".[55] Martin Pugh argues that "the movement was highly opportunistic in that it exploited issues which had local relevance, such as the presence of a Jewish community in Manchester, Leeds or the East End".[56] Like the Irish before them, poor Jewish immigrants tended to concentrate in large urban districts. In, Leeds and Manchester, however, they did not receive "the attention devoted to the East End".[57] Robert Benewick asserts that one important fact here is that the East End boroughs of the 1930s "still bore the scars of the rapid industrialisation and over-population of the preceding century".[58] This had left a stagnated East London with a legacy of derelict buildings which lined narrow crowded streets filled with dirt and smoke.

The concentration of Jewish immigrants generated accusations about their corrupt influence in slum clearance schemes and their poor hygiene. There were also allegations that Jewish immigrants exploited the labour force by running cut-price shops, opening on Sundays and running insurance frauds. The immigrants were accused of effectively running a white slave trade which lowered the tone of the area and devaluing British cultural life.[59] For example, in late 1936 the BUF's *East London Pioneer* investigated the labour conditions prevailing in the Jewish owned tailoring shops of East London. The *Pioneer* concluded that Jewish employers were exploiting seasonal trade difficulties in order to lower wages. They were also dismissing their British assistants and replacing them with younger immigrant Jews who were pouring into Limehouse and neighbouring districts from Continental Europe.[60]

In the East End there was a tradition of political anti-Semitism which dated back to the activities of the British Brothers League (BBL) in the Edwardian era. Richard Thurlow stated that "public opinion interpreted the BUF campaign as a last desperate throw of the dice of a declining movement which was deliberately trying to imitate Nazi success with the

---

[55] Pugh, op. cit. p130
[56] Ibid. p140
[57] Mandle, op. cit. p17
[58] Benewick, Robert, *A Study of British Fascism: Political Violence and Public Order* (1969) p217
[59] Pugh, op. cit. p228
[60] *East London Pioneer,* Jan 1937

issue".[61] W. F. Mandle suggested that Mosley "misjudged the possibilities of Fascism in England", and that he "bungled his campaign".[62] The collapse of Fascism can be seen through the damaging events at Olympia in which Mosley had failed to control the more violent elements in the BUF. Mosley also failed to "cement alliances with powerful men in both politics and industry" and he was not able to get his message to the people "partly because it was over-technical, and to an extent it was irrelevant".[63] Rather than take the blame himself, Mosley needed an external reason to explain his ultimate failure. In a pragmatic move he took an anti-Semitic stance in order to expose the alleged power of the Jewish population. In choosing areas to campaign:

> … the BUF deliberately chose predominantly Jewish areas for its marches, areas where its chances of attracting mass conversion would be slender, but where its presence would create tension.[64]

Stepney was characterised by overcrowding. At the time of the Census of 1931 it had a population of 225,238 spread over 1,766 acres which meant a density of 127.5 persons per acre.[65] 15.5 per cent of Stepney's population were judged to be living in poverty.[66] "Among the most significant concentrations of poverty were the dockland areas, Gill Street in the Limehouse area, Cable Street, and the neighbourhood centred on Duckett Street in Mile End".[67] It was the neighbourhood around Duckett Street, according to Linehan, "that was to become the BUF's principal recruitment centre in Stepney during this period".[68]

However, the stronghold of BUF support was to be found in neighbouring Bethnal Green. Although at 759 acres it was one of the smallest boroughs, the 1931 Census showed it had a population of 108,194 and an average population density of 142.4 persons per acre. Therefore the BUF's argument that the Jewish communities in Stepney were taking people's homes and jobs aroused considerable support in the area. For Jewish people, Bethnal Green was a place to be avoided. A "former

---

[61] Thurlow, "The Failure of British Fascism 1932-40" Thorpe, op. cit. p74
[62] Mandle, op. cit. p34
[63] Ibid. p34
[64] Ibid. p41
[65] *Census of England & Wales 1931* (1932)
[66] Smith, Sir Hubert Llewellyn, *The New Survey of London Life and Labour 1931-35* Vol III Survey of Social Conditions (I) The Easter Area (1931) Borough Summaries pp343-412
[67] Ibid. pp343-412
[68] Linehan, op. cit. p58

resident of Rothschild Buildings recalled that Bethnal Green 'was a Christian area and we avoided it because we were afraid of being beaten up'".[69] In *East London Pioneer* it was alleged that Bethnal Green furniture workers "were forced to accept hourly rates as low as 1s, 3d from 'their Jewish masters', who used 'Machines' and 'the labour of relatives' from 'Germany' to push down wages 'to the lowest possible level'".[70]

The Battle of Cable Street

The Battle of Cable Street occurred on Sunday, 4 October 1936. It was a significant moment in the history of Stepney, as it highlighted anti-Semitic feelings and centred on the collision of socialism with fascism. "They Shall Not Pass", the slogan of the battle, had a much earlier connection within Stepney. Arthur Foley Winnington-Ingram (Bishop of London) had used it in his Easter sermon of 1917. It was a slogan from Verdun, the embattled French fortress in the First World War. Tony Kushner argues that "the history of the East End of London reveals a tradition of immigration and ethnic and racial diversity that many in Britain would prefer to ignore or deny".[71] The streets of East London have been alluded to as a "patchwork quilt of settlements with interwoven sub-cultures".[72] This is a good analogy of the area with its mixture of English, Irish and Jewish cultures. Writing about the Battle of Cable Street, Kushner notes that "the very strength of the legend ... itself attests to its importance in East End history".[73] Neil Barrett suggests that, 4 October 1936 "represented not only a battle against fascist provocation in a predominantly Jewish neighbourhood; it also represented a battle between Jews themselves over the terms of their public representation".[74]

The largest concentration of British Jews was in the East End. Robert Skidelsky suggests that "... of the 350,000 British Jews, about 230,000 lived in London, 150,000 of them in the East End".[75] Of those in the East End, "Sixty thousand or so Jews were to be found in Stepney; another

---

[69] White, J., *Rothschild Buildings, Life in an East End Tenement Block 1887-1920* (1980) pp136-7
[70] *East London Pioneer* 5 Dec 1936
[71] Kushner, Tony, "Jew and Non–Jew in the East End of London: Towards an Anthropology of 'Everyday' Relations" in Alderman, Geoffrey and Holmes, Colin (ed.), *Outsiders & Outcasts – Essays in Honour of William Fishman* (1993) p32
[72] Fishman, W. J., *The Streets of East London* (1979) p8
[73] Kushner, Tony, "Jew and Non–Jew in the East End of London" op. cit. p46
[74] Kushner, & Valman, op. cit. p1
[75] Skidelsky, Robert, *Oswald Moseley* (1981) p393

20,000 or so in Bethnal Green; smaller numbers in Hackney, Shoreditch and Bow".[76] An example of anti-Semitic sentiment can be seen through a tenancy agreement that ended up being taken to Bow County Court thanks to one of its "very remarkable" clauses:

> Not to assign, under-let, or part with the possession of the said suite, or any part thereof, without the written consent of the landlords, such consent not to be unreasonably withheld in the case of a respectable and responsible person, but no Jews will be accepted as tenants.[77]

Benewick suggests that it was the constant political activity that occurred on a nightly basis that was more important than the periodical rallies. "The endless street-corner speeches and pamphleteering were bound to cause more resentment than large demonstrations where extra police could be detailed and the disorder minimized".[78] The East End was:

> … full of street corner meetings, you could hardly go to any area of the East End and not see a street corner meeting of one character or another, the Labour party, Christian organisations, and in the main street corner meetings held by the local communist parties.[79]

Another example of the number and variety of meetings being held can be seen in the Stepney police reports of "H" division. In five days, 14 meetings were held by various groups: the BUF, Communist Party, Social Credit Party, Protection of Civil Rights, Jewish Ex-Service Men, Young Communist League, Blue & White Shirts and the Democrats.[80] All these gatherings took place either on street corners, or in Victoria Park Square.

Watkins suggests young men may sometimes have had ulterior motives for joining the Fascists: "One said 'I ain't a Blackshirt, but they did give me half a crown and a pair of boots for joining'".[81] At night activities were running rife: "Fascists, Blackshirts and their rival blue and white shirts turned the East End into a No Go area after dark".[82] The Fascists used not only "knuckle dusters, but belts which were studded with

---

[76] Ibid. p393
[77] *East End News* 8 October 1936
[78] Benewick, op. cit. p222
[79] IWM Sound Archive ID Number 9157 David "Tony" Gilbert
[80] MEPO 2/3098 H division was the Stepney division and asked for additional support with any BUF meetings, because of anti-fascist feeling in the area.
[81] Watkins, Stephen, *How East Enders won the Battle of Cable Street* (THN, May 1991) Press cuttings Bancroft Local History Archives
[82] Ibid. May 1991

iron implements in the belt – in other words they became a terrible weapon";[83] Tony Gilbert remembered a group of Jews being "attacked and physically assaulted in such a manner that they were all taken to hospital".[84] The Chief Rabbi at one of the local synagogues, the Rev Zeffert, said "My people are terrified"; not surprisingly, in a climate where "elderly Jews were beaten and cut with razor blades, children thrown through windows and anti-Semitic graffiti covered wrecked shop fronts".[85] Many gentile children of the East End picked up on the slogan "The Yids, the Yids we gotta get rid of the Yids" and it was chanted regularly during processions.[86]

In June 1934, Mosley descended upon the East End when he marched the Blackshirts up to Victoria Park before giving a speech. This was to be the first outing of a completely new uniform, consisting of jackboots, breeches, military-style jackets, Sam Browne belts and officer-type hats. It was commented by J. Green that: "the uniform was seen by many to be in emulation of the Nazi SS".[87] On Sunday, 7 June 1934 the notorious Olympia meeting took place. On this occasion stewards of the BUF acted with great force in ejecting hecklers and interrupters, some of these had been organised to interrupt the meeting by anti-Fascist organisations, namely the Independent Labour Party and the Communist Party. Jack Gaster, a member of the Communist Party, was part of the outside demonstration at Olympia where he saw "blood and mayhem, mayhem!" It was, he said, "a really nasty one". Gaster organised a medical unit and support groups for the men who were brutally assaulted by the fascists.[88] One man who caused headlines was a Mr T. McNaulty who climbed up into the giant girders at Olympia. The audience watched breathlessly as a chase ensued over the girders and then outside the building on to the roof, although he was pursued, he managed to escape from the Blackshirts into a crowd of anti-Fascists.

On 26 September 1936 the announcement of a massive BUF march through a predominantly Jewish Stepney was greeted with alarm and dismay. The planned march was "seen as an act of calculated anti-Semitic provocation".[89] A debate ensued with the more conservative elements of

---

[83] IWM Sound Archive op. cit. 9157 David "Tony" Gilbert
[84] Ibid. 9157 David "Tony" Gilbert
[85] Watkins, op. cit. May 1991
[86] *Blackshirts* 17 October 1937
[87] Green, J., *A Social History of the Jewish East End in London 1914–1939: A Study of Life, Labour and Liturgy* (Wales, 1991) p463
[88] IWM Sound Archive ID Number 10253 Jack Gaster
[89] Cable Street Group, *The Battle of Cable Street* (1995)

the Jewish establishment and the British Labour movement urging their supporters to ignore it. The Communist Party, however, argued that to ignore the march was surrendering to Mosley and Fascism. The Jewish People's Council organised a petition that was signed by 100,000 people and which called for the march to be banned.[90] George Lansbury advised "those people who are opposed to Fascism to keep away from the demonstration".[91] The mayors of Stepney (Helena Roberts), Shoreditch, Bethnal Green, Hackney and Poplar were received, according to the *Daily Worker,* by the Deputy Under Secretary and after an hour's meeting they emerged reporting "that the matter was under consideration".[92] The consensus was that a ban would seem undemocratic. The response of the District Committee of the Communist Party was that Mosley was provoking civil war in East London. They urged people to:

> Protest against his military operations. Assemble in scores of thousands in the streets around Tower Hill. Remember the massacres at Badajoz and Irun, remember Olympia. Remember that Fascism means the destruction of free speech, of trade union, Labour, and Cooperative organisations. It means concentration camps and torture chambers. Londoners want no Hitler tortures or Franco butchery here. Assert your rights and end Fascist hooliganism in East London.[93]

As Essex Newspapers Ltd reported, the refusal to ban the march "left the population with no alternative but force and when the Blackshirts with their massive police escort reached Cable Street they found 300,000 East-Enders waiting for them".[94]

In response to the call of the Independent Labour Party and Communist Party that East-Enders should counter-demonstrate against Mosley "one of the most spectacular mass mobilisations of modern British political history" took place. According to the booklet *The Battle of Cable Street,* "half a million anti-fascist protestors took to the streets around Gardiner's Corner at Aldgate, the gateway to the East End".[95] Jack Gaster of the Communist Party, said that it was "highly organised and everyone was told where to go".[96] The Communist Party had a speaker van going round, calling for supporters, and Tony Gilbert witnessed the banners of various

---

[90] See *East End News* 2 October 1936 for the petition
[91] Ibid. 2 October 1936
[92] *Daily Worker* 1 October 1936
[93] Ibid. 1 October 1936
[94] *Essex Newspapers Ltd* 3 October 1986
[95] Cable Street Group op. cit. 4 October 1995
[96] IWM Sound Archive op. cit. 10253 Jack Gaster

organisations: "a great many communist banners, a fair number of Transport and General workers banners, also the anti-fascist printers ... and a great many of the tenants' organisations".[97]

On the morning of the confrontation, Kathleen and Alice Pingel-Holmes, "dressed in their Sunday best, began erecting a barricade in Cable Street in an attempt to stop Sir Oswald Mosley and his 4,000 Blackshirts marching through London's East End".[98] They broke into a builder's yard and dragged out bricks, ladders and planks of wood which they used to block the road. The East End was transformed with Red flags draped from windows and slogans of "They Shall Not Pass" adorning the walls throughout the district. Such slogans along with that of "No Pasaran" reflected the influence of the Spanish Civil War. There was an air of impending battle, and "loudspeaker vans, organised by the Communist Party and the Jewish ex-Servicemen's movement were touring all the morning"; "The Young Communist League band led by Harry Gross ... marched round the streets with slogan-banners".[99]

Charlie Goodman remembers the battle vividly: "it was fantastic to see all kinds of people united against racism. There were Irish Catholic dockers rubbing shoulders with Jewish rabbis".[100] As Ralph Finn recalls:

Being at school brought me into real contact for the first time with non-Jews – Goyim, as we called them. We mixed as though there were no barriers. Made close friends with boys of different religious beliefs. Worked and played together as if we were, which we were, all members of the human race.[101]

Evidence of this unification of the people of Stepney can also be found in the memoirs of Alexander Hartog. He writes that he was:

... born in a friendly neighbourhood where everybody knew everybody else and there were no enemies and there was no difference between colour and race – Jew, Gentile, Scotch, Irish, Welsh, Italian – and people in the main were hardworking and they wouldn't let you starve and, if there

---

[97] IWM Sound Archive op. cit. 9157 David "Tony" Gilbert
[98] Bain, Charlie, *Cable Street: They Shall Not Pass, People Power that beat the Fascists*
[99] Piratin, Phil, *Our Flag Stays Red* (1980) p22
[100] *Essex Newspapers Ltd* 3 October 1986
[101] Finn, Ralph L., *No Tears in Aldgate* (Bath, 1963) p76

wasn't an institution to do it, they would give you a cup of tea or a sandwich.[102]

However, in reality this was not always the picture. On another occasion when Hartog was playing with another little boy, the boy's uncle was teaching him anti-Semitism, in a subtle way, by saying "Tomorrow, you'll be going to church, won't you? Not like some people I know!" He was trying to create a wall. "I don't know where they come from. They're not clean like us. They're certainly not British".[103]

Faced with the prospect of the Fascist movement descending upon Stepney with Mosley's proposed march, the local community pulled together. Tens of thousands of anti-fascist workers assembled. The only route that was completely blocked by anti-Fascists was Cable Street. The police repeatedly charged the barricades in an attempt to clear the way for Mosley, but the defenders were too numerous and determined. Alice Pingel-Holmes, 81, recalled at a 60th anniversary march and rally, that "the police were very cruel and brutal that day and there were a lot of injuries".[104] Eventually the march was abandoned and this was celebrated as a great victory for the anti-Fascist movement.

At the Labour Party Conference, on Monday 5 October, Herbert Morrison suggested that the march led by Mosley "was consciously, deliberately and mischievously organised for the deliberate purpose of stimulating disorder and racial strife in the East End".[105] The Bishop of London, A. F. Winnington-Ingram, characterised the disturbances as "monstrous". He described the peacefulness of the area: "I lived in East London for nine years and except for occasional murders we were the most peaceable people in the country. There was no enmity between Gentiles and Jews".[106] He continued that it was "monstrous for a body of outsiders to come down and disturb the peace of East London and to force the Jews and Gentiles to make a common effort to oppose the interference".[107] He called upon Christians to "stand firm against all attempts to arouse anti-Semitic feeling for political or any other ends".[108] The Independent Labour Party wrote in a souvenir pamphlet:

---

[102] Hartog, Alexander, *Born to Sing* Recorded November 1973 to July 1974 (1978) p18
[103] Ibid. p19
[104] Bain, op. cit. *Cable Street: They Shall Not Pass*
[105] *East End News* 9 October 1936
[106] Ibid. 30 October 1936
[107] Ibid. 30 October 1936
[108] Ibid. 30 October 1936

The police said that Mosley was to march, the Home Office said Mosley was to march, His Majesty's Government said Mosley was to march, Mosley said through his own organs he was going to march! But the workers said No! And No It Was. Mosley Did Not March through East London.[109]

In the aftermath of the Battle of Cable Street, special police patrols were set up by Sir Philip Game, Metropolitan Commissioner of Police. This was only after Mrs Helena Roberts, Mayor of Stepney, complained about the situation. In order to maintain public order, the government banned the wearing of political uniforms, with the Public Order Act of 1937. The Labour and Communist Party had shown that they could organise the working class to keep the Fascists off the streets of Stepney even when the Government and the police had ignored the requests of the Stepney citizens. On the following Sunday, 11 October, the London District Committee of the Communist Party organized an anti-fascist demonstration through the streets of East London and the heart of the "blackshirt" area in Bethnal Green. The demonstration, according to Piratin was a huge success: "It ended in Victoria Park with a great meeting, and undoubtedly must have had a demoralising effect upon the fascists and their supporters in the parts of East London through which it marched".[110]

The so-called Mile End Road Pogrom followed, in which fascists resorted to acts of terror and provocation such as smashing windows of Jewish shops and homes; they also assaulted any Jews that they could lay their hands on. The *Jewish Chronicle* reported a Jewish shopkeeper saying, "I fear this is only the beginning".[111] Samuel Jelen, a resident in Mile End Road, described the following scene:

> I heard the noise, and went to the shop door. A crowd of about 200 youths rushed towards me. Four or five of the foremost members got me. One hit me across the face with a large piece of wood. Before I could get on to my feet again, I was seized and hurled through the window of Philip Levy's tailor's shop. The crowd then picked up a little girl and hurled her after me. Luckily she fell on me otherwise she might have been seriously injured. They then seized articles in the window.[112]

---

[109] Independent Labour Party, *They Shall Not Pass: 300,000 Workers Say Not to Mosley* A Souvenir of the East London Workers Victory over Fascism p3
[110] Piratin, op. cit. p26
[111] *Jewish Chronicle* 8 October 1999
[112] Ibid. 8 October 1999

Men were also "slashed with razors ... half-a-mile of shop windows [were] shattered ... [and] a car overturned and fired".[113] The presence of 2,000 special constables at a nearby Communist victory rally to celebrate Cable Street was not a deterrent. In the following days and weeks Jews continued to be beaten up and assaulted but the attackers were frequently not arrested. Thus it would appear ironic that the courts were filled with anti-Fascist demonstrators charged with breaching the peace at Cable Street.

So, why was Fascism unsuccessful in Stepney? Was it because Communists and Labour joined together in order to prevent the onslaught of Fascism? With a high density of Jews within the area, fascism was a very divisive force. It was not successful in Stepney because neighbours of all different ethnic backgrounds often lived in similarly miserable conditions.[114] However, neighbouring Bethnal Green was a Fascist stronghold. The people there lived on the breadline and they had "Jews on either side of them" geographically - people who "could be shown as owning shops, having businesses".[115] Therefore, Fascists in Bethnal Green could point over to neighbouring Stepney and say "They are stealing your houses. They are stealing your jobs".[116]

Joe Jacobs, Branch Secretary of the Stepney Communist Party, suggested that the Fascists were unsuccessful because they did not gain a foothold in Shadwell and Wapping "where lived the dockers of Irish descent with a strong Catholic background and a long history of working-class struggle behind them".[117] Another reason for the Fascists' failure was that the BUF were unable to establish an effective organisational presence within the Stepney trade union movement. An additional factor was the lack of cultural tensions "which characterise[d] Jewish-Gentile relations in north-east London during this period".[118] For Stepney, these tensions had been present in an earlier period but, although mutual suspicion still lingered, Jew and Gentile had learned to coexist. Thomas Linehan argues that:

> In this sense, Stepney fascism was partly an anachronism, the denouement of an ethnic politics that had first surfaced so aggressively in the Borough

---

[113] *Daily Herald* 12 October 1936
[114] IWM Sound Archive ID Number 9479 Solly Kaye
[115] IWM Sound Archive op. cit. 9157 David "Tony" Gilbert
[116] IWM Sound Archive op. cit. 9479 Solly Kaye
[117] Jacobs, Joe, *Out of the Ghetto* (1978) p114
[118] Linehan, op. cit. p91

at the turn of the century in the form of an anti-alien movement and the British Brothers League.[119]

Levels of Jewish-Gentile co-operation in Stepney are well illustrated by the rent strike movement of the STDL, as we shall discover. It is also worth noting that the Shops (Sunday Trading Restrictions) Act, 1936, was never "the controversial piece of legislation it was in Bethnal Green".[120] Fascism in Limehouse was essentially a working-class movement, "lacking the involvement of the middle strata of shopkeepers and traders which characterised the Mosleyite movement in Bethnal Green".[121]

The Spanish Civil War

In Spain, after the May 1936 elections a centre-left Popular-Front government came to power, which consisted of Republicans, socialists, syndicalists, anarchists, Marxists and communists. Army revolts broke out ten weeks later in several garrisons and the Spanish Civil War ensued from July 1936. General Francisco Franco emerged as the leader of the Nationalist rebels who were supported by "volunteers" from Nazi Germany and Fascist Italy. The war was seen by these two Fascist powers as a "dress rehearsal for a larger war, and might easily have become that war".[122] The British government's initial reaction to the outbreak of the civil war "was one of neutrality; and a policy of non-intervention was born".[123] *The Times* also adopted a position of neutrality, condemning both the "irresponsible butchery" by the republicans, and also the "ruthless cruelty" of nationalists.[124] However, it would appear from these "labels" that *The TImes* came down a bit harder on the nationalists than the republicans. The existence of these reports "produced a crisis of opinion in Great Britain" as:

> It widened existing divisions, between government and opposition, between right and left (terms hardly used in the political sense in England

---

[119] Ibid. p91
[120] Ibid. p91
[121] Ibid. p91
[122] Mowat, Charles Loch, *Britain Between the Wars 1918-1940* (Cambridge, 1987) p573
[123] Ibid. pp573-4
[124] *The Times* 8 September 1936

before this); it brought bitterness and class-consciousness into foreign policy, and so into domestic policies, to an extent unknown before.[125]

By August 1936 a Non-Intervention Agreement (NIA) was signed by 27 countries and a Non-Intervention Committee (NIC) was established, based in London, to monitor outside interference in Spain. Mowat suggests the Spanish Civil War "awoke people to political consciousness who had been indifferent to politics before; and [that] this consciousness found expression in new semi-political organisations, in intense activity in politics".[126] The British Communist Party was active in persuading British volunteers to join the International Brigade. With the party's success in Stepney there are many examples of people going to Spain in support of the Republicans. In all, about 2,000 British men and women fought in the International Brigades in Spain; most were "young and idealistic".[127]

Max Colin, for example, had joined the Communist Party after attending the Olympia meeting on Sunday, 7 June 1934. Outside Olympia policemen rode onto the pavements in order to try and gain control of the violent situation occurring. The level of force shown by the police shocked Colin. Whilst there, someone said to him "you want to know about it [then] join the Young Communist League (YCL)", which he did. From this point onwards he "began to pick up a political outlook".[128] Colin became an active member, attending "meetings, demonstration, what-have-you".[129] In 1936 Colin heard that Nat Cohen and Sam Masters, two of his friends, had taken a biking tour to Spain after which they had joined the International Brigade in the Spanish Civil War. Cohen and Masters had been members of the Jubilee Street cell, along with Joe Jacobs. Masters and Cohen, two East London garment workers, were the first to organise a group of British volunteers in Spain. They founded the "'Tom Mann Centuria', which was joined by half-a-dozen other Britishers who began to arrive during the first days of September".[130] The tiny British group was to join the "gathering of all International Volunteers at the newly-formed base of Albacete".[131] Nat Cohen fought on the Aragon front, where a bullet shattered his knee after he led an attack at Huesca. This injury

---

[125] Mowat, op. cit. p577
[126] Mowat, op. cit. p578
[127] Thane, Pat, *Cassell's Companion to Twentieth Century Britain* (2001) p363
[128] IWM Sound Archive op. cit. 8639 Max Colin
[129] Ibid. 8639 Max Colin
[130] Rust, William, *Britons in Spain: The History of the British Battalion of the XVth International Brigade* (1939) pp20-1
[131] Ibid. p21

removed him permanently from the war. Masters, however, was killed at Brunete in July. In *Britons in Spain* William Rust wrote of Masters that he was "one of the finest of the British volunteers and a true son of the working classes, [who had] died as he had lived, happy and resolute".[132] The involvement of Cohen and Masters in the Spanish Civil War from the start gave the Stepney Communist party a direct link to Spain. As news of this reached Stepney, others, like Colin, volunteered.

Colin believed, through attending YCL meetings, that if fascism could be stopped in Spain, then Hitler could be ousted from Germany. This was due to the fact that just under a half of the German population voted Left before Hitler had taken over. So, the people of Germany could tip the balance.[133] This thought process seemed logical to Colin. He believed what was happening in Germany was "absolutely heartbreaking and atrocious".[134] Previously, Colin had thought that the British Empire was "the greatest institution in the world".[135] However, his beliefs had changed after witnessing the brutal way the police acted at Olympia. Colin went to King Street, the headquarters of the Communist Party of Great Britain and joined the International Brigade.

Dr Tudor Hart, an orthopaedic surgeon, acquired an ambulance through the Spanish Medical Aid Committee to take to Spain and loaded it with as much medical equipment as it would take. Colin was the obvious ambulance driver Hart was seeking, as he had worked as a mechanic. On 23 December, 1936 Colin received a telegram from Hart and he left London for Spain on 28 December. Colin had a co-driver Gordon Davidson. As involvement in Spain was not a government backed venture, Colin and Davidson had no specific plans, only that they somehow had to drive the ambulance with its supplies to Spain. They arrived in Barcelona on 1 January, 1937 and from there went to Albacete, where they met up with Hart who was working with three trainee doctors - Kenneth Loutit, Reggie Saxton, Archie Cochrane, and three nurses. The group became attached to the 14th Brigade which was largely made up of French and Belgian soldiers. From Albacete they moved to Villarejo, which was near the Jarma Front. Charlie Goodman, another volunteer and member of the Stepney branch of the Communist Party, also saw action at Jarma in January 1937, along with Jack Louis Shaw who was a member of the 15th

---

[132] Ibid. p21
[133] IWM Sound Archive op. cit. 8639 Max Colin
[134] Ibid. 8639 Max Colin
[135] Ibid. 8639 Max Colin

International Brigade.[136] There was a call for unity. The political commissar at Villarejo said that it was the duty of those members of the Communist party and the YCL to join the International Brigade "to regularise our … point of view of discipline".[137] Colin believed in this and a couple of months later, volunteered to become a member of the International Brigade.

Another volunteer was Louis Kenton, who, after attending a meeting in 1937 decided to enlist for Spain as an ambulance driver - a legal route into the war. In June 1937 Kenton took his bike over to Spain and joined his friend and wife. David "Tony" Gilbert also volunteered after attending a meeting at the People's Palace at the end of 1936. He was persuaded by a story told by Isabel Brown, one of the leaders of the Spanish Aide Committee. She talked about a young man from Bethnal Green who had been killed. The young man was one of the ambulance team who had gone out onto the open fields to attend the injured. He was bragging "look they are not all that tough, look we can go and get them and he was killed".[138] On hearing Brown's words a man attending the meeting "jumped up and said that was my son".[139] The fact that it was a local young man stimulated the gathered crowd. For Gilbert, the story was to have a profound effect on his life. The next morning he asked his boss for some time off and went to the Communist Party headquarters to sign-up. Talking later of his experiences, Gilbert said:

> … when I encountered it, it was completely different to my experiences in the Second World War. The Spanish war to begin with was like the First World War trenches and moving across open ground to take territories, trying to learn the military methods of infiltration, so that you didn't go in one mass like they did in Europe 1914-1918.[140]

Sol Frankel's fight against fascism had begun when he worked as a volunteer at the refugee camp outside Southampton which housed "nearly 4,000 Basque children who had arrived in May 1937 following the bombing of Guernica by Hitler's Condor Legion".[141] Frankel was at the camp on the day it was announced that Bilbao had fallen to the Fascists.

[136] IWM Sound Archive ID Number 16612 Charlie Goodman & ID Number 13547 Jack Louis Shaw
[137] IWM Sound Archive op. cit. 8639 Max Colin
[138] IWM Sound Archive op. cit. 9157 David "Tony" Gilbert
[139] Ibid. 9157 David "Tony" Gilbert
[140] Ibid. 9157 David "Tony" Gilbert
[141] *The Independent* 24 May 2007

His seeing how distraught the children were left a deep impression on him. The older children rioted and broke up the camp in an effort to escape and go back to Spain to fight against Franco.[142] In December 1937, at the age of 23, Frankel arrived at the British battalion's base in Tarazona de la Mancha. He saw action in the Battle of Ebro in July 1938 and was wounded in the fierce fighting around Gandesa. This left his hand permanently partially paralysed.[143]

On 6 December, 1937 Clement Attlee, the Labour party leader, visited Barcelona, Valencia, and Madrid at the invitation of Prime Minister Negrín. This was after the Edinburgh party conference of October 1936 from which "the Labour party declared its support of the Spanish Republic and endorsed its right to buy arms wherever they could be procured, although the party continued to waffle on the issue".[144] The most significant decision of Attlee's Labour party was to visit the British Battalion itself. Attlee inspected the battalion which "was an impressive scene in a Spanish village by torchlight".[145] He also noted that "it was tragic that all the time the Communists were intriguing and seeking to divert the contest into a battle for Communism".[146] Attlee told the British volunteers "We are proud ... of the deeds of those who have died and those who still live".[147] Attlee further guaranteed the warmth of his welcome by calling the Non-Intervention Agreement, which prevented the Republic from buying arms, a "farce".[148] James Hopkins argues:

> In an unguarded moment, the future prime minister had evaded the caution of the trade union movement at home and had identified the parliamentary Labour party with the sacrifices of the British volunteers in Spain.[149]

As has already been mentioned, this would lead to the Communist Party suggesting in 1937 that without its support in Stepney the Labour

---

[142] Ibid. 24 May 2007
[143] Ibid. 24 May 2007
[144] Hopkins, James K., *Into the Heart of the Fire: The British in the Spanish Civil War* (California, 1998) p196
[145] Attlee, C. R., *As It Happened* (1954) p94
[146] Ibid. p94
[147] Hopkins, op. cit. p196
[148] "British Labour Delegation Visits Spain" *Volunteer for Liberty* 26, December 13, 1937, Attlee's account can be found in *As It Happened* op. cit. pp133-34
[149] Hopkins, op. cit. p196

Party would have been unsuccessful. The Communist's advocated the slogan "No Victory without Unity".[150]

On Attlee's return to England he was "criticised for returning the salute of the Spanish Forces with the clenched fist sign".[151] He argued, though, that, at the time, the salute was commonly used "by all supporters of the Republic whether they were Liberals, Socialists, Communists or anarchists".[152] Attlee did, however, see the Spanish struggle as "… the occasion for a very determined attempt by the Communist Party to get into the Labour Movement by devious methods … [But, he said] the majority of the Party were too experienced to fall into the trap".[153]

However, not everyone in the Communist party volunteered to fight in Spain. Solly Kaye, another Communist Party member, did not volunteer for the war as he had become Branch Secretary for Hackney and had his mother to look after. He thought he was better placed at home organising "the widest possible support for Spain" which involved putting "pressure on the Labour party to stop support for non-intervention and to give aid to Spain".[154] Kaye was involved with four great rallies that were to converge at Victoria Park Square. In order for the Communists to have a pitch at Victoria Park Square, Shorty Brooks, Secretary to the Bethnal Green Branch, along with "a few others pinched the pitch at Victoria Park Square and kept the meeting going".[155] The principle was that "if you had a meeting going then no-one could take the pitch".[156] Kaye supported Brooks in keeping the pitch until the rally arrived. Thousands participated according to Kaye.[157]

The last battle for the British battalion in Spain began on the night of 22 September 1938, which was the day before their evacuation from the Ebro. The British battalion was called "to face yet another Nationalist offensive against the crumbling Republican resistance".[158] This was a vicious and deadly struggle with 48 of the remaining 106 British volunteers being killed, taken prisoner, or declared missing in action. On

---

[150] Jacobs, Julie, *Discussion No. 12 The LCC Elections. Women in Co-ops. My First Six Months in the Communist Party* (London, Communist Party) February 1937 p4

[151] Attlee, op. cit. p95

[152] Ibid. p95

[153] Ibid. p95

[154] IWM Sound Archive op. cit. 9479 Solly Kaye

[155] Ibid. 9479 Solly Kaye

[156] Ibid. 9479 Solly Kaye

[157] Ibid. 9479 Solly Kaye

[158] Hopkins, op. cit. p310

24 September the British Battalion stood down for the last time. The
Republican forces were to struggle on until 16 November, when they were
finally pushed back across the Ebro. The defeat of the Republicans was
inevitable. In February 1939 the British and French governments
recognized Franco and his government as rulers of Spain. On 1 April 1939
the civil war was formally ended.

In Stepney and the East End, "it was the Communist Party's militant
stand against domestic Fascism in the 1930s which, more than anything
else, attracted many young East End Jews to the party".[159] It was this same
stand against Fascism which made many Stepney Communist Party
members volunteer for the Spanish Civil War. Also, since the Communist
Party had its stronghold of support in Stepney and the East End in general,
one would assume that a large number of the civil war volunteers came
from this area. The stories of the many volunteers were a great benefit to
the party's propaganda machine. However, as we have discovered, the
experiences of those who witnessed the battle of Cable Street also played a
major part in motivating people to volunteer for the war. The underlying
thought of many of those who supported the Republicans was that if
Fascism could be stopped in Spain then Hitler could be ousted in
Germany. However, in Stepney there was also the pressing domestic issue
of Housing, which the Stepney Tenants' Defence League was to tackle.

Stepney Tenants Defence League

The Housing Act of 1925 stated that "working-class houses shall be
kept in all respects reasonably fit for human habitation".[160] It was the
responsibility of the landlord primarily, and in default the local authority
would act. It was the need for fairer rents, along with the lack of keeping
working-class houses in a reasonably fit condition that saw the formation
of the Stepney Tenants' Defence League. The law was on the STDL's side
as it was stated in LCC by-laws that the "local authority is empowered to
deal with an unhealthy area (or 'slum') by requiring the owners to
demolish the unfit houses or by itself acquiring and demolishing them".[161]
In Stepney, overcrowding along with the poor conditions of the housing
was an on-going problem. In *Fire Under the Carpet*, it is stated
"practically the whole of Stepney is a slum" according to the housing

---

[159] Smith, Elaine R., "Class, ethnicity and politics in the Jewish East End" op. cit.
p363
[160] LCC 1932 *London Statistics* Vol 35 1930-31 (1932)
[161] LCC 1939 *London Statistics* Vol 41 1936-38 (1939)

committee who "officially and cheerfully commented" on this in the 1930's.[162] The promise held in the names of developments, such as Paradise Row and Fleur de Lys Street, was often contradicted by the squalor endured by those who lived in such places. In the Housing Committee minutes of 1930-31 a memorandum was received from the London Council of Social Service prohibiting the use of underground rooms for sleeping in. Although the council saw a fundamental difficulty in condemning such properties as people still lived in them, they still took the measure of closing "underground dwellings used for living and sleeping purposes".[163] Such measures highlight the housing problems faced by Stepney in this period.

In 1937 the STDL was set up to obtain fairer rents and necessary repairs to buildings. Lew Cherley lived near Langsdale Mansions and became involved in the rent strike which, like so many others, was over the lack of repairs to the building and the high rise in rents. The rents were supposed to be controlled, but for most of the time this was not the case in reality. The STDL's response was to find out what tenants were paying for their rent, establish what they should be paying and then fight for that rate as well as making the case for necessary repairs. What started as an instance of a few tenants not paying their rent soon became a widespread movement, which meant that, although bailiffs attempted to evict tenants, the people were able to prevent it. In 1939, a march to Leman Street police station was organised in 24 hours to protest at the police helping with the evictions. Twelve housing estates also held protests. The outcome was fair rent and repairs being carried out. Crab & Gold are often mentioned as the landlords, as they were the owners of many of the biggest tenement blocks in Stepney.[164]

Another large block to strike for improvements and rent control was Brady Street. The rents for the tenants paying controlled rents were 8s, for the decontrolled tenants the rents were 10s 6d with the landlords trying to increase them. The only way that this could be achieved was by installing decontrolled tenants when controlled tenants left. The new tenants could then be charged level of rent. 90 per cent of all the tenants in Brady Street joined the STDL and the rent strike began, lasting 26 weeks in total. Whilst out on strike many tenants received letters from solicitors saying that if rents were not paid they would be taken to court. This frightened

---

[162] Scaffardi, Sylvia, *Fire Under the Carpet: Working for Civil Liberties in the 1930s* (1986) p136
[163] Minute Book No. 8 of the Housing Committee of the Stepney Borough Council Dec 1930-Apr 1931 p394
[164] IWM Sound Archive ID Number 20649 Lew Cherley

people. In response to such threats the STDL made tenants safe from eviction by blocking off one end of the block, so that there was only one entrance through the gates, which was guarded. In the end the tenants were victorious and all rents were brought down to the controlled rates. However landlords had a part victory as they were able to demand rent in arrears, although this was only to be paid on a gradual basis. Max Levitas, says that Stepney was a real token of resistance for London, "a light" that demonstrated a way of getting rents reduced and necessary repairs done.[165]

Contemporaries often commented that there were a lack of repairs and improvements being carried out. An example that illustrates this is the report from Ellen House, Splidt Street, which shows the out-of-date planning of the flats. It was reported that on each landing there were four flats but that "only two are provided with a WC and scullery".[166] Thus "two tenants are forced to share these necessities to which every tenant is entitled".[167] The tenant whose flat housed the facilities could have no privacy and arrangements had to be made so that washing and sanitary arrangements did not overlap. There was also "no means of lighting the sculleries by electricity ... though the remainder of the flats are wired".[168] The WCs were of an out of date unhygienic pattern, with rusty cisterns which were in need of repair. It was recommended that electricity should be extended to the sculleries and the WCs should have light and the cisterns be replaced with modern versions. It was said that, eventually two flats should be converted into one which would be a "more advantageous way of using the existing space".[169] Within the block itself there were more problems. The staircases were ill-lit and the lights were always extinguished at 10.30pm, which was, the report said, "an entirely unwarrantable imposition".[170] The recommendation was that arrangements would need to be made for new lights to remain lit until daylight. The structure was also infested with vermin, which was a potential source of infection.

Another dispute arose at Felix Houses, Splidt Street. The outcome was that the rents of the controlled flats were reduced from 27 March (the date of the start of the dispute). Repairs were then carried out, with all lights

---

[165] IWM Sound Archive ID Number 20650 Max Levitas
[166] Groser Papers MS3428 *Ellen House, Splidt Street General Report on the condition of the building, with recommendations for repairs, re–decorations etc* by Patrick Wilson 15 April 1939
[167] Ibid. MS3428 by Patrick Wilson 15 April 1939
[168] Ibid. MS3428 by Patrick Wilson 15 April 1939
[169] Ibid. MS3428 by Patrick Wilson 15 April 1939
[170] Ibid. MS3428 by Patrick Wilson 15 April 1939

being kept on from dusk until midnight. This was not for quite as long as Ellen House had recommended, but it was an improvement for an agreement also came from the Landlord "to carry out from time to time all necessary repairs" and for "the stairways and landings to be cleaned once a week".[171] There was to be a five-year cycle for decorating the fronts, landings and stairways, along with the sculleries being white-washed once a year which would begin within two months of the strike ending.[172]

In October 1936 it was reported in a letter to *The Times* from Canon Sheppard that:

> ... the Stepney Housing Trust received financial support which enabled it to build two more blocks of flats – the second being part of a clearance scheme under the 1930 Act, which has swept away one of the worst districts in London.[173]

Once completed the scheme would re-house 290 people "who are at present living under terrible conditions".[174] With many pressure groups aiming for improvements in the housing conditions of Stepney, there were finally glimpses of hope that change was on its way. By September 1939, the Rent and Mortgage Interest Restrictions Act had been passed. This prolonged "existing Rent Restrictions Acts until six months after war is ended".[175] In celebration of winning rent controls, there was a large victory parade from Brady Street to Philpot Street, which took place on 9 July. In total, "6,000 participants heard Tubby Rosen declare that £25,000 had been refunded to tenants in lump-sum settlements for rent overcharges and that landlords had been forced to spend another £60,000 on repairs".[176]

However, with the onset of war, tenants issues did not cease. The 13 May 1940 marked the beginning of the Riverside Mansions Tenants' Strike. The Town Clerk reported that "the majority of the tenants had refused to pay rent and had, in some instances, displayed notices in their windows bearing the words 'Rent strike – no rent today".[177] On the same day, after consultation with the chairman of the finance and parliamentary

---

[171] Groser Papers MS3428 *Basis of settlement of disputes between the tenants at Felix Houses, Splidt Street, and the Landlords, the Norwich Union Life Insurance Society*

[172] Ibid. MS3428 *Norwich Union Life Insurance Society*

[173] *The Times* 20 October 1936

[174] Ibid. 20 October 1936

[175] *East End News* 29 September 1939

[176] Srebrnik, *London Jews and British Communism* op. cit. p41

[177] Minute book No. 16 of the housing committee of the Stepney Borough Council Dec 1939-Oct 1944 L/SMB/A/7/16 Tuesday, 28 May 1940

committee, "notices to quit were ... served on each of the defaulting tenants with the result that, save for 41 cases, the rent was paid and the notices consequently waived"[178] once again, this demonstrates the methods of intimidation often used by the council. Anyone who did not pay was issued with a summons 41 of these were issued in total. The tenants were striking due to the bomb damage to Riverside Mansions by enemy action not being repaired. However, Riverside Mansion was not the only estate to have been damaged by enemy action, other affected estates included:

> Gosling House, Roche House, Limehouse Fields, Williams, Jerome, Wilkinson, Aylward, Shaw, Orbell, Reidy and Besant Houses; 58 Three Colt Street, Newell House, 17-81 Elsa Street, St Annes House, Padstow House, Potters Dwellings, Ring House, Raphael House, 62 Clark Street, John Scurr House.[179]

It was reported that "first aid repairs are being carried out by the building works section of the borough engineer and surveyor's department".[180] However with the serious shortage of suitable housing accommodation within the borough the Housing Committee suggested that the Ministry of Health be approached "with a view to securing approval to carrying out ... more permanent works of repairs".[181] With the intense bombing of the Stepney area, the council was unable to do more than simple repairs. The issue of housing during the war will be discussed in the chapter on Mass Observation.

During the war the STDL, although continuing its work with Tenants rights, was to shift its attention to "wartime problems such as air raid precautions, food profiteering, and sudden increases in the cost of living".[182] The Communist Party was to have some success in the post-Second World War parliamentary elections, when Phil Piratin became one of only two Communist members of parliament.[183]

---

[178] Ibid. L/SMB/A/7/16 Tuesday, 28 May 1940
[179] Ibid. L/SMB/A/7/16 Tuesday, 28 May 1940
[180] Ibid. L/SMB/A/7/16 Tuesday, 28 May 1940
[181] Ibid. L/SMB/A/7/16 Tuesday, 28 May 1940
[182] Srebrnik, *London Jews and British Communism* op. cit. p41
[183] The other was Willie Gallacher.

Conclusion

At the beginning of this chapter the points of view of two historians were discussed. We considered Thurlow's assertion that the resurgence of the Communist Party was due to the activities of the tenants' associations and the recruitment for the International Brigade in support of the Republicans in Spain.[184] Smith's argument, however, was that the Communists' militant stand against domestic Fascism did more than anything else to attract young East End Jewish people to the party.[185] The Communist Party's role in the domestic fight against Fascism attracted people to become members of the party, as we have discovered from the evidence of the taped interviews with Max Colin[186] who joined the Young Communist League after witnessing the bloody scenes outside the Olympia Fascist meeting in June 1934. Many people were moved by what they witnessed on the streets – a fact illustrated by the numerous political street gatherings that took place in the meeting's aftermath. For Stepney the Battle of Cable Street was a unifying event for the community, as "... all kinds of people united against racism".[187] In the brief moment of the Battle of Cable Street Jewish people stood shoulder to shoulder with Gentiles against a Fascist incursion. Margaret Mullings asserts: "the political and community opposition to the BUF in the East End was closely intertwined because of the large Jewish membership of the parties of the left".[188] This political stand, no doubt, made the people of Stepney truly aware of their political power at street level.

The Battle of Cable Street was a complex event which "has been variously mythologised as a victory for working-class, political radicalism, cultural pluralism or local pride".[189] It was also "an important focal point for the exploration of the sensitive issue of the policing of ethnic minorities".[190] Kushner argues:

> It is ironic ... that the most remembered day in twentieth century British Jewish history should be the 'Battle of Cable Street' whose very title

---

[184] Thurlow, "The Failure of British Fascism 1932-40" in Thorpe, op. cit. p77
[185] Smith, Elaine R., "Class, ethnicity and politics in the Jewish East End," op. cit. p363
[186] IWM Sound Archive op. cit. 8639 Max Colin
[187] *Essex Newspapers Ltd* 3 October 1986
[188] Mullings, Margaret Mary, "The Left and Fascism in the East End of London 1932-1939" PhD (1984) p347
[189] Ibid. p1
[190] Ibid. p4

commemorates a pitched and bloody street fight between young Jews and others against the combined forces of the Metropolitan police.[191]

For Phil Piratin "the working-class had won the day. The Communist Party had shown itself capable of leading the working-class in keeping the fascists off the Stepney streets when the government and the police had attempted to foist the fascists upon them".[192]

In the aftermath of such an event many people joined the Communist party. Through meetings and discussion they appear to have felt that their political stand against Fascism could be effective in Europe, and namely Spain. With Communist Party strength increasing in the East End throughout the 1930s, one assumes that much of the support for the Spanish Civil War also came from the area. There are many examples of people from Stepney volunteering to go to Spain to aid the Republicans, as we have discovered. Their belief was that, if Fascism could be defeated in Spain, then it could be driven out of Europe.

Within an increasingly aggressive Fascist climate, the war in Spain brought a fear of wider conflict. Membership of the Communist Party in Britain rose from 8,000 in 1935 to almost 18,000 prior to the outbreak of war in 1939.[193] But the Communist Party obviously recognised its own weakness when it came to elections, and would openly throw its support behind the Labour Party claiming that: "Our central aim must be to maintain and extend Labour majorities, and to strengthen them by Communist representatives wherever possible" because "the stronger the Communist Party, the stronger the Labour movement".[194] In Stepney, on local social issues, the party was a strong force.

In Stepney the on-going issue of housing continued throughout the period. The Communist Party in Stepney was to address the issue through the foundation of the Stepney Tenants' Defence League in 1937. Fairer rents and improved housing conditions were striven for. It would appear that the STDL were successful in achieving both of these aims and that they had an impact upon Stepney citizens, improving their day-to-day lives. The election of Phil Piratin, the Communist Party candidate, at the

---

[191] Ibid. p5

[192] Piratin, op. cit. pp24-5

[193] Harmer, Harry, "The Failure of the Communists: The National Unemployed Workers' Movement, 1921–1939: A Disappointing Success" in Thorpe, op. cit. p30

[194] Manifesto of London District Congress Communist Party of Great Britain April 1937 *To the People of London! For Social & Industrial Advance for Unity to drive Fascism out of London* (London, Communist Party of Great Britain) p6

borough council elections later that year reflects the appreciation of local people for their efforts. The election of Piratin was unusual because one of the main problems for the Communist Party was that it was vying for the same electorate as the Labour Party: the working classes, who were largely and increasingly loyal to the Labour movement in elections. This was because Labour offered "industrially, the possibility of concession from the employers and, politically, the promise of a majority Labour government".[195] However, in Stepney Piratin was a successful candidate who was to achieve a good deal in the post-war years.

In conclusion, the Battle of Cable Street was to attract people to the Communist movement, which educated them not only in Communist party thinking but also in the ways of Fascism. This prompted people to volunteer in the fight against Fascism in Spain. However, domestically the Communist Party was to campaign for one key issue: housing. For Stepney this was a dominant issue, which the Communist Party was to challenge head-on with direct action such as rent-strikes. This action demonstrated what the party was doing and had a direct impact upon people's lives. This no-doubt aided the election of Phil Piratin to the borough council in 1937. With the outbreak of the Second World War, the STDL was to evolve and campaign for issues relevant to the new war conditions. Therefore, the case can be made that the Battle of Cable Street ignited interest in the Communist Party and that the Spanish Civil War was the European version of the battle. The STDL took on the domestic issues for improvements in day-to-day living conditions for the Stepney citizens.

---

[195] Harmer, "The Failure of the Communists", in Thorpe, op. cit. p29

CHAPTER SEVEN

THE SECOND WORLD WAR
AND THE EVACUATION
OF SCHOOLCHILDREN IN STEPNEY

In this chapter the experience of evacuation will be addressed through examining the initial evacuation of Stepney schoolchildren. With the imminent declaration of war against Germany, Stepney was to witness the largest concentrated movement of children away from the area that it has ever seen before or since. This was due to the implementation of the government evacuation scheme, which began on 1 September 1939, two days prior to the outbreak of war.

The idea for the evacuation scheme had its origins in the air raids of the First World War during which "1,400 civilians were killed in just over 100 raids, first by zeppelins then by heavy bombers".[1] In addition to the number of deaths, the psychological impact on the surviving community members was also great. A bomb had fallen on a council school in neighbouring Poplar and this event more than any other, according to Philip Ziegler, was to foster a doctrine of dispersal.[2] There was also a counter argument that "if people were dispersed throughout the city they would provide more targets for the bombers".[3] However, the vivid image of children's bodies being dragged from a shattered school won the day and the dispersal doctrine became the official policy. Such a policy would be essential, it was argued if the predicted bombing occurred at the outbreak of war. As Angus Calder states "in 1937, British experts reckoned that Hitler's Germany, if war broke out, would bomb Britain at once and carry on for 60 days. There would be 600,000 people killed and twice that number injured".[4] Evacuation would thus perform a crucial role

---

[1] Brown, Mike, *Evacuees: Evacuation in Wartime Britain 1939-1945* (Gloucestershire, 2000) p1
[2] Ziegler, Philip, *London at War 1939-1945* (Great Britain, 1995) p9
[3] Ibid. p9
[4] Calder, Angus, *The Myth of the Blitz* (1991) p60

in any defence scheme, as it would "minimise casualties by spreading the population as thinly as possible".[5]

The government was to concentrate on evacuating the poorest, as they lived in the areas most likely to be bombed and were less able to evacuate themselves. As Stuart Hylton notes, in "underpinning this decision were concerns about public order and the sanctity of property".[6] Three groups were identified as those most likely to panic: "foreign, Jewish and poor elements".[7] Stepney had many inhabitants who could find themselves placed within at least one of these categories and some even in all three, and it was claimed that these groups, according to Stuart Hylton would "turn out to be the classes of person most likely to be driven mad with fright".[8] It was therefore fundamentally the fear of people panicking which lay behind the decision to evacuate prior to the outbreak of war in order not to risk undermining morale.

The initial evacuation was swiftly executed on day one of the evacuation programme, 1 September 1939, with over 32,000 children being evacuated from the Stepney area (see attached table). The table shows the huge variation in the "final destinations" where evacuees from this one area, Stepney, ended up. It was not merely a case of all the children from the Stepney area being sent to one area; they could go to several. Exactly where they were to end up depended firstly on the underground station from which they began their journey, and secondly on the main-line station from which they left London. This system could take the school parties north, south, east or west of the capital. The exact destinations (as shown in the attached table) when related to the government's plans for the school evacuation scheme reveal how the planned destinations for Stepney's schoolchildren in fact turned out in reality.

There have been broadly two schools of thought about evacuation policy amongst historians. The first, asserted by Richard Titmuss, a seminal thinker on social policy issues, in the immediate post-war years, in *Problems of Social Policy,* suggests that evacuation along with bombing "stimulated enquiry and proposals for reform long before victory was even

---

[5] Macnicol, John, "The Evacuation of Schoolchildren" in Smith, Harold L. (ed), *War and Social Change – British Society in the Second World War* (Manchester, 1986) pp5-6
[6] Hylton, Stuart, *Their Darkest Hour: The hidden history of the Home Front 1939-1945* (Gloucestershire, 2001) p39
[7] Ibid. p39
[8] Ibid. p39

thought possible".[9] The experience of war brought "pressure for a higher standard of welfare and a deeper comprehension of social justice steadily gained in strength".[10] A. J. P. Taylor also adheres to this notion, in more striking terms: "the Luftwaffe was a powerful missionary for the welfare state for their bombs led to evacuation and evacuation to social revolution".[11] However, José Harris later questioned whether Titmuss's thesis needed some kind of refinement and modification, as she could find "little proof that war heightened government awareness of social welfare either as a tool of national efficiency or a means of enhancing solidarity".[12]

As the "classic" welfare state itself came under threat in the 1980s, a second school of thought appeared: a revisionist interpretation of evacuation. This interpretation sees the experience of evacuation itself as a multifaceted and sometimes contradictory event. For example, a positive point of evacuation had often been assumed to be the "health-giving properties" of country life. However, those sent to camp schools, did not necessarily gain weight. The children evacuated to these camp schools had a regimented lifestyle including much physical activity. Revisionists have also questioned the precise original state of health of the evacuees since no medical inspections were carried out before evacuation. Health officers were appointed to check evacuees on arrival, but their thoroughness is also open to question, as during the second wave of evacuation in 1940, health officers were "supposed to check 480 children per hour".[13] Also, the School Medical Service suffered much criticism for the state of health of the evacuees. The Chief Medical Officer at the Board of Education, Sir Arthur MacNalty, maintained the line taken by the Ministry of Health in the 1930s: that the school medical service was primarily educational.[14] MacNalty instead blamed the parents and home:

> The root cause of these conditions lies in the home. They mean that slum clearances still lack completion; that low standards of living still persist, and that the lessons taught in the school clinic, and good social habits, do

---

[9] Titmuss, Richard M., *Problems of Social Policy* (1950) p508
[10] Ibid. p508
[11] Taylor, A. J. P., *English History 1914-1945* (Oxford, 1965) p455
[12] Welshman, John, "Evacuation, hygiene, and social policy: the Our Towns Report of 1943" *Historical Journal* 42, 3 1999 p783 refers to Harris, José "Some aspects of social policy in Britain during the Second World War" in Mommsen, W. J. (ed), *The Emergence of the Welfare State in Britain and Germany* (London, 1981) p247-62
[13] Hylton, op. cit. p44
[14] Macnicol, John, "The Evacuation of Schoolchildren" op. cit. p21

not always survive the pressure of bad home circumstances when young people have passed from supervision.[15]

Many Stepney homes fell into the category of "bad home circumstances" as we shall discover. Finally, Titmuss suggested that the state accepted a greater responsibility for those in need, which for children included the provision of more free school meals and the milk scheme.[16] However, the wartime expansion of free school meals and milk were actually planned before the war rather than being a product of evacuation.[17]

The conservative interpretation has its roots in the *Our Towns* report generated at the time of evacuation, which studied the relationship between poor parenting and social inadequacy based on the condition of the children arriving at the reception areas. The evacuation provided "…a window through which English town life was suddenly and vividly seen from a new angle".[18] The report was "to take the accusations levelled against the evacuees one by one and examine what evidence exists to support them and whether they can justly be brought by the countryside against the town".[19] The report commented that evacuees were often infested and lacked knowledge in basic hygiene,[20] aspects that have since formed the basis of numerous historical enquiries.[21] Bob Holman states that the report's conclusion was that it was "not the evacuees to blame, not the residents of the cities from where they came, no the whole nation was to blame for allowing such deprivation".[22] As the report noted in the

---

[15] MacNalty to Sir Maurice Holmes (Permanent Secretary at the Board of Education) in Macnicol, Ibid. p21

[16] Titmuss, op. cit. pp507-17

[17] The Milk in School Scheme was introduced in 1934

[18] A study made in 1939-1942 with certain recommendations by the Hygiene Committee of the Women's Group on Public Welfare (in association with the National Council of Social Service) *Our Towns A Close Up: A Study made during 1939-1942* (Oxford) pxi

[19] Ibid. pxi

[20] The most famous example of this being: "'You dirty thing, messing up the lady's carpet. Go and do it in the corner", said one Glasgow mother to her child, in a story that has passed into the folklore of the Second World War" quoted from Macnicol, op. cit. p7

[21] For example: Welshman, "Evacuation, hygiene and Social Policy" op. cit. pp781-807; Welshman, John "Evacuation and Social Policy During the Second World War: Myth and Reality" *Twentieth Century British History* Vol. 9 No. 1 1998 pp28-53 Hygiene Committee of the Women's Group on Public Welfare, *Our Towns* op. cit.

[22] Holman, Bob, *The Evacuation: A very British Revolution* (Oxford, 1995) p144

conclusion: "… through evacuation the depth of our social failure can be appreciated, can any measures be found which seem to hold real hope for amelioration?"[23]

John Macnicol has suggested that "after bombing, evacuation was the most crucial life event experienced by the civilian population"[24] due to the disruption in family ties but also the appallingly early age that the children found themselves having to stand on their own two feet, in "a strange and often hostile environment".[25] For example, many Stepney evacuees encountered hostility towards their Jewish background, as in the case of Anita Truman, whose experiences are reported later.[26]

Many of the children from Stepney slotted easily into numerous stereotypes of what evacuees were like. As reported in the press and in reports to government departments, they were: dirty, lice ridden, foul-mouthed, bed-wetters, and undomesticated. When the children arrived at their destinations they were "hot, dirty and tired" and in the morning the discovery that a "proportion of the children had wetted their beds" caused considerable "emotional disturbance". [27] Some of the children "had never slept in a separate bed" and their manner of speech, Cockney, was "the laziest accent".[28] For example, it was noted that:

> … of 300 children being evacuated from Northwold Road Public Elementary School, in the East End, in June 1940, only twenty-five were marked as needing special attention (or 8%) comprising one with scabies, five with nits, eight with enuresis (bed-wetting) and eleven with other conditions.[29]

The evacuee's mothers were perceived to be "impossible to live with and having the vocabulary of a Billingsgate fish porter".[30] Also, the mothers were unable to cook, supposedly because both mothers and children preferred take-away food, such as fish and chips. Reception homes were unaware that many evacuees had little access to proper kitchens or that they had never before enjoyed "water ready at hand in

---

[23] Hygiene Committee of the Women's Group on Public Welfare *Our Towns* op. cit. p101
[24] Macnicol, op. cit. p7
[25] Ibid. p8
[26] See section entitled *Evacuee Experiences*
[27] St Loe Strachey, Mrs, *Borrowed Children: A popular account of some evacuation problems and their remedies* (1940) p18
[28] Ibid. p18
[29] Report of June 1940 ED 50/206
[30] Macnicol, op. cit. p15

unlimited quantities".[31] The answers to a questionnaire of the period show that, of 125 respondents from various parts of London, only "about one-half had a kitchen or kitchen-parlour to themselves, while two out of every five had no kitchen at all".[32]

Evacuation "was the first of those social developments from the imperatives of military and civil defence which scrambled the people together and acquainted them with each other as never before".[33] This "scrambling" of the people "thrust a better standard of living in front of a small town's children, and a far worse one against the noses of middle-class householders".[34] This was to produce a discourse concerning "the social question" as the consequences of urban poverty on its victims had now been brought to national attention. Also, evacuation highlighted the imagined "two opposing ways of life – urban and rural".[35] James Hinton suggests the placement of impoverished urban working-class children in rural homes "involved the negotiation of profound cultural difference, not only between town and country but also between class and class".[36] These differences were to have long-term consequences for both working-class and middle-class perceptions of social inequality.

Some historians, however, have suggested that the experience of evacuation did not dissolve class barriers, instead the "war hardened ... social distinctions".[37] *England Arise!* states that: "most people remained preoccupied with their private spheres and rejected initiatives to make them community-spirited".[38] For Stepney, the community had been partly destroyed by evacuation – schoolchildren and mothers with babies were spread all over the South of England. The concern for those remaining in Stepney was for the evacuated members of their family. Were they being cared for properly? There was also the physical destruction of the community due to the bombing raids to worry about. As we shall discover, there were broader ramifications because, in reconstructing the area, the

---

[31] Smith, Hubert Llewellyn, *The New Survey of London Life & Labour* Vol. VI (1934) p314

[32] Ibid. p314

[33] Calder, op. cit. p34

[34] Ibid. p34

[35] Rose, S. O., *Which Peoples War? National Identity and Citizenship in Wartime Britain 1939-1945* (Oxford, 2003) p56, 208

[36] Hinton, James, *Women, Social Leadership and the Second World War: Continuities of Class* (Oxford, 2002) pp147-7

[37] Morgan, Kenneth O., *Britain Since 1945: The People's Peace* (Oxford, 2001) p18

[38] Fielding, Steven, Thompson, Peter and Tiratsoo, Nick, *England Arise!* (Manchester, 1995) p213

community was altered due to the dramatic reduction in the number of Stepney residents' – from a population of 225,238 in 1931 to 94,000 to be housed in the County of London Plan.[39] The post-war reconstruction scheme thus rejected initiatives to make Stepney community-spirited – rather the government's reconstruction plans almost destroyed what had traditionally been a tight-knit community. Generally in Stepney, because of the lack of housing and the vast deprivation of the area, families across generations had often remained under one roof. However, the historian Roger K. Lee sees a direct relationship between the physical post-war planning for East London and improved social welfare. The "planned removal of population" relieved the intense pressure on space and facilitated the physical improvement of the urban fabric.[40] Thus the long-term improvements for Stepney were to come at the price of the community.

The evacuation of Stepney schoolchildren was to show evacuees a different way of living. Whether it was a rural life with a working-class family, a privileged life with a middle-class family or life in a school camp, it was unlike anything they had experienced before. The mothers left behind faced their own war back in Stepney, which will be discussed in the next chapter. After the initial evacuation, it should be remembered there was an almost immediate drift back to Stepney, due to the lack of predicted or expected destruction during the so-called Phoney War. This led to a recurring movement of evacuees between their homes in Stepney and various reception areas in the south of England. Such movement was very much dependent upon the extent of the bombing raids in Stepney, as shown by the "trickle system" of evacuation that occurred throughout the war. There was one final wave of mass evacuation after the V1 and V2 bombs struck Stepney in 1944, when once again fear and panic were instilled in a vulnerable population.

Planning for the Evacuation of Stepney

In 1938, the government was already seriously discussing the evacuation of some of the population. It involved the "co-operation of our local government bodies", and there was to be no need for secrecy concerning the government plans so that well organised schemes of

---

[39] Appendix C Comparative Population Figures and Decentralization Proposed in County of London Plan in Purdom, C. B., *How Should We Rebuild London?* (1945) p242
[40] Lee, Roger K., "Planning and Social Change in East London" *East London Paper* Vol. 14 No. 1 April 1972 p31

evacuation could be achieved.[41] Although the plan for evacuation in the event of war had first been made public in 1933, the development of the plan was very much carried out in secret. As a result "very little account was taken of the views of those whose cooperation would be vital to their success – the authorities in both the evacuation and the receiving area, and the evacuation families themselves".[42]

The government's first essential task was to compile a record of all available accommodation for evacuees. It was estimated that the number of children of all ages to be evacuated, in and around the Administrative County of London alone, would be approximately one million.[43] In fact "1,300,000 children and adults in the Metropolitan Area"[44] were in the end evacuated, after the previous figure was revised in May 1939.

The ideal plan was to have the evacuation take place two days prior to the actual outbreak of hostilities.[45] The first day would see the evacuation of children and school parties. On the second day mothers with babies and pre-school children would be evacuated. There was a suggested list of things to be sent along with each child. Their hand luggage would include: "the child's gas mask, a change of underclothing, nightclothes, house shoes or plimsolls, spare stocking or socks, a tooth brush, a knife, fork, spoon, mug and plate, comb, towel and handkerchief".[46] Also to be sent were: a warm coat or mackintosh, if the child possessed one, and food for the journey. The identity of a child and the school they attended needed to be visible. It was understood that not all parents would be able to meet all these requirements, but children were to be sent with as many of these items as possible in order to help the reception areas. "In Oxfordshire, the Schools Medical Officer noted of the London evacuees that 'a large number were under-clad and many poorly clothed with worn-out garments, including footwear'".[47]

Billeting officers were meant to find the necessary accommodation for the refugees and it was stated that "… the obligation to receive refugees

---

[41] MT 55/261 *Government Evacuation Plan 1938–1939* Emergency Organisation of Road Transport Evacuation Arrangements – General "A Conference on evacuation was held at the Ministry of Health on the 24th November 1938"

[42] Hylton, op. cit. p40

[43] MT 55/261 Circular 1759 *Government Evacuation Scheme* Ministry of Health 5th January 1939

[44] *East End News* 9 May, 1939

[45] Ibid. 5th January 1939

[46] Ibit. 5th January 1939

[47] Oxford Education Committee, *Report of the SMO, 1939* p11 in Welshman, John, "Evacuation and Social Policy" op. cit. p41

must be rigorously applied without regard to class or other distinctions".[48] In some cases, receiving homes that did not want evacuees and were nonetheless obliged to receive them could make the experience of evacuation painful thanks to their unwelcoming attitude. However, for other refugees, the experience of evacuation was a wonderful one. Unfortunately, as the personal accounts of evacuees show us, the experience they could expect when they left for the country was often left to a lottery of chance. Another problem that the Anderson Committee – a committee set up in May 1938 by the Home Secretary with four Members of Parliament under Sir John Anderson – did not anticipate was the hostility of working-class parents to the idea of sending their children to live with complete strangers. As the *East End News* reported:

> Children and mothers not wishing to come under the Government scheme could either remain at home or make personal arrangements for leaving, and if they remained at home no compulsory measure regarding them would be taken. Obviously it would be completely unjust and indeed impossible to go down to the homes of the people and drive them out.[49]

Also, for the hostesses and hosts seeing these "ill-clad, undernourished children" in their homes would have shown them, as nothing else could have done, the situation of many East Enders. It was reported that the "hostesses of today will not want to see their work undone" and that "they will have an interest which they could never have had otherwise in safeguarding the children temporarily committed to their care".[50]

With the international situation worsening rapidly, with the probable threat of Hitler's invasion of Poland,[51] tension in London increased. On 24 August 1939, the LCC recalled all staff from their holidays. On 25 August, the schools were instructed to re-assemble. This was followed on 26 August by the "get ready" signal. On Monday, 28 August, war diarist George Beardmore wrote: "… London schoolchildren are already labelled

---

[48] HLG 7/126 Ministry of Housing and Local Government, Evacuation of London Supplement Circular Amendment of Scheme *Draft Circular to the Clerk of the County Councils of Essex, Kent, Suffolk, Cambridge, Huntingdon, Isles of Ely, Northampton, Bedford, Hertford, Buckingham, Oxford, Berkshire, Wiltshire, Hampshire, Surrey and Sussex.*
[49] *East End News* 25 May 1939
[50] Ibid. 2 January 1940
[51] On 1 September 1939 Hitler invaded Poland. Chamberlain had entered a military commitment to defend Poland. After an attempt to patch up a last-minute compromise, however, Chamberlain declared war on Germany in a broadcast on 3 September 1939.

to be shifted out to the country in trains already assembled",[52] as schoolchildren were called to a massive evacuation rehearsal. The *East End News* reported that "... the response was [from] about 70 per cent of the pupils which was considered to be satisfactory".[53] Mr Lacey, head teacher of Upper North Street School, said that "the only thing that might upset their plans was if certain parents changed their minds at the last minute ..."[54] The Ministry of Health's response to the rehearsal was:

> The evacuation rehearsal which took place this morning in schools over an area containing some 11,000,000 inhabitants with a school population of over 1,000,000 was markedly successful. The response by both parents and children was very good.[55]

The Initial Evacuation

The first evacuation from London took place as planned two days prior to the outbreak of war on 3 September. Over 650,000 persons, including women and young children were moved according to the Government's Evacuation Scheme.[56] A government message received at County Hall at 11.07am on Thursday, 31 August ordered the commencement of evacuation the following day, 1 September. The transport authorities confirmed that they were fully prepared and the evacuation signal was given at 11.19am. It was to reach every one of the 78 "key" officials before noon and the operation commenced promptly the next morning, Friday, 1 September.[57]

Edith Ramsay, a Stepney councillor, was put in charge of a "non-school" party, which was evacuated on the first day of the war. When war was declared at 11am she was in the playground of Farrance Street School where those to be evacuated were gathered – schoolchildren, travelling with their families rather than their schools, and the very old. Edith's group of evacuees were taken to Paddington on buses en route for Bath.[58] The schoolchildren evacuated as a party from Farrance Street School,

---

[52] Beardmore, George, *Civilians at War: Journals 1938–1946* (Oxford, 1947) p30
[53] *East End News* 1 September 1939
[54] Ibid. 1 September 1939
[55] Ibid. 1 September 1939
[56] HLG 7/126 *The Government's Evacuation Scheme Plans V & VI* 10 July 1940
[57] ED 138/49 LCC Record of Evacuation 1938–1945. The Evacuation of September 1939
[58] Sokoloff, Bertha, *Edith and Stepney* (London, 1987) p95

found their destination was in the area of Somerton, Somerset.[59] Valerie
Gibbs was an eight-year-old child who was evacuated from the Stepney
area. She was among the children assembled in St George's School hall.
Later, she recalled being:

> ... marched down to Notting Hill Gate tube station, and eventually boarded
> [onto] a special train which took us to Ealing station, where we boarded a
> Great Western train which arrived at Chippenham, Wiltshire. After a short
> bus trip we were dropped off at Lacock, a small village about 13 miles
> from Bath, in Somerset.[60]

Those parties travelling by rail were to assemble at 1,589 points and
pass through controls to one of 169 entraining stations. "11 exchange
stations were used in the transfer of parties from the London Passenger
Transport Board (LPTB) system to the main-line railways" and the
"parties detrained at 271 stations in the reception areas".[61] According to
the remaining written records on the operation of initial evacuation, close
contact with key points such as railway stations and headquarters
organising the scheme was maintained. It is through such material,[62] that it
has been possible to piece together with some accuracy where the children
from the Stepney area were evacuated to.

So, where did the schoolchildren of Stepney end up? The final
distribution of London's children shows a close relationship to the main
line railways and the location of the schools they left from in London. It
was reported that:

> ... schools in South London are now to be found chiefly in Kent, Surrey
> and Sussex; those within reach of Waterloo Station find themselves in
> Dorset and Devon; those in the Paddington area are along the Great
> Western Railway line from Berkshire to Cornwall; while St Pancras
> schools are largely in Bedfordshire and Marylebone schools in
> Buckinghamshire.[63]

---

[59] See School Evacuation Table
[60] Wicks, Ben, *The Day they took the Children* (1989) p21
[61] ED 138/49 LCC op. cit. The Evacuation of September 1939
[62] LCC Government Evacuation Scheme, Directory of London Schools in the
Reception Area – December 1939; National Archives MEPO 3/2501 Evacuation of
School Children 1st day of evacuation
[63] ED 138/32 Education in Wartime. Evacuation and Education in London 1939–
1945. Distribution of the London Children

For London and the environs eastward of the Metropolitan Police District it was suggested that "the rural part of Kent, Surrey and Sussex should be considered as a reception area for the areas south of the river Thames; and that the rural districts of Essex, Suffolk and Norfolk should be similarly considered for the areas north of the river".[64] And for the Metropolitan Police District which included Stepney, "the area recommended for reception lies east of a line formed by, approximately, the western boundaries of Dorset and Wiltshire to Gloucestershire, with the exception of the area south of Winchester and part of the New Forest which will be required for Southampton and Portsmouth".[65]

The pattern of the evacuation of Stepney's schoolchildren can be seen in the attached table. It shows the number of children evacuated from each school, and from which underground station their journey commenced. It also reveals the main-line stations that took them out of London and onto their final destination. However, this research has raised some issues. Firstly, the exact movement of each school to the main-line station can not be determined. There was a tally of the numbers sent to the main-line stations: for example, from Stepney Green 2,880 schoolchildren were sent to Ealing, 740 to Richmond and 2,964 to Wimbledon. From which schools the children came, however, is unclear. What is shown is that batches of about 700 schoolchildren were sent to Richmond, Ealing, Wimbledon and New Cross Gate. The underground station from which their journey commenced determined which of the four main-line stations they were taken to.[66] From Mile End, Whitechapel, Aldgate East and Stepney Green, which all accessed the District Line, it naturally followed that the school parties were taken to Ealing, Richmond or Wimbledon. From Shadwell and Wapping the school parties were taken down to New Cross Gate.

A notable feature here is that, apart from Ealing, all the main-line stations (Richmond, Wimbledon and New Cross Gate) were south of the River Thames, which in the planning for evacuation, were distribution points for those residents south of the Thames, rather than north like Stepney. However, for Stepney, and the eastern areas, the District Line provided access to the main-line stations out of London and would thus be the reason why so many school parties ended up in south or west London. For those travelling out from New Cross Gate, their final destination was Sussex, Brighton and Eastbourne. Those travelling out from Wimbledon and Richmond went westwards to Buckinghamshire, Wiltshire, Gloucestershire, and Somerset. Some parties, though, who were taken over

---

[64] HO 186/128 General File. Evacuation of England and Wales. Government Scheme
[65] Ibid. Evacuation of England and Wales.
[66] MEPO 3/2501 Evacuation of School Children 1st day of evacuation

to Ealing ended up in Norfolk, Suffolk, Ely, Cambridge, Essex and Hertfordshire.

A second point to note is what the Ministry of Education described as an "outstanding feature of interest" in the distribution of school evacuees:

a) Neighbouring schools in London find themselves neighbours outside, although generally further apart, unless they happen to be in towns.
b) The density distribution has been very uneven. There is a great concentration of children in Sussex, which has one quarter of the total number evacuated from London. This is partly due to the abundance of accommodation in resorts such as Brighton, Hove, Worthing, Eastbourne and Hastings, but the heavy concentration is also present in rural Sussex much more than in rural areas elsewhere.
c) There are strong concentrations in Bedfordshire, Northamptonshire, Hertfordshire, Kent and Surrey.
d) Relatively few have gone to the more distant south-western counties such as Wiltshire, Somerset, Devon and Cornwall. East Coast counties, with the exception of Norfolk, have relatively few but even in Norfolk the distribution is by no means dense.[67]

Stepney, as can be seen from the table, had a presence in nearly all the above areas, barring Devon and Cornwall. For Stepney's schools, those evacuated from the same underground station appear to have ended up in similar areas, so that neighbouring schools would still be neighbouring in reception areas. However, members of a single school could be scattered over quite a large area, as one head mistress reported of an East End school relocated to Norfolk:

We are scattered in 7 villages and in 4 schools, Wroxham (33), Rachheath (34), South Walsham (84) and Upton (15). It is twelve miles between Wroxham and Upton, the two extreme villages; there is no railway or bus route. I managed to get a second-hand bicycle, and my daily rides are from 8-14-24 miles; it depends where I'm working.[68]

Sources show that discrepancies sometimes arose between the number of schoolchildren departing from the main-line stations and those arriving to start their journey at the underground stations of Shadwell and Wapping. Numbers of those arriving were often fewer. This could be due to miscounting at either end or it can be speculated that school parties

---

[67] ED 138/32 op. cit. Distribution of the London Children
[68] Ibid. ED 138/32 Report from the head mistress of an East End school now in Norfolk

were sent elsewhere, but neither hypothesis can be confirmed. It is worth bearing in mind that every other underground station in the area produced figures that tallied exactly with the main-line stations the evacuees passed through. Many of the schools were given a numeric code in order to identify them. For some of the schools, such as St Mark's Church of England, its numeric code was the only way to distinguish it from others of the same name, but in the chaos and confusion caused by such vast numbers of school parties passing through the stations distinguishing the schools by numeric code as well as name may not have occurred.

In this table, only the initial destination of the schools is shown. Some secondary destinations have been written in by hand,[69] but probably not all, as the book is dated December 1939 and it is questionable as to whether additional movements were added. Often teachers writing to the local newspapers at the time described that their pupils ended up in a city and its surrounding area, for example Upper North Street School ended up in Oxford and its surrounding area.[70] From the perspective of the LCC it was to prove an impossible task to keep a note of all the movements of the schools. Instead, the task fell to individual boroughs and the Divisional Dispersal Officer to keep track of their schoolchildren.

Frank Lewey, Mayor of Stepney, states: "… we were far too busy to keep records of the evacuees. It was … all we could do to get them out of London fast enough".[71] Generally speaking, keeping a record of where people ended up after evacuation, planned or otherwise, was one of the greatest problems for the authorities. The problem with keeping up with evacuees was highlighted by a LCC report on a visit to Stepney, as there was an "urgent need for some means of keeping track of people who have left the district so that their relations can get in touch with them".[72] Stepney council only knew "general figures such as [that] … one hundred and fifty had gone to Ealing, two hundred and thirty to Richmond, and so on".[73] They could not even tell relatives whether their relatives had been "evacuated or just buried under the local rubble by some bomb explosion".[74]

---

[69] See LCC *Government Evacuation Scheme, Directory of London Schools in the Reception Area* – December 1939
[70] *East End News* 2 January 1940
[71] Lewey, Frank R., (Mayor of Stepney during the London Blitz) *Cockney Campaign* (1944) p22
[72] HO 186/128 op. cit. General File Evacuation
[73] Lewey, op. cit. p22
[74] Ibid. p22

Communication between Evacuees and Stepney

The teacher and helpers who had been evacuated with the children also contacted the local newspapers, such as the *East End News,* in order to send back information about the local children. This was largely a propaganda exercise to try and boost morale at home. A common fear amongst parents left behind in Stepney and the rest of the East End is summed up in the words of one mother, talking to a reporter:

> I'm afraid my children will never want to come back home. They're in a lovely place, with a large bedroom and a bathroom next door. They have good food, with as much butter and cream and fresh milk as they like. I can't give them these things. It will not be surprising if they're discontented when they come back.[75]

A teacher who accompanied children from Upper North Street School wrote to the *East End News* saying that they had ended up in Oxford and its surrounding area, and where the children were happy and in comfortable homes. A school for the children to be taught in had not yet been provided, but the children would be getting together "as of Monday for walks and games".[76] Many of the foster-families possessed cars and so the children were enjoying rides out in the countryside. Some had been to the cinema and others were sharing bicycles. The children gained many new skills from the experience. They also had some memorable comments about the fruit and vegetables growing in their new surroundings, such as: "But they're in boxes where I live" and "ours grow in tins; they aren't dirty like that".[77] Children also became very resourceful and set up their own allotments; "they planted peas, potatoes, cabbages, and anything else they could make grow",[78] thus aiding the "Dig for Victory" cause. The children from the Mary Day Nursery, Tidey Street, Bow, found themselves living in a beautiful twelfth century Priory in Hertfordshire. The children's exam results were even published in the local newspaper.

Councillor Frank Lewey, Mayor of Stepney, and Councillor Dan Frankel, MP for Mile End, made a surprise visit to the evacuated children of the East End, in Alyesbury. Mr Lewey addressed the children and told them "... that they were in the country for their own safety and asked them

---

[75] *East End News* 2 January 1940
[76] Ibid. 2 January 1940
[77] Ministry of Information on behalf of the Board of Education *The Schools in Wartime* (1941) p9
[78] *Essex and East London Newspapers Ltd* 28 May 1976

to be on their best behaviour in their new homes".[79] Also, Mr Lewey brought with him news from Stepney. He told the children: "the people of Stepney are always thinking of you" and "with the help of the LCC we are doing all we can for your comfort".[80] Therefore, the newspapers and leading figures in the community tried to keep a two-way path of news and communication between the children of the borough and their parents.

The Camp Schools

Some schools were sent off to holiday camps, which were known as "Camp Schools". The boys sent to such camps ended up with a very regimented lifestyle according to accounts of their day-to-day life. Two hundred boys from north and east London were sent to the Golden Sands camp at Hopton-on-Sea, Norfolk, on the east coast. From the table of evacuation it can be seen that it was the special schools, Pigott Street Special, Tollett Special and Lowood Street Special, who were sent to the Hopton-on-Sea holiday camp from the Stepney area. It was reported that the boys would turn their hand to whatever was needed: "... if boots need mending the lads mend them. If clothes become shabby they are renewed".[81] A typical day for the boys would be filled with a mixture of work and play:

> He rises at 8.00, washes, dresses, tidies his hut and has breakfast at 8.30. During the morning he is at 'school' in the camp halls until dinner at 12.30pm. Following a rest he is busy once more till tea-time at 4.30; then he enjoys two hours of free recreation before supper at seven. Supper over he retires to his hut and reads or writes home till lights out at 8.30.[82]

One very important conclusion drawn by masters accompanying the children is that "in their three months of country life, the general health of the lads has improved enormously".[83] This shows how evacuation could bring improvements to the lives of evacuated children. However, this was unusual. Throughout the war, surveys were carried out by the Board of Education to assess the children's growth rates, which were often found to be "retarded".[84] The only explanation that could be offered by officials

---

[79] *East End News* 2 January 1940
[80] Ibid. 2 January 1940
[81] Ibid. 2 January 1940
[82] Ibid. 2 January 1940
[83] Ibid. 2 January 1940
[84] The reports, containing detailed statistical evidence, are in ED 50/211

was that "since children grew fastest during school holiday periods, the constant attendance at a camp school inhibited development: the regime of organised games, for example, caused children to burn up too much energy".[85]

The Trickle System

After the initial evacuation, there was a steady movement out of London by children, mothers with babies and pre-school children. Evacuations occurred three times a week. From July 1940, this was substantially reduced to once a fortnight in normal circumstances, but when there were heavy raids the number of evacuations was increased again.[86] It was hoped that there would be two advantages to this new "trickle" system:

> a) It will reduce the number of occasions on which local authorities in the reception areas have to be asked to receive parties, though the parties, when sent out, will naturally be larger than at present
> b) It will do something to discourage repeated re-evacuation. (There is evidence that some families are returning to London on the slightest excuse with the intention of at once registering for re-evacuation).[87]

With the lack of expected bombing, evacuees began to drift back home. By 31 August 1940, a total of some 765,000 persons had been moved from the London evacuation area since August 1939. This was in fact only 59 per cent of the original figure estimated for evacuation back in May 1939.[88] Of those unaccompanied schoolchildren, mothers with children and expectant mothers evacuated only 286,000 still remained in reception areas, thus some "480,000 persons (or over 60 per cent of the total number evacuated) had, therefore, returned to the evacuation areas or otherwise passed out of the scheme".[89] Between the end of August 1940 and February 1941, 350,000 schoolchildren were evacuated. Of this number almost 50 per cent had returned.[90] In a review of schools

---

[85] Memorandum by Bransby, E. R., "The Wartime Growth of Children", 6 October 1944, 50,211
[86] HLG 7/126 *The Government's Evacuation Scheme Plans V & VI* 10 July 1940
[87] Ibid. 10 July 1940
[88] 1,300,000 estimated figure in May 1939, *East End News* 9 May 1939
[89] MH 101/14 Ministry of Health War Diary Part B, Government evacuation scheme statement of position at 12 February 1941, Diary of events relating to evacuation 1939-46
[90] Ibid. Diary of events relating to evacuation 1939-46

evacuated it was found that of 216 children evacuated in 1939 from Morpeth St Central, to Bury St Edmunds, Suffolk only 49 children were on the roll on 31 July 1942.[91]

In September 1940 there were three distinct types of movement occurring:

a) evacuation to relatives etc outside the East End
b) evacuation to friends and relatives in other parts of the East End – families getting together under one roof
c) … movement to the West End at night. People stay in the West of London for the night.[92]

It is difficult to establish the extent of the movement. In Great Smithy Street, for instance – an area in the middle of the bombed area, that had not actually been bombed – about 50–60 per cent of the population were evacuated. The investigator, Nina Masel, an observer of the area who commented on everyday life through writing reports, distributing questionnaires and keeping a diary, had been left alone in the house where she rented a room on Great Smithy Street.[93] However, for those who had friends outside the borough who could accommodate them, "grants of money were given by the Assistance Board, to cover their fares".[94] Rachel Reckitt, who was in charge of the Citizens' Advice Bureau which was based at Toynbee Hall, was keen to see the elderly members of the population evacuated, so when she heard the Mayor of Stepney, Frank Lewey say that "he was giving out money to anyone needing it", Reckitt's response was to send him "all the hard cases I have in the next week with a note asking him to give them rail tickets etc".[95]

Schoolchildren were the responsibility of the LCC and the local office in Harford Street co-ordinated re-evacuation. Large-scale arrangements were officially in the hands of the Borough Council, located during wartime at the People's Palace. One thing that was not anticipated by council workers at the People's Palace, where Stepney citizens went for

---

[91] ED 138/32 Education in Wartime. Evacuation and Education in London 1939–1945. LCC Central Schools Review 16 October 1942. Also see School Evacuation table.

[92] MOA, TC Part 6 Reel 95 2/G East End Aug–Sept 1940

[93] Nina Masel was known as "the East End Unit" Ibid. Part 6 Reel 95 2/G Aug–Sept 1940

[94] Ramsay, Edith, *Life in Stepney: World War II, 1939–45* (1976) Pamphlet 080 Tower Hamlets Local History Archive p6

[95] Reckitt, Rachel, *Stepney Letters: Extracts from Written by Rachel Reckitt, from Stepney during the "Blitz" of 1940–41* (Cumbria, 1993) p14

assistance, was that evacuating mothers with babies were leaving their prams outside the People's Palace. When the Mayor, Frank Lewey, left work in the evening he was met with the view of "a great area of deserted prams in the evening light, with the drifting smoke of nearby burning houses dimming them".[96] This was because mothers were unable to take their prams on the overcrowded trains and so they abandoned them in front of the building. By the evening it was "hardly possible to get in or out except by climbing over a great expanse of them".[97]

Stepney's Deputation to the Home Secretary

By September 1940 it was generally felt by the churches of the East End[98] that the area was uninhabitable. On 17 September 1940, Rev E. G. Miles, a Presbyterian, sent Mr Malcolm MacDonald (son of Ramsay MacDonald former Labour Prime Minister) with a deputation to see the Home Secretary, Herbert Morrison. Instead they saw a Mr Lidbury, who was Controller of Civil Defence at Nottingham.[99] The deputation urged "most strongly that steps should be taken forthwith to evacuate all who were not required for essential employment in an area bounded on the north by the Mile End Road and running to Upton Park station in West Ham and bounded on the south by the river".[100] This area included Stepney, Poplar, parts of Mile End, Bow and West Ham. The deputation stated that:

> ... the population had been subjected to practically continuous bombing and that a breaking point was being reached. So far there had been no panic and no signs of any kind of rioting, but there was a deep resentment at the apparent absence of any government policy. It was the considered view of Mr Paton and Mr Grosen that a breaking point was bound to be reached soon when the population would stream out of the area and could not be held in check.[101]

However, in response to the deputation, Mr Dalton, the Commissioner of Police, found from his own observations that "... nothing ... would lead

---

[96] Lewey, op. cit. p20
[97] Ibid. p20
[98] Other members of the deputation included Father N. Grosen, Mr Millar of the English Presbytarian Church, Stepney, and Mr Paton of West Ham. HO 186/342 General File, Evacuation from East End of London
[99] *The Times House of Commons Guide* (1945) p89
[100] HO 186/342 op. cit. Evacuation from East End of London
[101] Ibid. HO 186/342 Evacuation from East End of London

me to the conclusion that a compulsory evacuation of the people ... is either necessary or desirable".[102]

Another major problem highlighted by the evacuation was the lack of understanding between those organising it and those participating in it. The organisers would have been high-ranking male civil servants of the upper middle-classes who would have been sent away as children to boarding school. Thus they would not have experienced much "family life". By comparison those evacuated would have been women and children from the working classes from tight-knit families, who would, in times of crisis, want to bond together and not be apart. Therefore, evacuation was a major upheaval for working-class people of the 1930s, overwhelmingly unused to spending nights away from home. The deputation felt that it was not sufficient to remove mothers and children, as in the East End it was common for several generations to live together and that "the only practical course was to move the family as a unit, less any essential workers, and also so far as possible to keep local groups together".[103] In another attempt to overcome this problem, the LCC introduced the cheap visits scheme, which enabled parents to visit their children by train at a reduced rate.

The deputation also criticised the fact that in the East End the local and government officials were keeping to a 10am to 4pm regime, six days a week, as "it was impossible to get a billeting officer on a Sunday".[104] This would have caused many problems, as the war on the homefront did not keep to office hours. Another criticism centred on the lack of petrol available to social workers transporting people away from the Stepney and the surrounding area. They could obtain cars and drivers "but there was no machinery for getting petrol for them".[105] However, even with these difficulties, the Commissioner of Police, Mr Dalton, found at Redman's Road School, Stepney Green – a Rest, Food and Collecting Centre for Stepney – "about 30 people waiting for billets; 150 had been evacuated from this School this morning".[106] At the main dispersal centre for Stepney and Poplar, the People's Palace, Mile End Road, "nearly 2,000 people had

---

[102] Metropolitan Police Letter 19 September 1940, Ibid HO 186/342 Evacuation from East End of London
[103] Ibid. HO 186/342 Evacuation from East End of London
[104] Ibid. HO 186/342 Evacuation from East End of London
[105] Ibid. HO 186/342 Evacuation from East End of London
[106] Metropolitan Police Letter 19 September 1940, Ibid. HO 186/342 Evacuation from East End of London

been evacuated" and "about 50 persons, mostly women and children [were] waiting for billets".[107]

The removal of refugees to isolated units in other parts of London was criticised by the deputies as it resulted in refugees feeling isolated and stranded and returning to the East End. The Commissioner of Police found that those who had been sent to Paddington and Wandsworth returned because "bombing had taken place in those districts and they preferred to remain in their own district unless they could be sent farther out".[108] An obvious place for refugees to be moved to was Epping, in Essex. Bus route No. 70 had a pick-up point at Cephas Street School, Stepney and a capacity of removing 500 people. In the event of Cephas Street School becoming full or being rendered unusable, the second pick-up point was Greencoat School, Whitehouse Road, Stepney, which had a capacity for 250 people.[109]

Evacuees' Experiences

What were the stories of the evacuees? Looking at many of the personal accounts of those evacuated from Stepney one can see that a recurring theme is that of re-evacuation. Joyce Lester for example went to Dagenham with her mother, returned and went to Mill Hill where they lived in two different homes, and then went to a requisitioned house in Hendon.[110] Kenny Micallef was evacuated to Guilford along with his mother, brother and sister. On their first evacuation they shared a big old house with fifteen families, where there were many rows over sleeping, rations and cooking arrangements. For his second billet, the family went to Bertha, just outside Guilford, where they had a two–bed roomed house. He felt that they were resented because they were the only evacuees in Bertha; there was another evacuated family in central Guilford, who they kept in touch with and then later another family moved in about a mile away. Kenny says that they would only associate with the other evacuees and felt that it was a case of "them" and "us". The local children seemed "snobby" to him and he says that the teachers treated them differently. There was not much money coming into the house as their father was away at sea, so as he put it, the children were dressed scruffily when they went to school. He

---

[107] Ibid. HO 186/342 Evacuation from East End of London
[108] Ibid. HO 186/342 Evacuation from East End of London
[109] MT 55/264 Movement of Refugees to Fringe Areas – Picking-up Points and Routes
[110] IWM interview ID Number 20091 Lester, Joyce Iris

recalls having thick bread and jam to eat whereas the locals had sandwiches and fruit – something that Kenny had hardly ever seen.[111]

Anita Truman, who was eight years old when evacuated, recalled that "it all sounded wonderful. We were going into the 'country'. We would see cows and sheep and trees and flowers. These things weren't exactly in abundance in London's East End".[112] Her adventure began at about nine o'clock, as she headed off on foot to Stepney Green Station. Once there, the children were ushered onto the waiting train by their teacher "I wasn't sad or unhappy – in fact I was quite looking forward to the adventure" recalls Anita.[113] As the train pulled out, neither the children nor their parents knew the final destination. Anita's parents had insisted that she must not be separated from her brother. It turned out that they were taken to Windsor.

On arrival "we were taken to a church hall and there we were given brown carrier bags with string handles. Inside we found sandwiches, a cold drink and a bar of chocolate".[114] There were lots of children in the hall. All the children were marched down a very long road, with rows and rows of houses and outside each stood a housewife. Then "as we walked along, the housewife would say, 'I'll have a girl', or 'I'll have two little boys'".[115] Anita ended up staying with Mr and Mrs Taylor, and their 12-year-old son, who one day asked if he could look at Anita's head. When she asked him why, "he told me that he had heard that Jews had horns!"[116] This shows that, even during the evacuation, there was no escape for many from anti-Semitic comments and prejudice.

Education for Returning Children

In the inner cities, schools had been closed so that any children who were not evacuated or who returned from evacuation "were free to roam the streets all day and, if they were so inclined, get up to mischief".[117] By Christmas 1939, "nearly 90 per cent of the mothers evacuated in September had returned home, compared with about 40 per cent of

---

[111] IWM interview ID Number 11835 Micallef, Kenny

[112] Schweitzer, Pam, and Andrew, Andy, & Fawcett, Pat (ed.), *Goodnight Children Everywhere: Memories of Evacuation in World War Two* (1990) p230

[113] Ibid. p230

[114] Ibid. p230

[115] Ibid. p233

[116] Ibid. p233

[117] Hylton, op. cit. p43

unaccompanied children".[118] The first official count of those who had returned occurred in January 1940 and "indicated that over 900,000 evacuees had returned in all, about 60 per cent".[119] With so many children back in London it was necessary for the LCC to organise some kind of teaching for the children. A Fabian Society report found that "eventually 12 emergency secondary schools were opened in April 1940, to give half-time education to a maximum of 250 pupils per school"[120] but this would still prove inadequate. The chief wartime education scheme in London in the autumn of 1939 was the "Home Tuition Scheme". Teachers were peripatetic in that they "collected small groups of children, and taught them in any room which could be borrowed".[121] The report stated that:

> Some teachers, when drafted to the staff of reopening schools, were actually sorry to abandon their groups, and the relative success of this strange experiment shows that there is scope for informal educational methods to be tried out in the elementary schools.[122]

It was a "humorous accident of officialdom" that many of the schools selected to be reopened were "frequently junior schools where the desks were too small for the senior children invited to attend!"[123]

With the schools being deserted, due to the evacuation of the schoolchildren, other purposes for the buildings had been found; many were now Rest Centres for those who had been made homeless during the bombing raids. Edith Ramsay, for example, was in charge of the Rest Centre at Dempsey Street School. She found it extraordinary that although many preparations had been made during the Phoney War, such as vast numbers of papier-mâché coffins being held at the Stepney Jewish Hospital in anticipation of the huge casualties anticipated, "the needs of the homeless – shelter, food and clothing – had not been envisaged; to these needs volunteers responded magnificently".[124] The Highways Club saw Lady Ravensdale and Vera Grenfell work tirelessly "helping the homeless, arranging evacuation and cheering all concerned".[125] At the Bernard Baron Settlement and the Stepney Jewish Club, the leaders, Rose

---

[118] Brown, op. cit. p36
[119] Ibid. p36
[120] Padley, Richard and Cole, Margaret (ed.), *Evacuation Survey: A Report to the Fabian Society* (1940) p200
[121] Ibid. p200
[122] Ibid. p202
[123] Ibid. p202
[124] Ramsay, Edith, *Life in Stepney: World War II* Pamphlet op. cit. p5
[125] Ibid. p6

and Basil Henriques and Phyllis Gerson, made the clubs into centres to help the neighbourhood. Toynbee Hall, under Dr J. J. Mallon, affectionately known as "our Jimmy" and assisted by his Secretary, Miss M. R. Kendall, "did magnificent work" according to Edith Ramsay.[126]

The Final Wave of Evacuation

The issue of evacuation was to span most of the war. A final wave of evacuation occurred after 13 June 1944 when the V1s or "Doodle Bugs" came. The V1 was a small pilot-less aircraft with a range of 130 miles, carrying an explosive warhead of two-thirds of a ton.[127] Of the 144 V1s that crossed the English Channel on the first day, 73 exploded in London and of these 36 exploded in Stepney with a further six exploding nearby.[128] Edith Ramsay estimates that, during this final wave of evacuation, "only 1 in 5 of the total London evacuees went officially – the others made their own arrangements, and I think this was true of Stepney".[129] Many people had formed relationships with their children's hosts, even though the children may have returned from evacuation, and used these relationships for private evacuation. With the deprivation of housing and lack of repairs "a large number of Stepney born and rooted families had moved and settled in new areas".[130] The Mayor of Stepney, Frank Lewey also commented on the many hundreds of people who walked away from Stepney "carrying their goods with them, but penniless".[131] The problem was that, once they had left the area, they could not be helped by the council. The Mayor heard that some got as far as Reading, which was 40 miles away, "… walking, carrying their goods. No home, no work, no money. Kind people took them in at night or they slept under a haystack".[132] All this underlines the fact that there was a relative lack of co-ordination in the evacuation process. Although it was a vast scheme, there were many cracks in the system. With people making their own arrangements, alongside official ones, there was much confusion, and no doubt those making their own arrangements felt let down by the official system.

---

[126] Ibid. p6
[127] Gardiner, Juliet and Wenborn, Neil (ed.), *The History Today Companion to British History* (1995) p774
[128] Ramsay, Edith *Life in Stepney: World War II* Pamphlet op. cit. p13
[129] Ibid. p13
[130] Ibid. p13
[131] Lewey, op. cit. p22
[132] Ibid. p23

Conclusion

In the year prior to the war there was much discussion officially, by the Anderson Committee, on how cities would be defended in the event of bombing, which was inevitably problematic due to the unknown length of the war or the exact nature of the bombing. As only so much immediate evacuation could be planned and carried out, they asked themselves what would happen next. How long would evacuees need to be kept away from their homes? Would they have homes to even return to? Such questions were unanswerable until such events occurred. Only then could solutions be found. The evacuation scheme itself was a scheme that would have to be implemented at short notice. So prior planning of how things could be carried out was the only way to necessitate any kind of smooth running of the system in the few short days of the initial school evacuation, which for Stepney saw the evacuation of some 32,000 schoolchildren to a wide variety of locations covering such areas as Buckinghamshire, Hertfordshire, Surrey, Gloucestershire, Somerset, Wiltshire, Berkshire, Sussex, Cambridgeshire, Suffolk, and Norfolk.[133]

What this study of the experiences of Stepney's schoolchildren reveals is the multifaceted nature of that evacuation. Some teachers who accompanied school parties described a happy country life for the evacuees, such as the children from Upper North Street School who ended up in Oxford. Other children were evacuated to "Camp Schools" and a regimented way of life ensued, with a strict timetable of activities. For those, such as Kenny Micallef, who was evacuated with his mother, when their first reception area proved unsuccessful, they returned to Stepney to be re-evacuated. Another factor for Stepney's Jewish evacuees was that the taunts they had received in Stepney also followed them to their reception homes, as seen through Anita Truman's experience. There was no "one experience" for evacuation, even when looking at a single area, such as Stepney.

The experience of witnessing the evacuation of Stepney brought the poverty and deprivation of the evacuees' home area to the attention of the residents of the various reception areas. It was evacuation that moved the poor families, such as Stepney's, into the reception area's living rooms. What came to the attention of the nation was the scale of the deprivation that many evacuees had endured, for example that "two out of every five had no kitchen at all".[134] The *Our Towns* report "echoed interwar debates

---

[133] See attached Table for more details of reception areas.

[134] Smith, Hubert Llewellyn, *The New Survey of London Life & Labour* Vol. VI (1934) p314

about behaviour and citizenship, but also reflected the ideas that would shape the welfare state in the post-war years".[135] The report suggested recommendations to address the issue of bad feeding habits, such as "a publicity campaign on the formation of good feeding habits in young children".[136] It also suggested that "education in cookery and dietary needs should be greatly extended".[137] Such assertions followed the argument that the condition of the children was the result of poor parenting and social inadequacy, which could be addressed through the rehabilitation and education of the parents.

The report also recommended that there should be: "a separate front door, water-closet, bathroom and kitchen to each 'let'".[138] Such ideals were striven for in the reconstruction plans for Stepney, as we shall discover in chapter ten. Thus evacuation was a factor in the reconstruction of Stepney in the post-war era. The subsequent social enquiry that evacuation brought to the nation also had its part to play in social reconstruction. The artificial conditions of war generated a basis for change, socially, through the welfare state, but also physically, through improved housing conditions, in the post-war era. The evacuation brought the social issues of housing to the fore. However, as we shall discover, it was the physical destruction of the area that allowed the reconstruction of Stepney to encompass a planned removal of the population, which relieved the intense pressure on space and facilitated improvements in welfare issues.

In this chapter, one is adding to the discourse on evacuation through the study of its impact upon one particular area, Stepney. This study has also reconstructed the movement of the Stepney schoolchildren from their home to their evacuation destinations, all over the South of England. One has found no previous example of such a study being undertaken, and am therefore adding a new perspective to the discussion. Studies have generally considered the evacuees once they have arrived rather than, perhaps more interestingly the journeys undertaken in order to arrive at reception areas. Upon arrival, schoolchildren experience at reception areas were multifaceted, as there were some who led a militaristic life-style at the camp schools, and some who lived an idyllic country life. However, for some, like Anita Truman, the taunts they thought they had been evacuated away from were once again present. Even with the study of one localised area, Stepney, there is no one experience of evacuation. It was therefore a crucial life event experience for many of Stepney's schoolchildren.

---

[135] Welshman, John, "Evacuation, hygiene, and social policy" op. cit. p786
[136] Hygiene Committee of the Women's Group *Our Town* op. cit. pp45-6
[137] Ibid. pp45-6
[138] Ibid. p110

Table 7-1 School Evacuation

Name & address of school	Number of children evacuated	Number of evacuees through each main-line station	Main-line station evacuees were to leave from	Department See *	Final Destination
Aldgate East - inner zone station					
0365 St Boniface, Adler Street E1	132				Aylesbury, Bucks
Mile End Central, Commercial Road East, E1	283				Aylesbury, Bucks
Commercial Street, Whitechapel High Street, E1	201				Aylesbury, Bucks
Myrdle Street, Commercial Road East	393				Chorley Wood, Herts & Rickmansworth, Herts
Fairclough Street, Back Church Lane	264			SB & SG	Chesham, Bucks & St Peters, Bucks
0369 Davenant, St Mary Street	224			G & I; B	Egham, Surrey
0379 Jews' Infants, Commercial Street	262				Ely, Cambs
0374 St Joseph's, Gun Street, E1	156	1,735	Wimbledon		Kings Lynn, Norfolk
0376 Tower Hill, Chamber Street, E1	397	867	Ealing		Aylesbury, Bucks
Total	**2,602**	**2,602**			
Mile End Station (district) Underground – inner zone					
Cyril Jackson, Northey Street, E14	295				Banbury, Oxon

Dalgleish Street, Salmon Lane, E14	278		Bristol, Gloucestershire
Farrance Street, Burdett Road, E14	473		Somerton, Somerset
Gill Street, West India Dock Road	349		Bristol, Gloucestershire
St Paul's Road, Burdett Road	428		***
Single Street, Bow Common Lane	344		Swindon, Wilts
Hanley Street, Aston St (Senior Girls from Southern Grove)	250		Bedford
Single Street, Bow Common Lane (Infants from Southern Grove)	168		Swindon, Wilts
Thomas Road Central Burdett Road	556		Oxford
0354 Guardian Angels, Whitman Road	362		Wellington, Somerset
0351 St Paul's C of E, Burdett Street	172		Wellington, Somerset
0344 Hamlet of Ratcliffe Cent., White Horse Street	152		Bucks
0346 Holy Name RC, Bow Common Lane	263	B & G & I	Farrington Gurney, Somerset (+ I); Bath, Somerset
0353 Holy Trinity, Solebay St	259	B	Moreton-in-Marsh, Gloucestershire
0347 Our Lady RC, (boys) St Anne's Row	140		Nr Bath, Somerset
0347 Our Lady (girls & infants) Copenhagen Place	198	G & I	Holcombe, Bath, Somerset
0348 Sacred Hart, Willow Row	55		Bath, Somerset

			Amalgamated with Westhill & Huntingfield	
0342 St Anne's C of E, Dixon Street	361			Reading, Berks
Pigott Street Special, E India Dock Road	55			Holiday camp, Lowestoft then Constitutional Holiday Camp, Hopton-on-sea, Suffolk
Southern Grove Special, Mile End Road	102	3,511 Ealing		Wantage, Berks
Coopers Secondary, Tredegar Square	440	2,800 Richmond		Frome, Somerset
Total	**6,224**	2,100 Wimbledon		
Plus Mile End 1a	**2,187**	**8,411**		
Grand Total	**8,411**			
Stepney Green underground – inner zone				
Geere House Open Air, 35 & 37 Stepney Green	39			South Ascot, Berks
Old Church Road Nursery, Commercial Road East	177			Bury St Edmunds, Suffolk
Tollett Special, Globe Road, E1	83		MD & PD	Hopton-on-Sea, Great Yarmouth
Cayley Street, Whitehorse Street, E1	594		JB & JG & I & DT	Slough, Bucks (2); Old Windsor, Bucks; Datchet, Bucks
0350 St Luke's C of E, Burdett Road, E3	230		JM & I	Addlestone, Surrey; Teddington, Middlesex
Ben Jonson, Harford Street, E1	736			Bucks/Berk
Raleigh, Ocean Street	456			Uxbridge, Middlesex

	No.			Code	Destination
Trafalgar, Trafalgar Gardens	541			SB & I	Weybridge, Surrey; Chertsey, Surrey
0345 Good Shepherd, Stepney Square	72				Windsor, Berks
0364 Red Coat, Stepney Green	316				Bucks
0366 Stepney Jewish, 71 Stepney Green	512	2,880	Ealing		Windsor, Berks
Total	**3,756**	740	Richmond		
Plus Stepney Green 1b	**2,828**	2,964	Wimbledon		
Grand Total	**6,584**	**6,584**			
Shadwell Underground					
Broad Street, The Highway	452				***
Heckfrod Street, Cable Street	414			JM & I	Haywards Heath, Sussex; Cuckfield, Sussex
Senrab Street, Charles Street	452				Haywards Heath, Sussex
0363 St Thomas Colet, Arbour Square	233				Brighton, Sussex
Blakesley Street, Sutton Street	424				Eastbourne, Sussex
The Chapman, Bigland Street	344				Eastbourne, Sussex
Christian Street, Commercial Road East	586				Brighton, Sussex
Highway, The Highway	388				Polegate, Sussex
St George-in-the-East, Central, Cable Street, E1	208				Hassocks, Sussex
0464 Johnson Street, Commercial Street E1	646			SB & SG & I	Brighton, Sussex
0527 St Mary & St Michael's, Lucas Street, E1	368				Bristol Rd, Brighton
0372 St Paul's C of E, Wellclose Square	280				Eastbourne,
Raines Foundation School, Arbour Square	666			B & G	Brighton 6; Hurstpierpoint, Sussex

	Total		New Cross Gate		
Lowood Street Special, The Highway	46	5400	New Cross Gate		Lowestoft, Suffolk then Hopton-on-Sea – Holiday camp
Total	**5,507**				
Wapping					
Brewhouse Lane, Wapping High St E1	121				Brighton, Sussex
Hermitage, Wapping High St E1	40				Hove, Sussex
0361 St Patricks R C (B&G) Green Bank, E1	294			B & G	Brighton, Sussex; Upper Drive, Hove 4
0523 St Peter's C of E, Red Lion Street, (SM)	66				Nr Reading or Burnham
0523 St Peter's C of E	215				Nr Reading or Burnham
0361 St Patricks (Infants) Red Lion Street	172	750	New Cross Gate		Upper Drive, Hove 4
Total	**908**				
Whitechapel underground					
Rutland Street, Ashfield Street E1	325			JB & I	Chertsey, Surrey; Virginia Water, Surrey
0524 (B) 0525 (G) St Bernard's Central, Damien St E1	416				Egham, Surrey
Buxton Street, Vallance Rd E1	171				Newmarket, Suffolk
Robert Montefiore, Vallence Rd E1	513			SM & I	Chatteris, Cambs; Wilburton, Ely, Cambs
Robert Montefiore, (J) Vallence Rd E1	178			JB	Haddenham, Ely, Cambs
0367 All Saints' Buxton Street e1	239			I & M	Ely, Cambs; Soham, Cambs
0375 St Anne's RC Buxton Street	293			B; G & I	Ely, Cambs; Bury St Edmunds

	No.	Total			
Dempsey Street, Partially Sighted, Jubilee St	51				Egham, Surrey
Davenant Foundation, Whitechapel Rd E1	182				Egham, Surrey
				SB & SG	Woking, Surrey; Englefield Green, Surrey
Dempsey Street, Jubilee Street, E1	334				
Cephas Street, Cleveland Way, E1	630				Bury St Edmunds, Suffolk
Essex Street, Globe Road	211				***
Redmans Road, Jubilee Street, E1	556				Egham, Surrey
0352 St Peter's Cephas Street E1	95				
Total	**4,194**				
Plus Whitechapel 1c	**3,368**	7,562	Ealing		
Grand Total	**7,562**	**7,562**			
Mile End 1a					
Millwall Central, Janet St, Millwall, E14	323				Campden, Gloucestershire
0264 St Edmunds, West Ferry Rd, E14	247				Stow-on-Wold, Gloucestershire
0259 St Luke's West Ferry Rd, E14	404				Weston-super-Mare, Sommerset
Chisenhale Rd, Auckland Road, Roman Rd, E3	485				Colchester, Essex
Cranbrook Terrace, Green St E2	475				Wellington, Somerset
Olga Street, (I), Medway Rd, Roman Rd, E3	200				Colchester, Essex
East London DCS, Olga Street School, Medway Rd etc	53		See Mile End	East London School for the Blind	Nr Brentwood, Essex
Total	**2,187**	**2,187**			
Stepney Green 1b					

Bonner Street, Green St, E2	341		Wroxham, Norfolk
Globe Rd, Green St, E2	369		Norwich, Norfolk & Wroxham, Norfolk
Morpeth St Central, Green St E2	216		Bury St Edmunds, Suffolk
Portman Place, Globe Rd, E2	801	JB & JG & SG & I	Bildeston, Ipswich; Naughton, Ipswich; Nr Hadleigh, Suffolk; Bildeston, Ipswich
Sewardstone Rd, Bishops Rd, E2	368		Mundesley, Norfolk
(029) St John's Peel Grove, Old Rod Rd E2	324		Hevingham, Norfolk
(0516) Our Lady of the Assumption, 33A Bonner Rd	169		Kings Lynn, Norfolk
Parmitters, Approach Rd, Cambridge Heath, E2	240	See Stepney Green	Walsham, Norfolk
Total	**2,828**	**2,828**	

Whitechapel 1c

Mansford Street Central Bethnal Green Rd E2	288		Kings Lynn, Norfolk
Mowlem Street, Bishops Rd, Cambridge Rd E2	408		Kings Lynn, Norfolk
Pritchards Rd, Hackney Rd, E2	448		North Walsham
Stewart Headlam, Somerford St, Bethnal Green E2	744	JB & JG & I	Bury St Edmunds, Suffolk
Teesdale St, Hackney Rd, E2	448		Kings Lynn, Norfolk
Wilmot St, Bethnal Green Rd E2	176		Colchester, Essex
Wolverley Street, Bethnal Green Rd, E2	296	SB & SG	Bury St Edmunds, Suffolk: Nr Ipswich, Suffolk
(037) St Patrick's RC Cambridge Rd, E2	104		Bury St Edmunds, Suffolk
(033) St Bartholomew's, Coventry Rd, E2	256	M & I	Hadleigh, Suffolk; Colchester, Essex

The Second World War and the Evacuation of Schoolchildren

			See Whitechapel	Coltishall, Norfolk
(034) St Jude's, Old Bethnal Green, E2	200	3,368	See Whitechapel	Coltishall, Norfolk
Total	**3,368**	**3,368**		
Aldgate				
Swan Street, Minories, E1	80			Chorley Wood, Herts
068 Sir John Cass Foundation, Duke St EC3	400			Aylesbury, Bucks
0378 Buckle Street Jew's (I), Leman Street E1	111			Aylesbury, Bucks
0370 St Mark's C of E, Royal Mint St, E1	147			Upton, Aylesbury, Bucks
Total	**738**			

Key

* DT = Detached Party; SB = Senior Boys; SG = Senior Girls; G = Girls; B = Boys; I = Infants; MD = Medical Deficiency

PD = Physical Deficiency; JB = Junior Boys; JG = Junior Girls;

*** = Unknown Destination

Sources

LMA LCC Government Evacuation Scheme, Directory of London Schools in the Reception Area - December 1939

National Archives MEPO 3/2501 Evacuation of School Children on the first day of evacuation

CHAPTER EIGHT

THE BOMBING OF STEPNEY:
THE LOCAL RESPONSE AND THE WORK
OF MASS-OBSERVATION

In this chapter the destruction suffered by Stepney during the Second World War will be discussed through the work of Mass-Observation (M-O), a national opinion polling movement, and the significant local organisation; the Stepney Tenants Defence League (STDL). The work of the social research organisation M-O, not only concentrated attention on the people of Stepney, but on the poor condition of the shelters too. In Stepney, the shelters were an issue throughout the war. One of the worst of these buildings was the notorious Tilbury shelter. Once the sub-standard quality of the shelters had been highlighted, improvements were striven for. These included limiting the numbers of people allowed into shelters at any one time. However, these aims were not necessarily achieved. Alongside the work of M-O, the STDL took more drastic actions in their campaign to introduce more deep shelters, which were thought to be safer. As we shall discover, the STDL took their campaign to the west side of London, to the Savoy Hotel shelter.

M-O was established in 1937 by Tom Harrisson and Charles Madge. The reason for M-O's existence was "to document popular life and belief in ways that would contribute to the democratization of sociological knowledge".[1] M-O was launched under the slogan "anthropology at home".[2] James Hinton suggests that M-O would probably have disintegrated had it not been for the war, due to its lack of focus and impetus. The war enabled M-O to develop a more coherent programme and practice.[3] Harrison wrote that M-O can be seen as a "several-pronged reaction to the disturbed condition of western Europe under the growing

---

[1] Hinton, James, "Mass-Observation (1937-1949)" in *Oxford Dictionary of National Biography* online edn, (Oxford) Feb 2009
[2] Ibid.
[3] Ibid.

threat of fascism".[4] As Angus Calder states, "Mass-Observation was part of the broad movement, typified by George Orwell, of conscience-stricken middle-class intellectuals trying, in days of wide unemployment, to meet and understand the working class".[5] Calder also questions "whether the primary aim was observation *of* the mass or *by* the masses".[6] This was due to the fact that M-O often seemed to address the "political classes" by offering them an improved understanding of public opinion, whilst at the same time representing itself "as a medium through which the Man in the Street can express himself, by-passing the MPs and pressmen who pretend to represent his opinions but don't".[7] However, in Stepney, the community's anti-fascist stance was to hinder the acceptance of Nina Masel (later Hibbin 1919-2004) as a Mass-Observer. Masel although Jewish herself was seen as an outsider, who encroached on a close-knit Jewish community. Through her reports and personal writings, Masel left an interpretation of the people she encountered in Stepney. Although her writing has faults, such as the account of making up answers, her work in Stepney provides a valuable insight into the area during the war.[8]

In order to analyse the issue of sheltering in Stepney, two main routes of investigation are used throughout this chapter. Firstly, I will look at first-person accounts of sheltering. Secondly, I want to explore the official government stance. In combining the two a clearer interpretation of the state of sheltering in the area can be achieved. In *London was Ours* Amy Bell analyses the first-person accounts of Londoners who wrote about the bombing raids on the city between September 1940 and May 1941. She shows how participants themselves wrote and rewrote the history of the London Blitz.[9] London's experience of the Blitz from a governmental perspective is reviewed in Robin Woolven's *The London Experience of Regional Government.* His paper explores the establishment of the London Regional organisation, how it operated and why, when the organisation was disbanded, the *status quo* was restored.[10] The regional organisation

---

[4] Harrisson, Tom, *Living Through the Blitz* (1976) p11
[5] Introduction by Angus Calder for 2nd Edition of Harrison, Tom and Madge, Charles, *Britain by Mass-Observation* (1986) (1st published 1939) pxiii
[6] Ibid. pxiii
[7] Ibid. pxiii
[8] Nina Masel admits to making up some answer in her questionnaires, see p188 of this chapter
[9] Bell, Amy Helen, *London Was Ours: Diaries and Memories of the London Blitz* (2008) p1
[10] Woolven, Robin, "The London Experience of Regional Government 1938-1943" *The London Journal* Vol 25 No 2 2000 p60

was an extra level of government inserted between Whitehall and the borough town halls. The reason for such a dramatic innovation was London's total lack of preparation for war which was demonstrated during the Munich crisis of September 1938.

As we shall discover, it is through the letters, diaries and memoirs of individuals, that an intimate glimpse into the private world of Stepney citizens is revealed, along with personal and family strategies for coping with the privations, stresses and dangers of war. What were perceived as safety precautions from gas explosions could be quite extraordinary. For example, Nina Masel's mother had read somewhere that the fumes from urine neutralised the effect of poison gas. Thus, she recalls, her mother made them:

> All solemnly ... pee into our chamber-pots, which were then placed beside every door in the house and that, fortified by this safety device, our family was now ready to face the war.[11]

The popular symbols of the blitz were of a nation taking cover in the shelters and the supposed camaraderie that could be found night after night as London, along with other great cities of Britain, was attacked by German bombs.

It was the Blitz, Bell argues, that provided the first test to the civilian morale of the nation. On the day war was declared the sirens sounded. Although the warning of an attack turned out to be a false alarm, it brought immediate panic to those who heard it. Thus, the Blitz "encompassed the historical themes that have come to characterize the Second World War in Britain: civilian fortitude under the bombing, and the emergence of a new national unity".[12] It was the Blitz that not only physically destroyed much of Stepney, but also tore the area apart in a social sense too, with the mass evacuation of the borough. Those evacuated ended up being distributed all over the Home Counties.

Edith Ramsay, a Labour borough councillor in the post-war years, commented that the "plans were clear ... we expected immediate German attack by sea, land and air".[13] In preparation for such an event, "the upper floors of the London Hospital were to be closed and the lower floor adapted for raid casualties".[14] With large numbers of casualties anticipated

---

[11] MOA, Hibbin, Nina "Occupational Risk"

[12] Bell, op. cit. p4

[13] Ramsay, Edith, *Life in Stepney: World War II, 1939-1945* (1976) Pamphlet 080 Bancroft Local History Library p1

[14] Ibid. p1

it was also expected that there were to be a lot of deaths and "vast numbers of papier-mâché coffins"[15] were held at the Stepney Jewish Hospital. This was under the direction of the Ministry of Health which in April 1939 had "very quietly issued a million burial forms to the local authorities, who in turn began stockpiling large supplies of coffins".[16] The coffins were made out of papier-mâché or stout cardboard, to ease the storage of them but also because "the authorities could not afford the £300,000 worth of coffin wood that they thought would be required in the first three months".[17]

Over 40,000 High Explosive Bombs fell on London along with "a quite incalculable number of Incendiary Bombs" during the first seven months of the Blitz.[18] Throughout London, a close watch on the German planes was kept by volunteers in every street - particularly in Stepney, as we shall discover. In her 1976 pamphlet *Life in Stepney,* Ramsay recalls doing a turn of fire-watching duty on a bad night, in the company of John Reardon, a borough councillor. She writes: "I said 'usually planes come in waves, but these go on all the time'. 'This ain't waves, it's a perm' replied Johnny".[19]

What the borough did not anticipate were the needs of the homeless – shelter, food and clothing. According to Ramsay, it was to these needs that "volunteers responded magnificently".[20] Examples of such generosity can be found in the Highways Club, where Lady Ravensdale and Vera Grenfell "worked night and day helping the homeless, arranging evacuation and cheering all concerned".[21] At the Bernhard Baron Settlement and the Stepney Jewish Club, the leaders Rose and Basil Henriques and Phyllis Gerson, made the clubs centres of help for the neighbourhood. There were also the activities of Dr J. J. Mallon, known as "Our Jimmy", assisted by his Secretary, Miss M. R. Kendall, who worked magnificently at Toynbee Hall.[22]

Mass Observation

The aim of Mass-Observers was to supply:

---

[15] Ibid. p5
[16] Hylton, Stuart, *Their Darkest Hour: The Hidden History of the Home Front 1939-1945* (Great Britain, 2001) p38
[17] Ibid. p38
[18] Ramsay, op. cit. p8
[19] Ibid. p8
[20] Ibid. p5
[21] Ibid. p6
[22] Ibid. p6

… accurate observations of everyday life and *real* (not just published) public moods, an anthropology and a mass-documentation for a vast sector of normal life which did not, at that time, seem to be adequately considered by the media, the arts, the social scientists, even by the political leaders.[23]

In order to continue their work M-O had "to produce more immediate and 'relevant' results".[24] It should be remembered that, although private diaries give us a sense of people's immediate personal responses to the war, many diary writers must have been at least partly subconsciously aware of the potential subsequent readers of their diaries. Harrisson's M-O raised this awareness, with the immediate reports that were being produced and also the talk of how these writings, surveys, and other sources would all provide valuable information for subsequent generations. As the M-O I.D. card stated, "Mass-Observation is a non-political, non-profit-making organisation which investigates and reports on public opinion, and finds the facts about what people are thinking saying and doing from day-to-day".[25]

This was not a completely new idea in the East End of London, as the area had been a focal point for social investigation in Britain since the time of Charles Booth's survey of *Life and Labour of the People in London* (1889 onwards). This was followed by the *New Survey of London Life and Labour* which was carried out in the 1930s. Alongside such investigation came some measures of social reform, for instance, the setting up of William Booth's Salvation Army and Thomas Barnardo's children's homes which had their origins in the East End. There was also the work of the university settlement movement. Toynbee Hall was established on Commercial Road, Whitechapel, in 1884 by students from Oxford and Cambridge. It was through such activities that Tom Harrisson first got to know the East End in the late 1920s, whilst he was still at Harrow public school. What was to attract Harrisson to the East End were "the dangers of racialism at home".[26] He was concerned with the activities of the BUF in the 1930s; this in turn led to Harrisson along with Leslie Taylor and Norman Cohn, carrying out "by far the biggest ever amassed [archive] of

---

[23] Harrisson, *Living Through The Blitz* op. cit. preface
[24] Ibid. preface
[25] MOA, op. cit. Hibbin, "Occupational Risk"
[26] Kushner, Tony, *We Europeans? Mass-Observation,"Race" and British Identity in the Twentieth Century* (England, 2004) p82

anti-Semitism in Britain".[27] However, Tony Kushner argues that M-O's more successful work "took place during its most difficult days, the blitz in 1940 and 1941".[28]

In late 1936 Harrisson had installed himself in Bolton, Lancashire, and had blended in with his cotton mill co-workers. He was also variously a lorry driver, ice-cream vendor and shop assistant. While working in these jobs "he discreetly took notes on the people around him".[29] This was to be the method he favoured for his fieldwork, focusing on what people did and not what they said. Harrisson joined forces with Charles Madge, a poet, and created M-O in 1937. They wrote *Britain by Mass Observation*, a work based on research into Bolton (Worktown) and London where Harrisson and Madge "induced small teams of M-O unpaid researchers to collect data by covertly observing people and asking open-ended questions".[30] This data was used along with contributions by hundreds of volunteer diarists whose anonymity was protected in order to encourage honest comment. The work of M-O pioneered tactics later adopted by the market research industry, asking questions about: "bathing habits, burial customs, smoking, drinking, sexual behaviour, attitudes towards current events, etc".[31] This was, according to Harrisson, a way of letting the ordinary people speak for themselves. Harrisson and Madge showed how much damage had been caused to public morale "by the lack of dialogue between the people and their leaders at the time of the Prime Minister Neville Chamberlain's decision to seek 'peace in our time' at Munich".[32] It was through the success of *Britain* by M-O that M-O became a household name, although its methodology was later condemned by academic social scientists for its lack of statistical rigour.

By 1939 M-O considered itself to have enough researchers. With the imminence of war the organisation asked its panel to keep diaries on a daily basis giving details of their everyday lives, which Nina Masel did for the month of September 1939.[33] Sandra Koa Wing highlights the fact that

---

[27] The archive of anti-Semitism now fills several boxes, see Mass-Observation: Topic Collection "Anti-Semitism". Kushner, Tony, *We Europeans? Mass-Observation,* op. cit. p84

[28] Ibid. p98

[29] Heiman, Judith M., "Harrisson, Tom Harnett (1911-1976)" in *Oxford Dictionary* op. cit.

[30] Ibid.

[31] Ibid.

[32] Ibid.

[33] MOA, D 5370. Masel then became "the East End Branch" of Mass-Observation. See Hibbin, Nina "I was a Mass-Observer" *New Statesman* 31 May 1985

the M-O diaries are "a particular hybrid of private diary and public research journal".[34] Due to the immediacy, the diaries also give an intriguing insight into British life and in this sense they differ from "the retrospective accounts we hear today in oral history interviews, in television reminiscences, on websites collecting testimonies, such as the BBC's *People's War* project".[35]

Diarists did not represent a true cross-section of British society: "although they came from a variety of backgrounds, and from different regions, most of them were middle-class, well-read and articulate".[36] Masel was, by her own admission, well-read. Her diary reveals that she was training to become a teacher and due to the war halting her studies and to her father's business declining, she felt that she ought to get a job. Instead, Masel went to the Town Hall and signed on for full-time Air Raid Precaution (ARP) work. Then another problem occurred which prompted her to change career path again. Masel received "a joyful postcard" which "announced that High School terms commencement is postponed indefinitely".[37] By, Monday, 11 September she had decided to go to see the head of an organisation she belonged to – one Tom Harrisson, of a group called "Mass-Observation".[38] After this she was to send Harrisson an ultimatum: "Either you give me a full-time job or else I stop writing my diaries".[39] Tom Harrisson was persuaded. At seventeen she was given a full-time job with him taking up digs in Stepney and becoming the M-O's "East End Unit". Essentially, Kushner argues, Masel was more or less from a working class background, having originated from Romford in Essex. Therefore, she was not a Stepney worker. However, she did have an interest in Stepney thanks to her own Jewish background which she had "some nebulous notion of exploring".[40] Her immediate work, though, would be concerned with recording her surroundings and day-to-day experiences.

Nina Masel's diary covers only the month of September 1939. On Friday, 1 September 1939, when the evacuation of Stepney's schoolchildren began, Masel was "pupil teaching" at a senior girls school, presumably near her home, Romford in Essex. With the announcement of the

---

[34] Wing, Sandra Koa (ed.), *Mass Observation Britain in the Second World War* (2007) pxiii
[35] Ibid. pxiii
[36] Ibid. pxiii
[37] MOA, D 5370 for Friday, 8 September 1939
[38] Ibid. Monday, 11 September 1939
[39] Hibbin, Nina, "I was a Mass-Observer" *New Statesman* 31 May 1985
[40] Ibid. 31 May 1985

evacuation of schools as "a precautionary measure" the school's history mistress "declared ... she had realised, as soon as they put the date forward that war was at hand".[41] That day also saw the departure of Miss M "who had joined the staff of an evacuating school".[42] By the evening, when a friend of Masel called on her to go to supper with her, she wrote:

> I was about to go, when my mother arrived, and unconditionally refused to let me go. 'You are not to go away from home' she declared dramatically, 'If we die, we all die together'.[43]

Also, the 1 September, saw the first serious attempts at black-out arrangements, which Masel, complained involved "the use of a light so small that it strains the eyes".[44] On 3 September, the first air raid siren sounded and Masel recalls:

> At eleven-fifteen, I was playing the piano in the front room, when suddenly my mother burst in, shouting 'stop that noise!' and then flung open the windows, letting in the scream of the air-raid siren, and the scuffling noise of neighbours in a hurry. Immediately, my father assumed the role of the administrative head-of-the-house, issuing commands and advice:- 'All get your gas-mask! Steady, no punch-up! Every man for himself! Keep in the passage!'[45]

The Masel family used the passage as they had no shelter. After a few minutes it was decided by the family that it was a false alarm, "so we went to the front gate (all except my mother and small sister, who kept calling us to come back) and remained there until the 'All clear' was given".[46] After this first false alarm, "we learnt for the first time about the declaration of a state of war".[47] The typical comment that Masel recorded was that "most people were glad. 'High time someone showed Hitler he wasn't such a god as he made out'".[48] The following evening more lasting black-out arrangements were made at the Masel home and their "wartime accessories" were gathered into one place. These included such items as

---

[41] MOA, D 5370 op. cit. Friday, 1 September 1939
[42] Ibid. 5370 Friday 1 September 1939
[43] Ibid. 5370 Friday, 1 September 1939
[44] Ibid. 5370 Friday, 1 September 1939
[45] Ibid. 5370 Sunday, 3 September 1939
[46] Ibid. 5370 Sunday, 3 September 1939
[47] Ibid. 5370 Sunday, 3 September 1939
[48] Ibid. 5370 Sunday, 3 September 1939

"torches, fire pails, and black paper".[49] Just before going to bed, warm coats were put in places where they could be easily found, just in case of an emergency. The outbreak of war also brought a new found harmony to the area. Masel describes how a female neighbour who the family had not been on speaking terms with for at least seventeen years, "offered us the use of her shelter, and demonstrated her method of blacking-out".[50] By 6 September the family was showing a far more relaxed attitude to the threat of air-raids:

> When we heard the sirens, we dressed, came down and had breakfast, and then sat in the dining room, listening to the wireless. After a time, we got fed up, so my father and I went into the street, and watched the aeroplanes. There were people at every front gate.[51]

When there was the sound of gun-fire, the Masel family went and sat in the passage. However, the family, with the exception of the mother, became bored again: "so we went into the back garden to see how people were enjoying sitting in the shelters" Masel writes. "None of them was in use".[52] Masel's diary gives an insight into one family's experience of the first few days of war and in particular the sense of intrigue surrounding the air raids. It was this kind of insight into her surroundings that Masel also displayed in her work on Stepney.

In Stepney, during the Blitz, people would shelter in the underground tube stations of Bank, Stepney Green and Mile End for example. Brick and concrete surface shelters with chemical closets were erected. Each of them was able to hold fifty persons. However, according to Edith Ramsay, most "people preferred and used large halls, some underground, but many linked with churches, warehouses, and firms".[53] The Tilbury was classified as an "unsafe" shelter and people were discouraged from using it, "but the people took the situation into their own hands, forced the gates and went underground, and it remained a place of shelter throughout the war".[54] On 5 May 1941, Edith Ramsay first recorded attending a meeting of the Stepney Shelter Sub Committee District 5 at Paddy's Goose, the Highway Club. Also present were Miss Moses (Chairman of the main Shelter Committee), Miss Greenfell (of the Highway Club) as Convener, along

---

[49] Ibid. 5370 Sunday, 3 September 1939
[50] Ibid. 5370 Monday, 4 September 1939
[51] Ibid. 5370 Wednesday, 6 September 1939
[52] Ibid. 5370 Wednesday, 6 September 1939
[53] Ramsay, Edith, op. cit. p9
[54] Sokoloff, Bertha, *Edith and Stepney* (1987) p107

with several members of the clergy and one or two others who had time in the day.[55] One issue raised by Miriam Moses at the meeting was bedding. The dilemma was, according to her, "that if people leave their bedding in the shelter there is the danger of theft. If by contrast they leave it for safety in a store or cupboard at the shelter it is never cleaned or aired".[56] What actually occurred in the shelter will be discussed later in this chapter. Edith was a marshal in her own small shelter, the Wadham Shelter that served the Toynbee flats where she lived.

By the autumn of 1941 the shelters were taking shape as bunks had been installed. New needs surfaced, though as Ramsay said: "primus stoves, kettles, cocoa are needed and lockers for storage".[57] The Shelter Committees also acted as "much wider welfare bodies, taking up people's needs, looking for improvement in conditions, [and] keeping up morale".[58] Doctors in the shelter, for example, would "talk to the people on health matters and a lot of good advice was given on food".[59] Feeding the people was an issue. Dr Jimmy Mallon was appointed by the government to "arrange provision of food in shelters and it was he who insisted that this must also be done in Tube stations". However, Ritchie Calder reported that John Groser, a local priest, "broke into an official food store to feed the homeless in his 'Second Line' (then very much 'First Line') centre",[60] perhaps indicating that the provision of food in the shelters was not good enough.

Diaries were treated by the diarists as confidantes. Masel noted in her diary that "... almost everyone carried a gas-mask. One in six of the men were not in civilian clothes".[61] On another occasion she wrote that:

In the streets, ninety-two percent of people were carrying gas-masks. I didn't carry mine, because of the inconvenience. I do, however, wear an identity disk on a chain round my neck, as instructed on the wireless.[62]

The one part of the work that Masel did not enjoy was the method of "indirect" questioning which involved trying to slip into general conversations questions like, "What do you think of the news?" Masel found this part of

[55] Ibid. p108
[56] Ibid. p108
[57] Ibid. p109
[58] Ibid. p110
[59] Ibid. p111
[60] Calder, Ritchie, "The War in East London" *New Statesman* 21 September 1940 p277
[61] MOA, D 5370 op. cit. Sunday, 3 September 1939
[62] Ibid. Tuesday 5 September 1939

the work difficult and took to making up the answers. Her admission does somewhat undermine her work, particularly since, as she notes, "nobody at 'HQ' spotted any discrepancy between my phoney reports and the real ones from the rest of the team".[63] However, this behaviour on Masel's part was only to last for a few weeks, since Masel found the work had its own dangers.[64] Now that the general public had become acutely spy-conscious, standing on street corners with a pad and pencil taking notes "was enough to send even the most imperturbable citizen scouring the streets for a cop".[65] In response to this, and in readiness for being approached by a policeman, Mass-Observers always carried their identity cards.

As Kushner argues, Masel's reports were used by the government to help monitor morale. For all their faults, they stand as some of the "most powerful writing produced by M-O in its social investigation work either in peace or wartime".[66] From 1939, the Ministry of Information, "engaged Mass-Observation to provide feedback on its (lamentable) efforts at propaganda to improve civilian morale".[67] By 1940 Harrisson and his team, which included Nina Masel, were observing people during and after heavy aerial bombardments. Living through the Blitz in Stepney pushed Masel into the "immediacy of East End life in a profound way".[68] Through her observations, many changes within the area can be seen such as "the changing language, gender relations, inter-generational conflict, contested identities and concerns of East End Jewry".[69]

In Stepney there was still a strong element of anti-Semitism. Prior to the outbreak of war, Willie Gallacher, the Communist MP for Fife, asked the Home Secretary why "two converging marches of the BUF were allowed to take place through the banned area of East London on Sunday, 16 April",[70] and whether more marches of this nature could be expected. Attlee asked if Sir Samuel Hoare (Home Secretary), was "aware of the great indignation caused in East London, owing to this provocative march", which led many to believe that the police condoned such marches. Sir Samuel stated, though, that the police were impartial. However, anti-

---

[63] Hibbin, Nina, "I was a Mass-Observer" *New Statesman* 31 May 1985
[64] The guilt was hurting Masel too much and she confessed all to Tom Harrisson. Hibbin, "I was a Mass-Observer" op. cit. 31 May 1985
[65] MOA, Masel, op. cit. Letter on Occupational Risk by Nina Hibbin
[66] Kushner, op. cit. p98
[67] Heimann, Judith M., Harrisson, Tom Harnett (1911-1976) *Oxford Dictionary* op. cit.
[68] Kushner, op. cit. p98
[69] Ibid. p98
[70] *Parliamentary Debates – Commons 1938-39* vol 346 April 13-May 5 1939 p499

Semitism continued through the war. Fascism also continued and Masel encountered her own allegation of fascism. One night Masel was summonsed to the local shelter, where she was accused of being the author of "vile fascist leaflets" which had recently been posted through the neighbourhoods letter-boxes. One of the leaflets had been found in her room and was used as evidence against her. In fact as part of M-O she had been collecting samples of material posted, along with recording shelter habits and other wartime behaviour patterns. She was locked into the shelter with angry arms pushing and jostling her. Through the crowd, as she noted in a letter, she heard ugly murmurs. Suddenly, she writes, she could see the situation from these people's point of view:

> A young girl sprung from nowhere, with no apparent family or immediately recognisable background, wandering the streets by day and typing into the small hours. Some cock-and-bull story about a fact-finding organisation that nobody had ever heard of. Nazi bombs by night; fascist filth by day.[71]

It was easy to put two and two together in such circumstances. Masel pleaded her innocence, but the only thing that convinced the crowd was when she began to recite a Hebrew prayer she had learnt as a child. This was a device to win the trust of the crowd and she was accepted.[72] Such an incident shows the weariness of the Jewish community towards strangers. It also shows how the Jewish community would often take matters into their own hands, rather than calling in the authorities. On the other hand Masel reported that she was often taken into police custody until it could be established that she was working as a Mass-Observer, further illustrating that her day-to-day work was not an easy task.

The incident in which Masel was locked in a shelter was set against a back-drop of anti-Semitic and anti-Alien feeling. By May 1940 there were M-O reports, based on questionnaires, that the general public's view of aliens was becoming more hostile. It became imperative that the Home Secretary should investigate large-scale internment. All Category B aliens of German or Austrian origin were ordered to be rounded up and arrested on 27 May. This was followed by the arrest of all Category C males in the weeks following 21 June. In Stepney, widespread unhappiness was caused by the internment of aliens in the area. There was much press campaigning for the release of aged aliens, many of whom had come to Britain in the first few months of their lives. The next generation of these internees were

---

[71] MOA, Masel, op. cit. Hibbin, "Occupational Risk"
[72] Ibid. – See "Occupational Risk" for the full story of this incident.

"almost out of their minds" as they had not received any news of their parents. The STDL sent letters to the Under Secretary of the Home Office on behalf of residents who wished to have neighbours released.[73] With such tension and uncertainty surrounding the Jewish quarters of Stepney, it was therefore hardly surprising that Masel had such an experience. The fact that Masel was also a young woman, on her own in the area, with no family connections and only distant Jewish ties is likely to have further deepened any suspicions against her.

The Physical Destruction

Stepney was described by *An A. A. Brigade* as:

> ... a vista of gashed streets, with the ambulances slowly moving and ARP men frantically digging like dusty little terriers, ... and the bitter, bitter smoke of our burning London drifting chokingly over all and a six-year-old girl, puny and weazened – a shame on the England that bore her – wearing a too-large yellow apron and lustily sweeping up debris with a broom taller than herself while she sang like a startled canary at the top of her voice.[74]

The letters of Edith Ramsay describe the conditions as being "past belief. Large parts of the whole area are comparable only to Ypres after the last war", she wrote.[75]

In Stepney the destruction to the area was extensive. When looking at maps of the bomb damage the main colours upon the area are black and purple denoting total destruction and damage beyond repair.[76] These maps show that the entire borough was covered with general blast damage. One can see that V1 bombs struck: near Fenchurch Station, St Katherine's Dock, London Dock, Commercial Road Goods Depot, Adler Street, The Highway – near London Dock, The London Hospital, Ratcliff Wharf, the Generating Station for the borough of Stepney, Commercial Road by Dalgleish Street, Mountmores Road, Aylward Street, Exmouth Works, Stainsby Road, and twice by industrial sites on Bow Lane. The V2 bombs hit Stepney High Street, Pole Street and Goulston Street. It was therefore mainly the V1 bombs that struck the area. One can conclude, if we

---

[73] MOA, TC London Survey Part 7 Reel 134/65/1/A Survey of Political Activity 30 July 1940

[74] *An A. A. Brigade at War!* 2 April 1944

[75] Sokoloff, op. cit. p97

[76] Maps of bomb damage to London at the London Metropolitan Archives

consider the positions of these blasts, that the bombers were aiming for key positions within the borough: the docks, the hospital, the gas works and industry in general. In aiming for these key areas, more widespread destruction of the borough occurred, causing chaos for residents.

The destruction of homes and the conditions in which people had to live afterwards was hard to accept. At 31 Commodore Street, for example, an explosion left the "... whole house except kitchen and scullery more or less in chaos". As a M-O reporter of the time describes it:

> Upstairs there are holes in the roof mattresses and bedsteads leaned against the wall, the floors soaked with water in most parts. Downstairs furniture is stored in the two front rooms, everything piled higgledy piggledy on top of each other.[77]

At 21 Commodore Street, where destruction had also occurred, the council came and did first aid building repairs but said that they could not do anything else. The Sanitary Inspector visited too. When he was asked if it was safe to live in the house, he said "No" because the house needed major repairs. When the tenants went back to the council, however, they were still told that nothing else would be done. This illustrates the kind of squalid conditions in which people had to live, in part because of the lack of resources, and also because many of these areas would be totally reconstructed in the post-war era. Therefore, only temporary repairs would be carried out until the council repossessed these people's homes.

Since 7 September 1940, the People's Palace had been used as a rest centre, because "this place was big enough to give us elbow-room in handling the masses of homeless who were already tramping in like a retreating army". The People's Palace was universally known, in central Stepney, and accessible by plenty of roads.[78] Originally, the council offices of Stepney were situated on Wapping Island, adjacent to the docks. This island was only accessible by two bridges, one of which was made of wood. It was obvious that the borough's affairs could not be conducted during the Blitz from such a position due to the possibility of being "cut off by any well-placed bomb".[79] It was decided by the council that St George's Town Hall, which held council meetings, would be used instead. However, after the first raid on London, Frank Lewey comments that "the Germans moved us again". This was because the Germans had dropped "some 'heavies' near enough to the building for the blast to render it

---

[77] MOA, TC Part 5 Reel 70 Housing 1938-1948 4 April 1941
[78] Lewey, Frank R., *Cockney Campaign* (1944) p20
[79] Ibid. p20

unsafe".[80] As a result the council moved briefly, for a mere three days, to offices in Raine Street, but:

> The rooms there were so clouded with smoke from the dock fires that it was difficult to see across from one desk to another; there was an unceasing barrage of coughing from smoke-seared throats. A warehouse containing spices from the East had caught light and burned steadily.[81]

Finally, the decision was taken to use the People's Palace. The People's Palace became the hub for sorting out the evacuation of Stepney citizens.[82]

With the people of Stepney being bombed out of their homes they made their way to the People's Palace to seek help with accommodation. People waited in trepidation to be "passed" to one of the tables at the entrance, where the Women's Voluntary Service (WVS) or other official seated behind it could give them help and recommend evacuation. Here is one example of what could happen:

Man: I want to be evacuated
WVS: In what condition is your house?
Man: I can't get into it; the ceiling's fallen down
WVS: Is the house itself still standing?
Man: Yes but it's no use to us
WVS: I'm sorry, but we can't do anything for you, unless your house is burnt right down, or bombed out.
Man: But the children...
WVS: They can go away under the evacuation scheme for school children. How old are they?
Man: One is 15 and one 9.
WVS: I believe they're both all right for it. That's the best thing to do. Go to their school, and find out about it.
Man: What about us? Where shall we go to?
WVS: You could stay with friends for the night. Have you got friends or relations here? Well, stay with them, if you have.
Man: What about the house?
WVS: The landlord will come and see to that. If you really think it's uninhabitable, you can ask the demolition squad to come along, but if it's still standing ... good day.[83]

---

[80] Ibid. p20
[81] Ibid. p20
[82] See the work of Mayor Frank R. Lewey in Ibid.
[83] MOA, TC Box 9 23/9/T 21 September 1940 People's Palace M 50 C & WVS 60 B conversation

Such an exchange was probably typical for Stepney. The people of Stepney were trapped. The council would not undertake major repairs, when the house was likely to be damaged or destroyed with the next attack. The council had no other accommodation to offer residents as the entire borough was at the forefront of the Blitz. Ritchie Calder also comments:

> … as I went through wrecked streets I saw rent-collectors on the doorsteps of houses where gaps were covered with tarpaulin and windows were cardboarded, where there was neither gas, light or water and where a bomb, streets away, might shake down the remains. It was rent day, raids or no raids.[84]

Both of these examples show how life continued in Stepney. They also give us an insight into the harsh treatment of those who were bombed out. If there was the remotest possibility of tenants remaining in destroyed buildings they would still be charged rent as usual. The council was unable to deal with the volume of destruction Stepney encountered, which is clearly evident in Stepney Council's failure with regards to Air Raid Precautions.

In looking at London's regional government experience, the responsibilities of the Air Raid Precautions (ARP) are considered. They were divided between the London County Council (LCC) having the county-wide task and the City and metropolitan boroughs who had local ARP services. Locally these services included first aid posts, stretcher parties and gas decontamination centres.[85] The ARP in Stepney had its first meeting on Thursday, 5 May 1938. Councillor Morris Harold Davis was nominated and seconded as Chairman, and J. C. Lawder, JP became Vice-Chairman. The borough, for the purpose of the scheme, was to be divided into the three parliamentary divisions of Limehouse, Mile End and Whitechapel & St George's, with each division under a Divisional Warden. For Mile End and Whitechapel & St George's, 160 Air-Raid Warden Posts would be allocated, while 80 of these posts would be allocated to the Limehouse Division.[86]

By the summer of 1939, since the prospect of war was looking like turning into reality, rehearsals for such an event were vital. As discussed in

---

[84] Calder, op. cit. p277
[85] Woolven, Robin, "The London Experience of Regional Government 1938-1945" *The London Journal* Vol. 25 No. 2 2000 p61
[86] Minutes of the Air Raid Precautions Committee May 1938-July 1940 Thursday, 5 May 1938 L/SMB/A/19/1

the previous chapter, children in the area were called into school to practise the evacuation process, so that, in the event of war being declared, people knew what to do. The ARP Department of the Home Office sent a communication to Stepney, dated 29 June 1939 stating that:

> ... the Royal Air Force proposed to conduct an exercise on an extensive scale between 8pm on Tuesday, 8 August, and 7pm on Friday, 11 August, over an area including London; that it would be of value to the Royal Air Force and provide a good test of lighting restrictions of darkness as is practicable on the night of 9 to 10 August, between the hours of 12.30am and 4am; that, if weather conditions were unfavourable the blackout would be postponed until the same time on the following night.[87]

The council recommended that the Heads of Departments affected would be instructed to take steps necessary to secure "as great a degree of darkness as practicable"[88] on the nights requested.

With the international situation rapidly deteriorating, climaxing with Germany invading Poland, the local authorities were asked to appoint a small Emergency Committee, ideally consisting of three people who would undertake council business and appoint an Air Raid Precautions Controller. Stepney appointed the elected Labour Party Leader, M. H. Davis, a decision which would later be regretted, as the Stepney ARP services required executive action by the Regional Commissioner.[89] From the Minutes of the Meeting of Monday, 5 September 1939, M. H. Davis, "reminded the committee that, by the resolution passed by the council on 11 May 1939, he had been appointed as ARP Controller on the understanding that his appointment would take effect from such time as the Lord Privy Seal might formally direct".[90] Thus, upon instructions received from the London Regional Headquarters of the Home Office on 31 August 1939 at 16.20 hours he assumed the duties of ARP Controller. Davis was also chairman of the special Emergency Committee, so he was in a domineering position.[91]

At the date that Davis assumed his duties of ARP Controller, "8,250 of the 9,745 'Anderson' shelters required in the borough had been consigned by the Home Office to the Railway companies for delivery within the

---

[87] Ibid. L/SMB/A/19/1 Thursday, 20 July 1939
[88] Ibid. L/SMB/A/19/1 Thursday, 20 July 1939
[89] Woolven, op. cit. p65
[90] Minutes of the Air Raid Precautions Committee op. cit. L/SMB/A/19/1
[91] Also on the committee were Mrs K. O'Connor, R. Silkoff, S. Singer and F. B. Tyrrell Minutes of the Air Raid Precautions Committee op.cit. L/SMB/A/19/1

borough".[92] Approximately 1,800 had been erected but, with the state of emergency, outside contractors would be used in order to accelerate the work. The question that still remained was that of how many people needed to be accommodated within these shelters. At the last census in 1931 the population had been 225,238. By the middle of 1937, however, it was estimated that the population had dropped to 203,100. By October 1939, 67 basements had been requisitioned across the borough with the purpose of civil defence. These would provide shelter for a maximum of 40,324.[93] The largest basement was LMS Railway Depot, Commercial Road which could hold a maximum of 7,034 people and in contrast the smallest was at 61 John Fisher Street, which held a maximum of just 30 people. Railway arches were also to be used which would provide shelter for 4,058 peoples, thus providing a total of accommodation for 44,382 people in public shelters. The 9,745 "Anderson" shelters were capable of accommodating six persons, providing shelter for 58,470 persons. Overall, the borough had provision of shelter for some 98,794 people, which was less than half of the population. However, revisions were made in order to accommodate the entire population.

After re-assessing Stepney, it was found shelter could be provided for 223,100, or the entire population of the borough. This would be done in the following fashion:

---

[92] Minutes of the Air Raid Precautions Committee Ibid. L/SMB/A/19/1
[93] Minutes of the Air Raid Precautions Committee Ibid. L/SMB/A/19/1

Place	No. of persons
In cellars of buildings	100,000
Under railway arches and viaducts	70,000
Under the north half of Rotherhithe Tunnel	10,000
Upon the following railway stations –	
Aldgate East	
Whitechapel	
Stepney Green	1,400
Mile End	
Shadwell	
Wapping	
St Mary's	
In conveniences – 20 at 10 persons each	
Underground shelters in the following parks –	
Albert Square, Arbour Square, Beaumont Square	
Brickfields Gardens, Carlton Square, Ford Square	41,500
King Edward Street Playground, Mile End Gardens	
Ratcliff Churchyard, Sidney Square, Stepney Green	
Trafalgar Square, Wakefield Garden, York Square	
Tredegar Square	
Total	223,100

Fig. 8-1 The Provision of Shelter for Stepney from MOA, TC 207/848 *Stepney Metropolitan Borough ARP Scheme*

Thus Stepney gained, in the cellars of various buildings, accommodation for almost 60,000 people. Underground stations were also being used, and a figure had been put on underground shelters in the parks. The next issue would be the cost of all the above provisions, which was estimated as follows:

Summary	£
1. Rescue parties and clearance of debris	4,316
2. Repair of damaged roads	462
3. Repair of damaged sewers	1,057
4. Provision of shelters for the protection of	
the public	300,000
Total	305,835

Fig. 8-2 The Cost of the Provision of Shelter for Stepney from MOA, TC 207/848 *Stepney Metropolitan Borough ARP Scheme*

The Blitz was to make well-known characters of individuals who otherwise would have been unknown. Micky Davis, for instance, was a "gallant little dwarf" who ran "Micky's shelter" in Spitalfields.[94] Another such personality was Dr Hannah Billig, who was practising in Cable Street during a bad raid when a serious bomb fell. It was said that "she stayed in the street tending casualties, operating and binding torniques, with bombs falling within 20 yards of her".[95] It was also reported that one family sheltered in what, with hindsight would seem the most dangerous place, but at the time obviously seemed quite sensible: "we ourselves would … shelter in the wharves, amongst the tea, rubber, spices, canned goods, wine, brandy and other spirits" Alice Beanse recalls. She continues "this cocktail of goods and the obvious target they presented was to make ours one of the most dangerous areas of the world under attack".[96]

The ethos of "getting on with it" can also be seen in the memories of William Kidd who was a five year old boy at the outbreak of war. He recalls:

> … my mother doing up the buttons on my coat, shoving my hat on my head and saying 'Now listen to what I'm telling you. Go straight to school and see if anyone is there. If there's no-one there, or if the school is gone, come straight home … D'you hear me?'[97]

At the end of a raid Kidd remembered his Gran saying "I'll go and see if the gas is working, and make a cup of tea". What she really meant, according to Kidd, was to "see if the house is still there".[98] The following morning "… would see everyone in the streets carrying buckets of ceiling plaster from their bomb-damaged homes and dumping it in the gutter for the council to collect later".[99] Kidd goes on to comment that "this was done in stoic good humour, no-one crying, no-one complaining, just a simple philosophy of 'get on with it'; we're all in this together".[100] Despite the fact that the people of Stepney may have felt they were "getting on with things", the government was watching the area closely at the time and preparing to take appropriate action.

---

[94] Calder, Ritchie, op. cit. p277
[95] Ibid. p277
[96] From the BBC's World War Two People's War Website "My Mum's War: Life in the East End" by Alice Beanse A1143820 and put on 11 July 2005
[97] *East London Advertiser* 6 March 1997
[98] Ibid. 6 March 1997
[99] Ibid. 6 March 1997
[100] Ibid. 6 March 1997

The Regional Commissioners and the Minister of Home Security felt it necessary to show their wrath over the state of the huge "Tilbury" shelter, off Commercial Road. There was massive overcrowding and insanitary conditions created by the number of shelterers, regularly up to 16,000, according to Ritchie Calder writing in the *Daily Herald* and the *New Statesman*.[101] Prime Minister Winston Churchill insisted that Davis be superseded as ARP Controller and in October 1940 the Town Clerk E. Arnold James was appointed. He resigned two months later however, due to what he saw as a dilemma. Robin Woolven has written that, "to strictly conform to the directions of the Minister of Home Security without regard to the views and policies of the Council was incompatible with his position as Town Clerk and his consequent duty to the Council".[102] In this situation, drastic action was called for, and Herbert Morrison, the Minister of Home Security, removed the ARP responsibilities from the Council and appointed the Town Clerk of Islington, W. Eric Adams, as the new ARP Controller for Stepney. Adams, against a backdrop of problems, in the form of the Council withdrawing its goodwill and many resources, managed to turn Stepney around. After six months he returned to Islington, with an OBE. His replacement was Captain A. R. Beaumont.

The Ministry was to remain in control of Stepney's civil defence affairs until 1943. This was due to Morrison refusing to return control of the ARP in Stepney to its elected representatives or officers whilst Councillor Davis or Mr James remained in office.[103] The experience of Stepney within the regional government shows not just the lack of faith felt by the Minister of Security, in two particular people, M. H. Davis and Arnold James, but also Stepney Council's inability to carry out its ARP services. What was assumed to be best for the people living in Stepney had to be considered by Morrison. What he concluded was best for them was to involve outside assistance from nearby boroughs and to ask people he trusted to execute ARP services. This episode resulted in severe damage to the image of the Labour Party in Stepney, from which they would take several years to recover. Mile End was particularly hard hit, as Phil Piratin the Communist candidate was elected MP in the 1945 General Election. As Geoffrey Alderman notes, during this difficult period for the Labour Party, "the Communist Party was able to reap a predictable harvest in

---

[101] Calder, Ritchie op. cit. p277

[102] Stepney Council, Minutes 6 December 1940

[103] HO 186/2228 Gowers to Morrison with Morrison's manuscript annotation dated 23 June 1943

terms of seats both on the Stepney Council and on the LCC".[104] But, how did the Communist Party achieve these gains? To answer this one must look at what the Communist Party was physically seen to be doing for the people.

Calder comments that the "Communists remained faithful to their long-standing interest in the ARP as a potential revolutionary flashpoint".[105] In Stepney there were approximately 400 air-raid warden's posts which would require manning, with two relief's of three air-raid wardens per relief so that a total number of 2,400 air-raid wardens was required. The definition of an air-raid warden was of a person who has "volunteered to perform a number of important duties in time of air attack", someone who augments and relieves "the normal resources of the civil authorities for safeguarding the general public".[106] Phil Piratin was one of these people and became a Senior Air Raid warden who served on various committees. He was in charge of the Philpot Street Synagogue shelter which held about 500 people.[107] The ARP in Stepney successfully gained a number of deep shelters for the area. However, such behaviour came at a price. Councillor Piratin was dismissed as air raid warden, due, according to the district warden Mr A. Garmen, to the adverse manner in which he had "conducted the duties allocated to him".[108] But what could have possibly caused his dismissal? The root cause may possibly have been his involvement in the Stepney Tenants' Defence League, or perhaps the incident, described below, that occurred at the Savoy Hotel.

Shelters and the STDL

The Stepney Tenants' Defence League brought about significant change to the situation of sheltering in Stepney. At a meeting of the Executive Committee of the STDL on Sunday, 25 February 1940 it was stated:

We have now waited one month and it is our duty to review the position in Stepney as regards the provision of shelter for the people against air raids. So far we see that only the Borough Council and the LCC flats are being actively provided for and also one or two places where the militancy of the

---

[104] Alderman, Geoffrey, "M. H. Davis: The Rise and Fall of Communal Upstart" *Jewish Historical Studies* Vol XXXI 1988-1990 p265
[105] Calder, Angus, *The People's War* (1995) p167
[106] MOA, TC 207/848 *Stepney ARP Scheme* op cit.
[107] IWM, ID Number 10210 Piratin, Sherwood Philip
[108] Minutes of the Air Raid Precautions Committee op. cit. L/SMB/A/19/1

people and the Committee would make it urgent that the shelter should be built.[109]

It was therefore envisaged that an immediate campaign should be carried out to:

… bring protection to the people of Stepney and will force the government and its nominee the ARP controller either to get on with the job or else for him to get out and give a person who commands the confidence of the people a chance to get on with the job.[110]

This campaign was highlighted by the incident at the Savoy Hotel. The Savoy Hotel was chosen because it took the issues of the East End directly into the West End. Also, at the Savoy Hotel's shelter, the hotel experience had been transported underground, as people were still being served there.

The Savoy Hotel[111]

The lack of deep air raid shelters in Stepney was highlighted when at 8pm on the night of 14 September 1940, the Savoy Hotel shelter was taken over by the STDL. It had been decided that there would be four group leaders who each brought ten people to the shelter. On that Saturday evening, Piratin and four black-suited men went through the back entrance to the shelter to give an official presence to the STDL. Three of the men who accompanied Piratin were lawyers. Other groups came in at specified ten second intervals, but instead of the forty people expected, some seventy people turned up, including Ward Marshalls from Stepney, children and a couple of dogs. The STDL stated that they wanted the tube stations to be opened as public shelters. Piratin said that he wanted tea and milk for everyone, and that they would only pay the same price as at Lyons, where tea cost 2 pence per cup. The Savoy Hotel staff agreed to this and brought in tea and served the Stepney tenants. Once the all clear had been sounded, the STDL left peacefully.

To intensify this protest, the following Tuesday, George Caffel, who led the Camden Tenants' Defence League, broke open the gates of Goodge Street underground station when the sirens sounded. A couple of crow bars

---

[109] Groser Papers, MS3428 *Report of the Organising Secretary of the League to the Executive Committee meeting* Sunday 25 February 1940
[110] Ibid. MS3428 Sunday 25 February 1940
[111] An article based on this section was produced in the BBC History Magazine October 2010 "Going Underground"

had been strategically left outside by the entrance for this purpose. Once in, Caffel used a megaphone to encourage others to come and shelter and to argue for the use of underground tube stations as shelters for all. Two days later, on the Thursday, Mr Morrison announced in Parliament that tube stations would be used as shelters and fitted out for the occupation of people, with refreshments being provided. Piratin recalls, in an interview he gave in 1988 for IWM sound archives, that if the announcement had not been made in Parliament, then more events that would have caused even more disruption would have gone ahead as planned.[112] Therefore, the STDL's protest was successful in securing a number of deep shelters for the population of Stepney. Piratin also suggested that the use of deep shelters could help alleviate housing issues as people who had been bombed out in Stepney could find friends to stay with or visit during the day but had nowhere to go at night. With the successful opening of deep shelters people could safely stay their over night.

However, according to the Parliamentary Debates from the time, we can see that the issue of deep shelters was an on-going one. James "Jimmy" Hall, Labour member for Whitechapel & St George's, in the early days had asked the Lord Privy Seal, Sir John Anderson, whether he was "prepared to consider the advisability of providing underground bomb-proof shelter in those congested areas near to docks and works which can be regarded as highly dangerous districts in wartime?"[113] To this Anderson had replied that deep bombproof shelters could only be considered as part of a long-term policy and that at the present time main shelter problems were being tackled instead. Hall continued his tirade, by asking if the Gentleman was "aware of the very meagre protection that is provided". He noted that, "in my own district many people would have to travel quite a mile through a labyrinth of streets in order to find even shelter of that character".[114]

After the Savoy Hotel incident Morrison stated that:

> So far as is consistent with public safety and with the over-riding necessity of maintaining the London Underground system, the public are now allowed to use tube stations at night for shelter purposes. The amount of accommodation available, must, however, be limited by the paramount need to preserve the tubes as a means of transport for the workers.[115]

---

[112] This story is taken from a taped interview with Phil Piratin at the IWM op.cit. 10210, Piratin, Sherwood Philip
[113] *Parliamentary Debates – Commons 1938-9* Vol 342 Nov 28-Dec 22 1939 p870
[114] Ibid. p871
[115] Ibid. p264 8 October 1940

This statement was made on 8 October 1940, which was a little later than perhaps Phil Piratin's memory was allowing for. According to his interview, the use of deep shelters would have been announced in parliament on 16 September, but there is no such announcement on that day. However, the victory over deep shelters for Stepney was short lived. In January 1941, Hall took up the question of deep shelters for Stepney again, asking if the Secretary of State, Mr Herbert Morrison, had "considered the plans for deep shelters submitted to him by the Stepney air raid precautions controller; and whether he is prepared to sanction the provision of the shelters?"[116] Morrison answered that, due to a lack of resources, it would not be possible to provide Stepney with the deep shelters they had requested.[117] As the Mayor of Stepney, Frank Lewey, notes in his memoirs:

> Undoubtedly, local morale suffered because we all knew that the construction of sufficient shelters had not been pushed forward fast enough. There was, of course, a great spurt of official activity in building shelters while the raids were actually in progress; but that did not help us much.[118]

During the Christmas period of 1940 a group of students worked in the rest centres and shelters. There were approximately 1,000 shelters in the area, of which over 90 per cent were small brick surface shelters that held 30-60 people. When these were not available to people they sheltered in trench shelters, railway arches and private shelters (which were either converted business premises or basement shelters, or shelters attached to blocks of flats) as previously shown. Others chose to use private shelters not open to the public, family shelters, church crypts, converted coal holes and basements, or, of course the Tilbury.[119] The main conclusion drawn from the survey was that there was a major safety issue. The report stated that: "there is not a single bomb-proof shelter in Stepney" nor one that "has any sort of protection against gas".[120] There was also criticism of the lack of comfort in the shelters, with the main sources of discomfort being "bad lighting, bad ventilation, cold, damp, lack of sleeping accommodation

---

[116] Ibid. p279
[117] For a full version of the debate between James Hall and Herbert Morrison see *Parliamentary Debates – Commons 1940-41* Vol. 368 Jan 21-Feb 13 1940-41 p279
[118] Lewey, op. cit. p22
[119] MOA, TC Box 9 23/9/T
[120] Ibid. Box 9 23/9/T

and often of any form of benches and chairs and ... the most primitive,
filthy and insufficient lavatory arrangements".[121] In addition to these
concerns, it was noted that there were no canteen arrangements, or even a
supply of water in the smaller shelters. In the large shelter where canteens
did exist they were often run by private enterprises. The poor lighting
mentioned might be either too strong or too dim. It was felt that there
needed to be good lighting combined with areas of dimmed light which
would allow people to sleep.

Another observation was that many of the shelters were disused due to
the majority of shelters in Stepney being "unsafe, unhealthy, and appallingly
uncomfortable". In Oriental Street, for instance, there were 8 surface
shelters unused.[122] In the reports summary it was asserted that:

a) the policy adopted has been to cover the area with a large number of
small brick surface shelters
b) it is therefore impossible to provide decent standards of comfort and
hygiene in this large number of small shelters
c) consequently the people do not use the small shelters, but crowd into
the large one, where some degree of comfort and organisation, however
scanty, exits
d) the necessary facilities for comfort and health outlined in the section
above can only be realised economically by building large, well-equipped,
bomb-proof shelters.[123]

It was proposed that the "Haldane" type shelter should be adopted.
This type of shelter was built of reinforced concrete rather than brick and
was also equipped with gas-proof entrance locks, a ventilation system,
electric light, and heating. In addition to these provisions, medical facilities
and lavatories were also addressed. The STDL ran a special drive for the
Haldane shelters, during the summer of 1940. As a M-O survey noted at
the time:

... the window of the main offices of the Stepney Tenants' League,
Commercial Road, is devoted to Haldane shelter propaganda. In the centre,
there is a card-board model of the shelter in section form, so that the initial
and the progressive stages can be demonstrated. The Daily Worker cutting
describing the shelter is plastered to the window. A hand-painted poster
shows up the weak points of Anderson and street shelters, with simple and
striking sketches of each. The news that John Anderson granted permission

---

[121] Ibid. Box 9 23/9/T
[122] Ibid. Box 9 23/9/T
[123] Ibid. Box 9 23/9/T

for beginning Haldane shelters, in certain areas, is announced under the heading VICTORY![124]

For Stepney, it was the Tilbury Shelter that lured the people in, as we shall now discover.

The Tilbury Shelter

The Tilbury Shelter was originally planned to hold 1,600 people but by the later stages of the Blitz it was holding over 10,000 people per night. The Medical Officer of Health for Stepney made a visit to the shelter on 22 September 1940. Part of his report suggests that:

> Much of the shelter consists of a roadway used by horse traffic, with horse manure on the floor. The ground of the shelter is insanitary and difficult to keep clean, owing to the cartage and traffic carried on during the day. Many dark alleyways and corners, especially near the railway line, were soiled by human excreta and urine. I searched all corners with torchlight, and found large pools of urine and excreta in several places. The two toilets and male urinals on the south side were constantly used by queues of women, and were flooded with urine and unclean.[125]

This shows the poor conditions that people in Stepney would endure in order to stay beneath the ground, with company, whilst sheltering from the bombs. These conditions it was feared would be a breeding ground for illness. The report continues:

> Typhoid may be expected from the probable presence of human carriers, the pollution of the ground with excreta, and the habits of the people in eating their supper and breakfast in these premises.

It was also stated that:

> Epidemic Infantile Diarrhoea may similarly be expected, with its large mortality. Typhus or Jail Fever, so common in Russia after the last war may similarly be expected. Hunger and cold are predisposing to this

---

[124] Ibid. London Survey Part 7 Reel 134 65/1/A Stepney Tenants League 29 July 1940
[125] *Medical Officer of Health for Stepney* visit made to the Tilbury Shelter on 22 September 1940

complaint, and it is transmitted from one individual to another by means of the louse.[126]

The Tilbury shelter was a notorious example of a large shelter which was ill-ventilated over-heated and intolerably stuffy. But this provides us with just one example of the poor conditions of shelters in Stepney.

In such a large shelter there were unwritten laws which most people adhered to. One was that it was an unpardonable crime to tread on anyone's blanket. It was felt that music and singing should be stopped at 10pm in the main part of the shelter, and 12pm by the entrance. Officially there was a "no smoking" policy, but people generally smoked by the back entrance. The Metropolitan police did not have any authority in the shelter because it was not a public building, so it was down to the warden, shelter marshals, and soldiers to keep order. People were bound to take advantage of their new found authority. One particular young soldier would take bribes to get people "good places". If they put a bit of silver rolled up in their blanket, when they returned the next day it would be spread out in a relatively comfortable position.[127]

What did the users of the shelter make of its conditions? One woman who used the shelter every night for three weeks commented that "… it's much better than it used to be. It smells of all these disinfectants, but that's violets to what it used to be".[128] This could have been due to the people of Stepney signing a petition "requesting improvement in the Tilbury where thousands … take shelter".[129] It was said that the Salvation Army provided the food, which was "not very sustaining" as it was usually "tea and cake".[130] A man who commented on the canteen observed that "It's alright, get a cup of tea for a penny. That's what they're all here for (indicating people strolling down the gangways). They're not going to stop here. They're just going to have a cheap supper, and off again. Just come for a look round and a meal".[131] The conditions of the shelter may have been appalling, as the Medical Officer found, but it still attracted the people, perhaps because it was somewhere that the community could come together and "fight" the blitz.

---

[126] Ibid.22 September 1940

[127] MOA, TC Box 9 23/9/T How Order is Kept in the Tilbury Dock Shelter

[128] Ibid. Box 5 23/5/1 F 25 C

[129] Ibid. Box 7 23/7/A Mr Davis (ARP Controller for Stepney) refuses to speak to deputation from the Tilbury

[130] Ibid. Box 5 23/5/1 F 25 C

[131] Ibid. Box 5 23/5/1 M 35 D

Conclusion

Edith Ramsay, describes the situation in Stepney as follows:

During the 7 months of the Blitz, before Hitler turned the Luftwaffe on Russia, 40,000 High Explosive Bombs fell on London, and a quite incalculable number of Incendiary Bombs. These rained down from the German planes, and throughout the raids close watch had to be kept for them by volunteers in every street throughout all London, most of all in Stepney.[132]

From this description of the bombs raining down on Stepney, it is no wonder that the people of Stepney were keen to be underground in shelters, so that they could not see the destruction happening all around them. Their entire world was falling apart around them, the children were being evacuated away from the area and those left behind were watching their homes and community being destroyed. But, of those left behind were some new public faces, such as Micky Davis, who ran his shelter in Spitalfields and Dr. Hannah Billig who carried on attending casualties even though the raid continued all around her. They can be regarded as the unsung heroes who played a vital part in those dark days of war. However, there were those who had already been in the public eye such as M. H. Davis, who the Home Office did not trust. Another individual, Phil Piratin, campaigned tirelessly for the opening of deep shelters in Stepney. He was later to receive acclaim in the post-war elections, but during the war his behaviour was rewarded with his dismissal from his ARP duties. Therefore, it can be argued that the war could bring about the worst as well as the best in people.

Nina Masel encountered these extremes of behaviour when she was observing those she lived with. Her encounter with the community she thought had accepted her understandably frightened her. It also highlighted the tense atmosphere which surrounded the Jewish community and that there was considerable anti-Semitic feeling still present in the area. Fascist movements were still present and strong, sometimes organising marches through the streets of Stepney. There was also the internment of "aliens", many of whom were part of the older generation of Jews living in Stepney who had not taken British nationality. In times of war they were seen, by British nationals, as the enemy which would have brought much distress to the relatives they left behind. It must be noted that at the outbreak of the war "although the proportion of Jews in the East End was beginning to

---

[132] Ramsay, Edith, op. cit. p8

decline ... they still represented nearly half of Stepney's total population of 200,000".[133]

The war played its part in shaping local identity. Through M-O, "the reality of living through the Blitz pushed Nina Masel into the immediacy of East End life in a profound way".[134] In early September 1940 she wrote that "No-one is talking about *anything* except the bombing" and not surprisingly her daily reports were dominated by the impact of the blitz.[135] Such reports demonstrated the mass destruction to the area, for example Masel's visit to Commodore Street. Also, how people were treated at the People's Palace can be seen in the overheard conversations she witnessed about what people were meant to do when their homes had been destroyed and they wanted help from the council.[136]

Some of the most important work done by the Mass-Observers was their reporting on the deplorable conditions at the Tilbury Shelter, and also the conditions within the other shelters across the borough. The main conclusion the M-O drew from the surveys was that there was an issue of safety. There were no bomb-proof shelters in Stepney nor was there any sort of protection against gas. Another major issue was comfort, or the complete lack of it, in the shelters. In highlighting the poor condition of the shelters in the area, M-O's reports and surveys brought Stepney into the limelight. Ritchie Calder also highlighted the conditions of the area in his report in the *New Statesman* in 1940.[137] Without such volunteers as Nina Masel, who lived and commented upon the community of Stepney, so much insight into the day-to-day conditions of living through the Blitz could not have been achieved.

So, what was the role of Regional Government during the war with regards to the Blitz? For Stepney, the Regional Government, the LCC, was effective in aiding the borough through the issues raised by the Tilbury Shelter. The ARP Controller, M. H. Davis did not address the issues, which were highlighted through the reports from M-O but also the Medical Officer in the area. With no action from the ARP Controller, intervention from a higher level was thought to be the only way to be able to implement change. With mass destruction happening throughout Stepney, it is no wonder that the LCC had to intervene. Having consulted the records of two neighbouring boroughs, Bethnal Green and Poplar,

---

[133] Kushner, op. cit. p86
[134] Ibid. p98
[135] Ibid. p98
[136] MOA, See the conversation at the People's Palace M 50 C & WVS 60 B TC Box 9 23/9/T
[137] Calder, Ritchie, op. cit. 21 September 1940

records for the Air Raid Precautions survive throughout the war period.[138] For Stepney though, the records stop in July 1940. It was not until October 1940 that the Town Clerk E. Arnold James was appointed, shortly followed by Islington's Town Clerk. Such intervention was severely damaging to the image of the Stepney Labour Party, which was reflected in the 1945 General election results, as Phil Piratin was elected Communist MP for Mile End.

A vast achievement for the population of Stepney, particularly due to the efforts of the STDL, was the right to be able to use the underground system to shelter in. The STDL saw that the provision for shelters in the area was appalling and campaigned tirelessly for improvements, and for people to be able to use the underground system as it was a deep shelter. Their campaign took them to the Savoy Hotel, to draw the attention of the West End to the conditions those in the East End were enduring. Neighbouring boroughs were also involved in the campaign. Such events were to force Morrison to retract earlier statements about not allowing people to use the underground system as a shelter, and for the underground system to be opened as a deep shelter. With hindsight, one can see that one of the most powerful images of the Blitz is of people sheltering on the platforms of the underground stations of London. It was due to the campaigning of the STDL that such an image is possible.

---

[138] The records for both Bethnal Green and Poplar survive for the duration of the war at the Bancroft Local History Library (Tower Hamlets)

CHAPTER NINE

POST-WAR STEPNEY:
LABOUR IN POWER AND LABOUR RELATIONS

With the end of war in Europe came the General Election of 1945, which resulted in a landslide victory for the Labour Party. Yet, in Stepney, there was the return of its first Communist Member of Parliament: Phil Piratin. Through the subsequent borough and LCC elections one can see the Communist party's electoral success. This chapter will assess why this Communist success occurred, when Stepney had been a Labour heartland during the interwar years. However, by the 1949 borough election clear signs of the party's demise were evident. The following year Piratin lost his seat in parliament. Also, this chapter will address why the Communist party's success was only brief. With the return of the men to many of their pre-war trades, the poor conditions of the dock workers were highlighted through the strikes in the post-war years. By focusing on the dockers' strikes, the issue of employment conditions will be addressed. Another important issue for Stepney, which the dock trade highlights, was the arrival in the area of another foreign community: immigrants from Britain's Empire.

The end of the German War instigated a dilemma for the coalition government: should it continue working until the end of the War with Japan or dissolve immediately? Churchill's advisors favoured an early election in order that he might benefit from his image as victor in Europe, whereas Labour favoured a lapse of a few months. Things came to a head at Whitsun, 18-21 May 1945, when the Labour Party held its annual conference. On that Friday, the 18 May, when Attlee was preparing to leave London, the Prime Minister sent him a letter offering either an early dissolution or continuation of the coalition government until victory over Japan. By 3pm Attlee had sent an amendment to the letter, making the coalition appear more agreeable to the National Executive Committee of the Labour Party. On 23 May Churchill announced the termination of the coalition government. Churchill opted for an early election chiefly in order to benefit from his image as victor. The coalition government was dissolved in June and the election was set to take place on 5 July 1945. The outcome of Labour's landslide victory put Clement Attlee into No. 10 Downing Street. This was an ultimate victory for the East End: an "East Ender" was now Prime Minister.

In Stepney, Attlee's constituency was Limehouse, an area "devastated by bombing"[1] which had seen the electorate reduced to 44 per cent of the pre-war figure, from 37,020 electors at the 1935 General Election to 16,367 electors in 1945.[2] This was an important factor in the return of Phil Piratin for Mile End. Attlee's supporters were confident that he would have no difficultly in retaining his seat. He had been Limehouse's Member of Parliament since 1922 with an average majority of 23.7 per cent. As Attlee described it, his supporters "willingly set me free so that I might undertake an electoral tour throughout the country".[3] This was the first election in which radio broadcasting was effectively used. Attlee delivered the first of the Labour election speeches in a broadcast electoral series, following Churchill. Attlee concluded his speech by referring to the representative nature of the Labour Party by saying:

> Forty years ago the Labour Party might, with some justice, have been called a class Party, representing almost exclusively the wage earners. It is still based on organised labour, but has steadily become more and more inclusive. ... The Labour Party is, in fact, the one Party which most clearly reflects in its representation and composition all the main streams which flow into the great river of our national life.[4]

On polling day, 5 July 1945, Attlee witnessed "the electors of Limehouse walking to vote through wide open spaces which had once been streets crowded with people".[5] There were still "three weeks of suspense"[6] to wait until the results would be announced, in order to collect all the votes from the forces overseas and then commence the count. However, in the interim weeks, Attlee joined Churchill and Anthony Eden in Potsdam for talks with Britain's, American and Russian allies.[7] The

---

[1] Attlee, C. R., *As It Happened* (1954) p141
[2] Craig, F. W. S., *British Parliamentary Election Results 1918-1949* (Chichester, 1983) 49
[3] Attlee, op. cit. p141
[4] Ibid. pp142-3
[5] Ibid. p145
[6] Ibid. p145
[7] Ibid. pp145-6

talks were interrupted in order "that we might return home to hear the result of the General Election".[8]

Attlee's wife Violet acted as a counting agent at the elections and "had already seen the opening of the boxes of the Service voters and had a good idea of how the land lay, but kept it to herself".[9] Attlee won in Limehouse with a majority of 6,780 or 67.6 per cent of the vote. Overall he gained 8,398 votes or 83.8 per cent of the total votes cast,[10] his greatest victory yet. In Whitechapel, both the Liberal and Tory candidate lost their deposits. There W. J. Edwards also had a landslide victory for Labour with 10,460 or 83.4 per cent of the votes and a majority of 9,347 or 74.5 per cent.[11] Attlee notes that "the only drawback was the loss of Mile End to a Communist".[12] Labour only gained 3,861 or 36.2 per cent of the vote for candidate Dan Frankel. Phil Piratin, the Communist Party candidate, gained the majority of the votes with 5,075 or 47.6 per cent, which gave him a majority of 1,214 or 11.4 per cent.[13] In Mile End it was felt by the Labour movement that Piratin was the better representative. Piratin was described as "a great fighter for unity" which would have persuaded otherwise Labour voters to support his nomination. Once again during this period, according to Henry Srebrnik, the Communist party was trying to affiliate to the Labour party.[14] Frankel was seen as a rather shy and retiring candidate. Piratin was a well-known figure who campaigned tirelessly throughout the war for Stepney issues, such as the use of deep shelters. He was also recognised due to his work as an ARP warden. Also, the influential Jewish population of Mile End saw the Communist party as "a worldwide alliance of workers' parties led by the USSR".[15] The Jewish vote was probably the crucial point in Piratin's success.

For Attlee, the dominant picture for the election campaign was of his wife, Vi, driving him to all his various appointments. Attlee had spent most of the campaign travelling up and down the country to make speeches and "Vi drove him everywhere in their own small car".[16] In

---

[8] Ibid. p147

[9] Ibid. p147

[10] Craig, op. cit. 49

[11] Ibid. 51

[12] Attlee, op. cit. p147

[13] Craig, op. cit. 50

[14] Srebrnik, Henry Felix, *The Jewish Communist movement in Stepney: Ideological Mobilization and Political Victories in an East London Borough 1935-1945* PhD (Birmingham, 1983) p203

[15] Ibid. p203

[16] Harris, Kenneth, *Attlee* (1982) p258

contrast, Churchill "was driven in a cavalcade and was accompanied by a massive entourage".[17] When Attlee flew back to London on 25 July, Vi picked him up and drove him to Stepney, where Attlee learnt of his victory in Limehouse. As we have seen, this was Attlee's greatest victory in Limehouse as he gained 8,398 or 83.8 per cent of the votes.[18] At Transport House, Attlee and his family learnt that "there were indications of a landslide in favour of Labour".[19] Labour gained 47.8 per cent of the national vote and a majority of nearly 150 seats. Attlee received a summons to the Palace. He commented at the time: "My wife drove me there and waited outside for me".[20] The King commissioned Attlee to form a Labour Government.

In a Gallup poll "58 per cent of the electorate thought it had been a bad thing for the country to hold an election at that time and only 28 per cent regarded it as a good thing", nonetheless the "public saw Labour as intending to carry out what it had promised".[21] Gallop also found that prior to "nomination day as many as 84 per cent of the persons questioned in the poll declared that they had already made up their minds how to vote".[22] There were also the millions of men and women set free from the war and the "ten year harvest of young new voters".[23] The most urgent problem was that of housing and 63 per cent of those polled said the government should turn its attention towards this issue, with one in three saying "that they were looking for fresh accommodation".[24] By the end of 1945, 95 per cent of those polled had heard about the plans for nationalization and 59 per cent approved of them.[25] However, Labour's popularity soon started to wane. By 1946 the cracks were starting to appear as "only 36 per cent thought that the authorities were doing everything possible to relieve the housing shortage and a majority, 56 per cent, thought Labour was not doing so".[26] It should be noted that this was the first time that opinion polls had been used in a general election and that "they were not widely

---

[17] Ibid. p258
[18] Craig, op. cit. 49
[19] Harris, op. cit. p262
[20] Attlee, op. cit. p148
[21] Wybrow, Robert J., *Britain Speaks Out 1937-1987 – A Social History as Seen Through the Gallup Date* (1989) p19
[22] McCallum, R. B. and Readman, Allison, *The British General Election of 1945* (Oxford, 1947) p 269
[23] Ibid. p 269
[24] Wybrow, op. cit. p20
[25] Ibid. p21
[26] Ibid. p23

trusted".[27] What the opinion polls did show was "the importance of class in voting and the appeal of Labour to the young".[28] Notably, wartime propaganda aided the Labour party. Nowhere was this more evident than in areas of reconstruction and social reform which were "pushed [for] so forcefully after the publication of the Beveridge Report".[29] It was found by Mass Observation that "by far the main reason for voting Labour was class identity: 43 per cent gave this as their reason".[30]

The Labour government had two central aims: economic recovery and the international containment of communism.[31] *"England Arise!" The Labour Party and Popular Politics in 1940's Britain* asserts that the "prime objective" of the Labour government was to "boost output and exports, whilst restricting home consumption and imports".[32] Home restrictions can clearly be seen with the introduction of bread rationing in July 1946. Labour was to alter the face of Britain through its policy of public ownership. By the summer of 1947 there had been "six great measures of public ownership ... the Bank of England, cable and wireless, civil aviation, coal, electricity, and road and rail; gas and iron and steel were scheduled to follow".[33]

In the East End overall, Labour experienced a landslide victory. Bethnal Green, Poplar and Stepney all saw Labour triumphs. The only exception to Labour's successful run occurred in Mile End, Stepney. A reason for this Communist victory was mentioned in the *Mile End Enquiry*. The "Labour Party has suffered" it commented, from "the grave reduction in the population of the division since the intensive bombing of London started"; the population had dropped from 34,000 to 15-16,000[34] of which some "2,000 were in the services".[35] For all three constituencies of Stepney there had been a dramatic reduction in the electorate. Limehouse had experienced the greatest reduction in population by 45.5 per cent, with a loss of 20,653 voters or 55.8 per cent. Mile End lost

---

[27] Eatwell, Roger, *The 1945-1951 Labour Government* (1979) p36
[28] Ibid. p37
[29] Ibid. p38
[30] Ibid. p43
[31] Phillips, Jim, *The Great Alliance: Economic recovery and the problems of power 1945-1951* (1996) p131
[32] Fielding, Steven, Thompson, Peter, and Tiratsoo, Nick, *"England Arise!" The Labour Party and Popular Politics in 1940's Britain* (Manchester, 1995) p169
[33] Morgan, Kenneth O., *Britain Since 1945: The People's Peace* (Oxford, 2001) p33
[34] *Mile End Enquiry* ACC24/7/E/3/61
[35] Piratin, Phil, *Our Flag Stays Red* (2006) p79

20,117 potential voters or 55.4 per cent. Whitechapel & St George's lost 19,739 voters or 51.1 per cent.[36] For Limehouse, the loss of population was evidently not an issue for Labour as Attlee had his greatest victory yet. In Mile End there had been a drive to re-establish the Labour Party in 1945. They had managed to secure 400 new members but when the election came the votes did not materialise and the Labour Party lost morale. Another factor was Dan Frankel's re-nomination as Labour candidate for Mile End. He was hindered by a general public view of the Labour Party. Many saw them as "fixers" and "bosses";[37] Pelling considered Frankel to be "of indifferent quality".[38] Dan Frankel was retiring as a Member of Parliament.[39] The other candidate was a Conservative, Squadron-Leader Motion, who gained 1,722 votes or 16.2 per cent and was therefore no major threat.

The strength of the Communist Party was demonstrated in July 1945 when Phil Piratin won votes at the General Election through his popularity and effectiveness as a borough councillor. He was interested in the problems of the people: housing was a key issue. Piratin was active in the formation and continuation of the Stepney Tenants' Committee. Father Groser, the Chairman of the Stepney Tenants' Committee and a keen Communist, aided the election campaign. The party also sought actively to encourage tenants to start making their needs known to the authorities. They argued that people should pull together telling each person to:

> Come together with your neighbours and go along to see the responsible officers at the Council. Don't just let them know what you want, but find out from them what they believe to be the obstacles that are holding things up.[40]

In Stepney, "Jewish Communism flourished as Jewish Communists were encouraged to assume political and moral leadership of a broad alliance within the Jewish community".[41] Phil Piratin was Jewish and a key figure in the fight against the BUF. Both of these factors contributed to his gaining the Jewish vote in Mile End. In the 1937 borough elections,

---

[36] Craig, op. cit. 49-51

[37] Srebrnik, op. cit. p204

[38] Pelling, Henry, *The British Communist Party – A History Profile* (1958) p 131

[39] Piratin, op. cit. p79

[40] Shapiro, Michael, *How to Speed up the repairs* (London, London District Committee, Communist Party) *The Labour History Archives* CP/LON/CIRC/03/1(1)

[41] Srebrnik, Henry Felix, "Communism and Pro-Soviet Feeling Among the Jews of East London, 1935-45" *Immigrants and Minorities* Vol. 5 No. 1 1986 p286

in the aftermath of the Battle of Cable Street, it was felt by many that "Marxism offered the only solution to the 'Jewish question'".[42] In Whitechapel and Limehouse the Communists presumably supported W. J. Edwards and Attlee, since the Communist Party advocated the support of Labour candidates if there was no Communist standing in the election. In 1945 the Stepney Reconstruction group had discovered that just under half the population was Jewish[43] thus their vote was significant in the elections. Henry Srebrnik argues that the Jewish Communists were interested in Mile End because of its small constituency, which was about a third of the size of an average constituency, and also because of the area's increased Communist Party membership throughout the war years: from 807 in late 1941 to 2,450 in January 1943.[44] The Jewish Communists were significant in gaining votes through their influence in the Workers Circle and the Jewish unions, such as NAFTA and NUTGW. The Jewish vote was the key in Mile End to electoral success or failure.[45] Out of the three constituencies for Stepney, Mile End had the only Communist candidate standing to be a Member of Parliament.

Piratin noted that much of the support that the Labour Party would have received "was lost because of the ineffective record both of the local Labour Party, particularly on the Stepney Borough Council, and of their candidate".[46] The Communist Party candidate (Piratin), it was reported, used "superb organisation – always his peculiar genius". However, Piratin's perceived estimated votes required to win, "turned out to be altogether too high".[47] As the campaign progressed, the Labour Party began to realise their loss of ground and "introduced slander and lies" about the Communist Party and Piratin himself.[48] Piratin went on to comment: "On the very last day of the election, posters were stuck up throughout the constituency, containing the vilest slanders against the Communist Party".[49] On polling day Piratin said that the "Communists were everywhere".[50] It was to be a further three weeks until the count of the votes was completed, but estimates on the day, were quite accurate.

---

[42] Ibid. p286
[43] Stepney Reconstruction Group, *Living in Stepney, Past & Present & Future* (1945) p44
[44] *London District Bulletin*, January 1943
[45] Srebrnik, *The Jewish Communist movement in Stepney* PhD op. cit. pp202-6
[46] Piratin, op. cit. p81
[47] *The Times* 11 December 1995 Phil Piratin's Obituary
[48] Piratin, op. cit. p81
[49] Ibid. p81
[50] Ibid. p81

For the Stepney Wards the count took place at the Peoples Palace. The triumph of Piratin in "Mile End owed much to Labour's local complacency".[51] As Phil Piratin says "Gallacher and I were elected in 1945 on the communist ticket". Piratin adds that they were recognised because they had stood on that basis.[52] Willie Gallacher had been elected as MP for West Fife in 1935. An earlier Communist Party MP was Shapurji Saklatvala for Battersea North between 1924 and 1929. Saklatvala was sole Communist representative in parliament during this period and in order to forge links with the wider labour movement the Communist Party published some of his speeches as pamphlets.[53] However, Gallacher and Piratin had each other. Looking back on Gallacher and Piratin's relationship in 2006, Piratin comments:

> There are two of us as you well know, and Gallacher is the elder and therefore automatically I moved and seconded that he should be the leader. He then appointed me as Chief Whip .... Comrade Gallacher decides the policy and as Chief Whip I make sure he carries it out.[54]

Piratin affectionately describes their relationship as being like that of a "father and son". Gallacher was sixty-four by the time Piratin entered Parliament. Piratin was a mere thirty-eight years. In Parliament Piratin was nick-named "Lucky Phil". In his maiden speech, on the second day of Parliament in 1945, he stated that he represented "the people of Stepney", and that therefore he was "concerned to introduce certain points about the people of Stepney".[55] He also declared the line of the Communist group in Parliament and how they would continue to back Labour.[56]

The practice of allowing Private Members Bills was stopped with the onset of war in 1939. It was not renewed until 1949. It worked on a lottery system, so both Piratin and Gallacher put their names forward. They decided whoever was chosen first would put forward a bill for safety at work, as the interests of the working classes were paramount. In his interview Piratin gleefully announced that it was "Philly" whose number was pulled out of the hat first.[57] He put forward a bill called the "Safety in Employment Bill". It called for a minimum standard of safety at work with

---

[51] *The Times* 11 December 1995 op. cit. Piratin's Obituary
[52] Interview with Phil Piratin 31 August 1988 CP/HIST/02/07 p116
[53] Squires, Mike, "Saklatvala, Shapurji (1874-1936)" *Oxford Dictionary of National Biography* online edn. (Oxford, 2004)
[54] Ibid. CP/HIST/02/07 p116
[55] Ibid. CP/HIST/02/07 p141
[56] Ibid. CP/HIST/02/07 p119
[57] Ibid. CP/HIST/02/07 p116

the use of safe equipment and premises. The first clause placed "an obligation on every employer whatever the trade or wherever the place of work to take all practicable steps to prevent injury at work".[58] The second clause gave "the Ministry of Labour power to make regulations for minimum standards of safety in any particular trade or occupation".[59] It was hoped that the Bill would "reduce the accident rate because among other things", it would be "financially worthwhile to employers".[60]

Piratin was to prove to be an active Member of Parliament; he asked 325 questions and 185 supplementary questions during his career.[61] He raised many East End issues in the House, such as concerns about Fascism and housing. In spring 1946 he was, along with other London MP's such as Louis Comyns (Silvertown), "openly critical of the lack of progress being made"[62] fighting for better social services. He also spent a vast amount of his time on individual cases. In 1949 alone he dealt with 388 cases of which 266 were based on personal interviews.[63]

Thanks to the party's electoral victory, with Piratin's success at the General Election and the party's successes at the borough elections at the time of the AGM in April 1946, the Stepney Communist Party saw its position as strong. The party's weakness was its "extreme lack of experienced comrades capable of staffing the Party Organisation".[64] However, there was a confidence that the decisions taken at the AGM in March 1947 would assist the Communist Party to win increasing support. The Communist Party was to win support by showing "the correctness of [their] policy", and the "perspective of a Communist majority on the Stepney Borough Council in 1949".[65] This did not occur as Labour won the majority of the votes. The "lack of experienced comrades" was a huge disadvantage. The party peaked in 1945, with Piratin's electoral victory and membership being 520. Two years later, instead of the number of

[58] Protection at work: Phil Piratins fight for safety of employment 1949 – Private Bill: The safety of employment (Employers Liability) Bill

[59] Ibid. Private Bill: The safety of employment (Employers Liability) Bill

[60] Ibid. Private Bill: The safety of employment (Employers Liability) Bill

[61] *Jewish Clarion* No. 44 February 1950

[62] Bullock, Nicholas, "Re-assessing the Post-War Housing Achievement: the Impact of War-damage Repairs on the New Housing Programme in London" *Twentieth Century British History* Vol. 16 No. 3 2005 p280 – see *Parliamentary debates, Commons Session* 1945-46 Vol 419, 1276-7

[63] *Jewish Clarion* op. cit. February 1950

[64] *Report of the Stepney Borough Communist Party Committee* 1 April 1946 to 31 January 1947

[65] Ibid. 1 April 1946 to 31 January 1947

members increasing, the total had decreased to 504.[66] The following
breakdown shows where the Communist Party's votes came from:

**Table 9-1: Occupational breakdown of Communist Party voters in
Stepney**

Occupation	% of vote	Occupation	% of vote
Housewives	29	Distribution	2
Clothing	26	Docks & Seamen	1.75
Clerical	6	Transport	1.75
Electrical & Engineers	5	Printing	1
Government & Local Govt.	5	Unemployed	1
Building Trade	3	Forces	0.5
Food	3.5	Miscellaneous	12
Woodworkers	2		

Figures taken from *Report of the Stepney Borough Communist Party Committee* 1
April 1946 to 31 January 1947

It was also noted in the report that, of those surveyed, "128 comrades
work in the borough" and "98 comrades work outside the Borough".[67]
This shows the impact a housewife could have upon election results.
Stepney was said to have the "highest proportion of Party Members per
capita in Great Britain: 1 member per 175 of population".[68] The reason for
the subsequent decline in the popularity of the Communist Party can be
found by looking at the European scene. The "British soldiers returning
from occupation zones in Europe brought back unfavourable reports of the
behaviour of Russian troops and their comrades";[69] thus a growing
unpopularity for the Soviet Union arose which had inevitable effects upon
Communist Party membership.

In the Borough Council elections also held in 1945, the Communist
party won 10 seats - a gain of 7 seats from Labour. Interestingly this
election saw electoral success for Edith Ramsay for Labour and Bertha
Sokoloff for the Communist Party. These two women were to become
great friends, working closely together. In future years, Sokoloff wrote

---

[66] Ibid. 1 April 1946 to 31 January 1947
[67] Ibid. 1 April 1946 to 31 January 1947
[68] Ibid. 1 April 1946 to 31 January 1947
[69] Pelling, op. cit. p138

Edith Ramsay's biography *Edith and Stepney: the life of Edith Ramsay*. Although they followed different political ideologies both were deeply interested in the welfare of Stepney's citizens. Edith Ramsay devoted her life to the welfare of Stepney and was particularly concerned with prostitution in the area, housing issues, immigrants and the settlement of colonial dockers in the post-war years.[70] In Mile End Old Town North, after his defeat at the General Election Dan Frankel was again crushed in the borough council elections, gaining only 390 votes or less that 26 per cent of the votes cast.[71] However, Frank Lewey the ex-Mayor of Stepney was unopposed in his seat for Mile End Old Town South East. His tireless work for Stepney during the war, in aiding evacuees and finding accommodation for those remaining in Stepney, secured his seat.

In *Labour keep faith with London* it is stated that in the Borough elections of November 1945 23 out of 28 Metropolitan Boroughs returned Labour councils.[72] In Stepney a majority of Labour councillors were returned, but for Mile End Old Town North and West, St George's in the East North West, Spitafields East, and Whitechapel East Communist candidates had the majority share of the vote. Phil Piratin was a candidate for Spitalfields East.[73] By 1949 Piratin lost his majority but the Communists were still prevalent. They had majorities in Mile End Old Town West, Whitechapel East and Whitechapel Middle.[74] On polling day 29.9 per cent of the people voted, which continued to mark the steady decline in voters: 33.4 per cent in 1945 and 41.2 per cent in 1937.[75] Interestingly, when looking at the hourly break-down of voting during polling day, we can see that only in the latter stages of the day did the majority of people cast their vote. Between 7 pm and 8 pm the greatest numbers of votes were cast in Stepney and throughout London, indicating that the majority voted once they had finished work.[76]

In the LCC elections of the following year, 1946, Dr Hastings and Mrs Janner, both Labour candidates for Mile End, were defeated by Jack Gaster and T. Bramley, the Communists candidates. The Communists gains were due in part to the euphoria of Piratin's success in the General Election the previous year. Although nationally, the Labour Party were

---

[70] See Edith Ramsay's papers P/RAM
[71] Willis, Alan and Woollard, John, *Twentieth Century Local Election Results* vol 2 1931-62 (2000)
[72] Pamphlet *Labour keep faith with London* ACC24/7/C/2-8
[73] Willis, and Woolland, op. cit. p112
[74] Ibid. p142
[75] LCC *Metropolitan Borough Council Elections 1949*
[76] Ibid. 1949

successful, with Attlee leading a Labour government into the post-war world, on a local level the Communist party was embraced as part of the mainstream political scene. The Labour Party manifesto highlighted that on 8 March 1934 they had gained control of the LCC. Labour held 731 seats out of 1385, holding 50.8 per cent of the seats on the LCC.[77] From then until the outbreak of the War, Labour made "the biggest onslaught of all time ... upon the slum plague".[78] However, in Stepney in 1937 Piratin gained a seat for the Communist party and penetrated the previously Labour only council. In five short years the Labour Party claimed that "80,000 slum-dwellers were re-housed in healthy homes and [that] nearly 13,000 slum houses were demolished ... a rate of progress five times as great as that of the Tories".[79] If this course of action had continued, the Labour Party suggested that "practically all of the London slums existing in 1934 would by now have been swept away".[80] War had instigated a temporary halt on this progress, however. In the postwar LCC election campaign of 1946, Labour pledged to make housing a priority. In Limehouse and Whitechapel this brought them success. R. Coppock and A. Reeve gained 79.7 per cent of the vote. In Whitechapel, J. Oldfield and R. Clements gained 62.1 per cent of the vote.[81]

During the 1949 LCC election campaign, Labour emphasised its achievements in housing; the LCC had "provided over 28,000 homes" with "another 10,000 LCC homes ... already under construction" and a "further 12,600 to be begun in 1949".[82] It was reported in a letter from the London Labour Party, Westminster, that the Tories were to exploit the London housing waiting lists.[83] Candidates were encouraged to draw attention to the housing lists and suggest that it would have been "surprising if there were *not* a heavy waiting list in view of 80,000 London homes [being] destroyed by bombing".[84] In *London the LCC and You* the Conservatives stated that between 1919 and 1934 they had cleared away over 100 acres of slums, but according to LCC official records the total cleared between 1919 and 1947 was 345.67 acres. This would suggest that

---

[77] Willis, and Woolland, op. cit. p198
[78] LCC Election 1949 – Manifesto of the Executive Committee of the London Labour Party ACC2417/C/1 Election Notes from the London Labour Party
[79] Ibid. ACC2417/C/1 Election Notes from the London Labour Party
[80] Ibid. ACC2417/C/1 Election Notes from the London Labour Party
[81] Willis, and Woolland, op. cit. p35
[82] LCC Election 1949, op. cit. ACC2417/C/1 Election Notes from the London Labour Party
[83] LCC Election 1949, Ibid. Letter dated 21 March 1949 ACC2417/C/1
[84] Ibid. ACC2417/C/1 Letter dated 21 March 1949

246 acres of clearance could be accredited to Labour's efforts – meaning that Labour had been responsible for two and a half times as much clearance in only a third of the time.[85] Since housing was such a pressing issue this would have been foremost in the minds of the electorate. By 1949 electoral ward boundaries for the LCC elections had changed and Stepney had become a single ward. This probably aided the Labour party and hindered the Communists since Labour had a landslide victory.

7 April 1949 was polling day for the LCC Election. The main electoral issues were housing and mothers and children, which appealed to women voters. Women were encouraged to be involved in the LCC. As *London Pride* stated at the time:

> Women play a big part in running Labour LCC … Almost everything the LCC does has a special interest for women. So it's only right that women should have a big say in deciding LCC policy and under the Labour LCC they do have a big say.[86]

Mrs A. L. Reeve was an LCC member for the Stepney Labour Party. The London District Organiser of the Labour Party visited Stepney Borough to see how the 1949 election campaign was progressing. It was difficult to gain a clear picture of progress but it was suggested that "canvassing here, as elsewhere, is less than it should be, but this is not universally true as in some parts of Stepney a good deal has been done".[87] Anxiety was felt by Labour towards the progress the Communist Party was making although the impression gained was "that the Communists had made less headway" than presumed.[88]

The Communist Party concentrated its efforts on the local borough elections, also in 1949. A grand total of 59 Communist candidates stood in this election. The Communist party had representatives on the council from Whitechapel Middle, Whitechapel East, and Mile End Old Town West. After the party's previous electoral successes, Communists expected no doubt their rise to continue in this election. Previously, in 1945, all 10 candidates who stood for the local borough elections had gained a seat on the council. It would therefore be expected that with 59 candidates standing in the 1949 local borough election that the party would add more seats to the previous success. However, only 9 candidates made it onto the

---

[85] Ibid. ACC2417/C/1 Letter dated 21 March 1949
[86] *London Pride* ACC2417/C/2-8
[87] ACC2417/E/3/59 Letter Dated 29/30 March 1949 From the London District Organiser to the Stepney Labour Party
[88] Ibid. ACC2417/E/3/59

council. This was a crushing blow for the Communist Party, who no doubt thought that concentrating their energy on the borough election would have led to them experiencing greater levels of victory. Previously, a serious obstacle for the Communists was the party's lack of experience, which although the party had gained some experience in the world of politics, the electorate turned their back on the Communists in favour of the Labour candidates. Labour fought a very strategic campaign concentrating on the issue of housing, which for Stepney was a pressing issue.

The Docks

The Dockers, Timmins writes, "discovered the strike weapon and turned themselves into the shock troops of the working class, producing the first manifestations of the 'I'm All Right Jack' philosophy".[89] Both the TUC leaders and Labour Party ministers took a "tough-minded attitude towards unofficial strikes",[90] due to the docks being of vital importance to the government's trade-based programme for economic recovery. The Attlee government was successful in increasing export volume. It rose "nearly 70 per cent between 1947 and 1951".[91] There was a frustration at "the frequency and disproportionate extent of unofficial action in the docks"[92] as it undermined the authority of the main docker organization, the Transport and General Workers' Union. Kenneth Knowles asserted that although the dockers' strikes were increasing in number in the post-war era, the miners' strikes were declining. Between 1948 and 1949 the proportion of strikes that did not last more than 1 day was 69 per cent for the docks and 43 per cent for all other industries.[93] One major issue was the continuation of the Order 1305 which prohibited the right to strike. It was passed in 1940 as a wartime measure. Order 1305 lays down that "a worker shall not take part in a strike in connection with a trade dispute unless":

---

[89] Timmins, Nicholas, *The Five Giants: A Bibliography of the Welfare State* (1995) p172
[90] Taylor, Robert, *The Trade Union Question in British Politics* (Oxford, 1993) p40
[91] Jay, Douglas, "The Attlee Government" *Contemporary Record* Vol. 2 No. 4 Winter 1988
[92] Phillips, Jim, "The Postwar Political Consensus and Industrial Unrest in the Docks, 1945-55" *Twentieth Century British History* Vol. 6 No. 3 1995 p 304
[93] Knowles, Kenneth, "The Post-War dock strikes" *The Political Quarterly* July-September 1951 Vol. xxii No. 3 p269

1. The dispute has been reported to the Ministry of Labour
2. Unless 21 days have been elapsed since the date of the report
3. Unless the Ministry has failed to refer the dispute during that time in accordance with Article two of the Order.[94]

However, more serious was the issue of wage-freezing during a period of generally rising prices.

In the *Port Workers' News* it was reported that the working week was 64 hours, excluding travel. The men were working at excessive speeds which resulted in record after record being broken with the amounts of tonnage being handled in London. At what price did this come, though? The number of accidents occurring also broke records, therefore begging the questions:

> Is it in the National interest to permit enormous profits at the expense of workers wages? Is it in the National Interest to have shops filled with goods that workers cannot afford to buy? Is it in the National interest for workers to work 64 hours a week and be worse off? Is it in the National interest to drive down the living standards of workers?[95]

The workers' demands were for a 40 hour week and 25 s per day, which they felt was long overdue. The strikes resulted in a sacrifice of wages which led to great hardship for the wives and families. As the Arthur Deakin, General Secretary of TGWU, said in a memo to the London Dock Branches: "In addition there has been a great loss of public sympathy and support for the dockers".[96]

In response to the Canadian Seamen's dispute it was felt that the British dockers "… should never have become involved". It was the first time in the history of the dockers' organisation that "a platform was given to trade union leaders from another country".[97] The London dockers had refused to unload *SS Beaver Brae* and *SS Argomont*. Even though the British Government ordered them to unload the vessels the dockers refused. They did offer to continue unloading non-Canadian ships, however. Jack Dash recalls Willie Gallacher and Phil Piratin receiving a deputation of dockers. Piratin had contacted all the dockside MP's to listen to the case of the dockers, who:

---

[94] Order 1305 and the Right to Strike ACC/3287/02/46-51
[95] *Port Workers News* October 1949
[96] Transport and General Workers Union Memo From: General Secretary – Arthur Deakin To: London Dock Branches
[97] Ibid. Memo From: General Secretary – Arthur Deakin To: London Dock Branches

... had come to urge the dockside MP's to demand the moving of the two strike-bound Canadian seamen's ships to berths in a backwater until such time as the Canadian seamen's dispute ... had been settled.[98]

The following day in Cabinet, the MP's put questions to George Isaacs, the Minister of Labour, but to no avail. The Dockers' Labour Board recognised that there was no legitimate Canadian dispute and therefore said that there could be no discrimination. This was how a deadlock arose. 15,000 British stevedores were out on strike within two weeks. One major crisis that soon occurred was that food for Britain was not being brought into the country. Equally important was the fact that Britain could not export goods either, which it needed to do, particularly in view of the massive dollar debt.

The Ministry of Labour and National Service issued an order which brought into operation a permanent scheme for the decasualisation of dock workers in the principal ports.[99] This was generally known as the Dock Labour Scheme. The Scheme was based upon the following principles:

a) limitation of entry to dock work by the registration of both Port employers and dockworkers and the restriction of employment on dock work to registered dockworkers
b) centralised hiring of dock labour
c) payment for reporting for work if no work was available
d) a guaranteed minimum weekly wage for all who reported regularly for work.[100]

There were four major unofficial strikes between 1947 and 1950. The first was the "zinc oxide" strike of June 1948. On the 27 May 1948, 11 daily workers, employed by the Grand Union (Stevedoring & Wharfage) Co. Ltd. at Regents Canal, began to load 100 tons of zinc oxide from barge to ship. The men felt that some consideration should have been given considering the exceedingly dirty nature of the packaging, which were open-weave Hessian sacks. As Joe Bloomberg commented at the time; "when picked up, the oxide seeped through and when they were lifted by the crane, they smothered everyone with zinc dust and made breathing

---

[98] Dash, Jack, *Good Morning Brothers!* (1969) p69
[99] Ministry of Labour and National Service – Press Notice 20 June 1947 order under the Dock Workers (Regulation of Employment) Act 1946
[100] Connolly, D. J., *International Review* Vol 105 No. 6 June 1972 from the Ministry of Transport UK *Report of the Committee of Inquiry into the Major Ports of Great Britain* (Cmd 1824, 1962) p133

very uncomfortable".[101] There was no agreed piece-work tonnage rate laid down for zinc oxide and the men enquired as to what their rate of pay would be. Their reply was 3s, 4d per ton, which was an appropriate scheduled rate for such commodities. The gang unloading the zinc oxide claimed that the cargo was noxious and thus disputed the rate. Representatives of the Short Seas Trades were called in but they agreed that the rate was fair. Joe Bloomberg remarks that the "officials viewed the discharging ... on the quayside so as not to get covered or have to breathe in the zinc dust".[102] However, the men refused to handle any more of the cargo unless the rate of pay was increased, which did not happen. Two days later the same gang were employed to unload the zinc oxide, but they again refused. This time the men were reported to the Dock Labour Board for being in breach of the scheme. Eventually, on the 8 June, the gang completed the job at a rate of 3s, 4d. Their action was at a price, for the London Dock Labour Board stated that the gang of 11 men were in serious breach of the Dock Labour Scheme and were to incur the penalties:

   a) 7 day suspension from Scheme without pay
   b) 3 months disentitlement to attendance money and guarantee make-up.[103]

The gang appealed but before they could be heard a stoppage of work was called. By the 17 June, an amendment had been added to the penalty and the three month disentitlement was reduced to two weeks but the strike continued.

On 24 June, with the men still striking, troops were moved into London to handle perishable goods. This was reminiscent of the General Strike, when the troops and strike breakers had unloaded ships at the docks.[104] The newspapers reported: "oranges will rot in the port if they are not moved quickly".[105] "1,500 soldiers were drafted to the docks today bringing the total number to 3,000" with the prospect that "another 2,000 soldiers will be arriving at the docks tomorrow".[106] With no sign of the strike ending, the Attlee government implemented the 1920 Emergency

[101] Bloomberg, Joe, *Looking Back: A Dockers Life* (1979) p31
[102] Ibid. p31
[103] Ministry of Labour and National Service – Unofficial Stoppages in the London Docks *Report of a Committee of Inquiry* May 1951
[104] See Chapter Five of this book "The General Strike of 1926 – profile of Stepney; how the strike was organised locally" pp80-91
[105] *The Empire News* 4 March 1945
[106] *Evening Standard* 5 March 1945

Powers Act which proclaimed "a state of emergency and [the sanctioning of the] use of troops as strike-breakers in unloading vessels in London, Liverpool, and Avonmouth".[107] It was claimed by Lord Ammon and the Dock Labour Board that the "active hand of the Communist Party amongst the stevedores" could be seen.[108] An example of the Communists at work can be seen in the *Report of the special committee* for the Transport and General Workers Union in which it was stated:

> ... we desire to record that in our considered opinion the agitation leading to the unofficial London Dock Strike of June & July (1949) and the attempt to extend the strike on a national basis was part of a wider plan inspired from Communist sources, the object of which was to dislocate the trade of the country and so add to our economic difficulties.[109]

With a state of emergency being declared, Dockers took part in meetings. The outcome was that on the 30 June the men resumed work.

The average age of a docker at the time was 47, whilst the average age of a miner was 39. Kenneth Knowles writing in *The Political Quarterly,* acknowledged that the age of the labour force was increasing.[110] This was a cause for unease for the dockers. The second strike, the "Ineffectives" Strike of April 1949 was organised in response to an attempt by the dock owners to try and rid the docks of men who were "unwilling or unable to fulfil their obligations".[111] There was to be a review of the Port Register to select those with failing health or permanent physical incapacities, from which a list of 33 unfit men would eventually be compiled. A couple of examples from this list are as follows:

> 19 No. D.O.B 22 August 1876 [93 years old] Incapable of dock work. Unable to find own work. No longer able to carry out obligation scheme.

---

[107] Minutes of Cabinet Emergencies Committee, 21 June-22 July 1949 CAB 134/176

[108] Ibid. p98

[109] Transport and General Workers Union *Report of the special committee appointed under the terms of the decision recorded in minute No. 1125 of the General executive council* dated December 15 1949 Unofficial London Docks Strike (1949) Committee of inquiry W. Pinnell, E. Slavin, H. C. Young, E. E. Fryer, A. Deakin General Secretary HE557.6

[110] Knowles, op. cit. p269

[111] Transport and General Workers Union op. cit. December 15 1949 Unofficial London Docks Strike (1949) HE557.6

24 No. D.O.B 11 June 1908 [41 years old] 1 turn of work in 47 weeks. Considerable sickness over the years Tonsillitis, Bronchitis, Rheumatism, Fibrosis, bad legs. "C" man. Prove 134 turns.[112]

Most of the 33 men on the list fell into a similar category as No. 19. Most were in their 80's or 90's and incapable of dock work. The collective response appears to reflect the close-knit community of the dock workers helping their own to keep on earning in order to live. The dockers decided to call a strike in protest against these dismissals; it was felt that the register should be reduced by ordinary wastage and without replacement. Joe Bloomberg, who worked for Regents Canal, suggested that "... if we had to sack the old men from the industry then we should start at the top. Lets begin with the Chairman of the National Dock Labour Board who is 76 to begin with!"[113] Finally on the 16 April there was a full resumption of work. Of the 33 men issued with notices, 12 appealed. In a single case, a man had his notice overturned. "The man concerned was [allowed] to return to work, but the remainder [were] not, and their position was in no way altered as a result of the strike".[114]

The "Expulsions" Strike of April 1950 was triggered by the conduct of eight members of the Trade and General Workers' Union who made up an unofficial committee, the London Central Lock-out Committee. They sympathised with the Canadian lock-out strike. A special committee was formed and they recommended that three of the men should be expelled; four others were barred from office; and one was warned as to his future conduct. The men appealed, but their complaints were rejected. A mass meeting was held at which the dockers stated that they were against the TGWU's decision to expel three of the men: Dickens, Saunders and Constable. A stoppage began and work did not resume until 1 May.

There was also the Lightermen Strike of May 1950. On 14 April *SS Baron Renfres* docked with a cargo of bulk sugar, which the lightermen were supposed to discharge in two shifts between 6am and 10pm, but the men refused to work outside their normal hours of 8am and 5pm. The 14 men were reported to the Dock Labour Board as the union had accepted the two shift system. The Dock Labour Board issued each man with a seven day suspension from the scheme without pay. They appealed against these terms, but they were unsuccessful. The Silvertown Lightermen went

---

[112] Examples from Trade and General Workers Union Area No. 1 Docks Group 11 April 1949
[113] Bloomberg, op. cit. p30
[114] Transport and General Workers Union op. cit. dated December 15 1949 Unofficial London Docks Strike (1949)

out on strike in protest and were threatened with dismissal. This provoked a mass stoppage in support of the Silvertown Lightermen. There was a resumption of work on 5 June.

Overall, between 1945 and 1951, 2.89 million days were lost to dock strikes.[115] According to Jim Phillips, the disruption caused by the strikes would "delay the process of Western European economic stabilisation".[116] Also, with the economic stabilisation the government perceived that the first steps in halting communism's post-war progress, would have been taken.[117]

As we have discovered earlier in this section, the Communist Party was to suffer crushing defeats in the 1949 borough elections. In the case of Stepney, they marked the beginning of the demise of the party locally. By the borough election of 1953, no Communist candidate held a seat on the council. In that year, only 12 candidates stood for election and they were all defeated. Labour was once more victorious throughout the borough of Stepney.[118] In the previous year there had been the LCC elections, which had seen Labour easily keep hold of Stepney with 73.0 per cent of the vote.[119]

Edith Ramsay, a Labour councillor, was keen that Stepney council should provide for the immigrants from the colonies who were arriving in London, as they tended "to congregate in the East End [and] predominantly in Stepney".[120] Although the number of colonials arriving was small, it was said that "the treatment given to them and the training they have here, will have repercussions throughout the whole Empire".[121] The problem was that although there was a provision of hostels for "British seamen", since the "colour bar" was in operation, there was "no place for coloured colonials".[122] As a token gesture, Colonial House, Leman Street, provided sleeping accommodation for 12 men and a recreation room. In the past, individual cases had been left to the local agencies serving the community.

---

[115] Phillips, Jim, *The Great Alliance: Economic Recovery and the problems of power 1945-1951* (1996) p131
[116] Ibid. p132
[117] Ibid. p132
[118] Willis, and Woollard, op. cit.
[119] Ibid.
[120] Memorandum on the Welfare of colonials in East London. P/RAM/3/2/2 Folder entitled "Leading to Action: Official provision for arrival of Colonial Seamen in Stepney. Hostel in Leman Street. Organised by Dr Jimmy Mallon". Circa 1945-50 Edith Ramsay Papers, Bancroft Local History Library (Tower Hamlets)
[121] Ibid. P/RAM/3/2/2
[122] Ibid. P/RAM/3/2/2

These had sometimes had terrible consequences – something which the following example shows:

> In June 1945 Amara Forana, an orphan boy aged 14, arrived in North Shields as a stowaway from Freetown. He came to London in December 1945. In February 1946 representations were made to the colonial office that Amara should be repatriated. This was ruled out of order and Amara was left to fend for himself in Stepney. Last month the boy was charged with 'shooting with intent to kill'. Fortunately it was possible to convince the judge at the Central Criminal Court of the boy's youth and he is to be sent back to Freetown in the near future. But during his time in London there was no official charged with responsibility for this child and the care that would have been given to an English boy of his age was denied to him. It is only a fortunate chance that the bullet that Amara fired did not kill the man at whom it was aimed.[123]

It was feared by many local residents that colonial seamen constituted "a danger to the area in which they live". Edith Ramsay commented that they "learn much that is evil and little that is good from their stay".[124] The colonials appear to have faced two main problems. Firstly, following the decasualization of the docks, 200 discharged men were forced to seek work elsewhere. Unsurprising, employers preferred "to take Londoners if they have to choose between them and coloured colonials".[125] Secondly, those local employers who had been persuaded to take a quota of colonials found that the men "frequently gave up their work for inadequate reasons, or proved undesirable".[126] In the long-term this was to close doors to future colonial men who might have prospered. It was found in Stepney that "a high proportion [of colonials were] … employed in Beckton Gas Works, in Glass Firms and as kitchen-hands and porters in West End Restaurants".[127]

In the post-war world anti-Semitism was "much less acute … in Stepney and Bethnal Green than it was before the war".[128] Ramsay recalled that "over and over again I have been told about the streets and districts where ten years ago it was not safe for a Jew to walk".[129] There were three main reasons why this had changed:

---

[123] Ibid. P/RAM/3/2/2
[124] Ibid. P/RAM/3/2/2
[125] Ibid. P/RAM/3/2/2
[126] Ibid. P/RAM/3/2/2
[127] Ibid. P/RAM/3/2/2
[128] Ibid. P/RAM/3/2/2
[129] Ibid. P/RAM/3/2/2

a) The comparative prosperity of the East End
b) The reduction of the population
c) The passage of time.[130]

Ramsay advocated the all inclusive "community" of which the colonials were now a part, stating that, "I do not think it is right or desirable to restrict our work entirely to the Christian and Jewish communities".[131] It was on the basis of this inclusiveness that she desired for the community of Stepney that she was elected to the governing body of the People's Palace in 1945. She also championed housing issues, as we shall discover.

Conclusion

Throughout the elections in the postwar world of Stepney, the Communist party enjoyed a short period of success. Phil Piratin had the greatest electoral success for the party, when he became Communist Member of Parliament for England. The reason for his electoral victory was due in part to the dramatic decrease in the population of the Mile End constituency and also the perceived weakness of his opponent Dan Frankel, who was viewed as an indifferent candidate. In the aftermath of their victory in the General Election, the Communist party was successful at the borough council elections (also held in 1945) with 10 of their candidates gaining seats on the council. The following year saw two out of the six Stepney seats on the LCC being held by Communists who represented Mile End. However, although the Communist party put forward their greatest number of candidates in the LCC and borough council election of 1949, the public did not vote for them. The electoral tide had turned back to Labour once more.

It was feared that the Communist party would find support with the striking dockers, who wanted improved working conditions. The Labour government took a tough stance against the strikes, according to Jim Phillips, as a way of halting Communism's postwar progress.[132] In Stepney, many people worked for the docks. Communist activists were often at the heart of the dockers' strikes. Jack Dash, a shop Steward was one such activist. Because of the lack of lasting achievements brought by the Communist-led strikes, it is not surprising that by the 1949 elections the people of Stepney were turning their back on Communism. The industrial action of the dockers' meant that for many families, money

---

[130] Ibid. P/RAM/3/2/2
[131] Ibid. P/RAM/3/2/2
[132] Phillips, op. cit. p132

would have been tight. The Labour government's promise to deliver locally on the issue of housing – a critical issue for the borough – is likely to have won them many voters.

The Communist allegiance to the striking workers was to have a detrimental effect on their fortunes in the elections. In the 1930's striking was one way to bring changes. The party had effectively used strike action to attain better rates of rent and housing improvements through the Stepney Tenants Defence League. During the war the STDL had campaigned vigorously and successfully for the use of the underground system as a place of public shelter. It can be argued, however, that after the 1945 election and Piratin's success, that the party should have followed traditional means of enacting improvements, using the governmental system rather than its traditional tactics of strike action and anarchy to force change. Although Piratin and Gallagher pushed for their "Safety in Employment Bill" in 1949, it would appear that it was too little too late. The damage to the party had already been caused in Stepney with the dock strikes.

CHAPTER TEN

STEPNEY AND THE FESTIVAL OF BRITAIN, 1951: A BRAVE NEW WORLD?

In this chapter, aspects of the Festival of Britain and the reconstruction of Stepney in the initial post-war years will be discussed. During the Second World War, Stepney had suffered severe bomb damage. This gave the planners a clean canvas on which to reconstruct the area and attempt to bring Stepney up to modern standards of living. Stepney no longer needed to be the slum-ridden district of its past. Finally, it could be a modern area, with planned neighbourhoods, proper road access, open spaces, recreational facilities and work all close to people's homes. The nagging question for planners though was whether Stepney would be able to realise and implement the plans and become a modern space to live in, finally casting out its former issues of overcrowding and poor housing.

The Festival of Britain was planned to be a national showpiece, with numerous exhibitions and celebrations. Its task was "to display the British contribution to civilization, past, present and future".[1] There were two travelling exhibitions, one by land and the other by sea. There was a Science Exhibition at the South Bank and a separate Science Exhibition at the Science Museum. A Heavy Engineering Exhibition was on display at Kelvin Hall, Glasgow, and an Architecture and Town Planning Exhibition (the Lansbury Estate) in the East End of London. The science fiction writer Brian Aldiss, called the Festival "a monument to the future".[2] However the festival was also seen by some as conveying "a retrograde message as a meaningless display of British chauvinism". It was, according to the authors of A Tonic to the Nation, "the moment at which we stopped trying to lead the world as an industrial power and started

---

[1] Festival of Britain, *The Festival of Britain 1951* Pamphlet 18316 (1949) p2
[2] Banham, Mary, Firmstone, Christopher, and Hillier, Beris, *A Tonic to the Nation* (England, 1976) intro

being the world's entertainer, coaxing tourists to laugh at our eccentricities, marvel at our traditions and wallow in our nostalgia".[3]

The Lansbury Estate

In 1948, the LCC was invited to contribute an "Exhibition of Live Architecture" in the forthcoming Festival of Britain. It was decided that a part of the development in Stepney-Poplar neighbourhood would be completed in time for the Festival and "displayed to the public as a demonstration of the potential of planning".[4] This neighbourhood was number nine. Neighbourhood nine was named the Lansbury Estate in honour of the pioneer East End socialist and Labour Party Leader, George Lansbury. The "area was intended to be a kind of planning laboratory wherein the experience gained could be used not only in the rest of the Reconstruction Area, but throughout the County of London".[5]

The Lansbury estate was "a full-scale neighbourhood unit which [was] in various stages of completion" at the time. It could, it was said, "demonstrate the best that current British architecture, town planning and building technique has to offer".[6] There were to be various pavilions on display. The Town Planning Pavilion displayed the principles of town planning and argued for the urgent need for new towns. The Building Research Pavilion explained how science successfully aided building technology. Finally, there was Gremlin Grange, which was "a full-size demonstration of how many things may go wrong when scientific principles in building are ignored".[7] Below is a map of the exhibition site, in which all the various pavilions and buildings are depicted.

The Lansbury estate was criticised by some for being too modest and "lacking in exciting 'architectural statements'".[8] However, the estate was immensely important to those who were involved in rebuilding post-war Britain as they were influenced by its development. As soon as the exhibition finished the Lansbury estate became a living organism, which continues to this day. Unfortunately, the exhibition did not set the trend for the East End as a whole. The pressures of party politics took over and the ambitious visions for the area did not become protocol, as we shall discover.

---

[3] Ibid. intro
[4] Addison, Paul, *Now the War is Over* (1985) p76
[5] Johnson-Marshall, Percy, *Rebuilding Cities* (Edinburgh, 1966) p179
[6] Festival of Britain, op. cit. p6
[7] Ibid. p8
[8] Banham, Mary and Hillier, Bevis, (ed.), *A Tonic to the Nation: The Festival of Britain 1951* (1976) p141

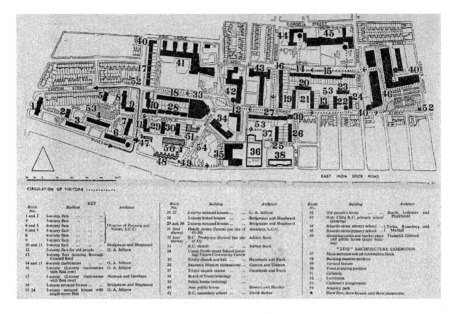

Fig. 10-1 Taken from *The Builder* 16 June 1950 (Tower Hamlets Local History Library and Archives)

Background to the Festival of Britain

Housing in Stepney was a long-standing issue which was still a prevalent concern during and after the war. Mass Observation (M-O), for example, was organising questionnaires on the issue of housing. One particular survey was carried out along Commodore Street, Stepney. This was a fairly poor working-class street, which had many dwellings with more than one family sharing a house. The questionnaire was intended to establish what the people thought of the housing they were currently living in, and more interestingly, how they desired to live. When Stepney residents were asked the question "Would you rather live in a house or flat?" 75 per cent said they would like to live in a small house.[9] As to what kind of garden they would prefer, an extraordinary 100 per cent opted for a separate garden, rather than a communal, grass only or balcony garden.[10] Given the choice of owning their own property or renting, the majority

---

[9] MOA TC Welfare and Social Conditions 1939-49 Part 5 Reel 70 Housing 1938-48 Housing Questionnaire 16 May 1941

[10] Ibid. Reel 70 Housing 1938-48 Housing Questionnaire 16 May 1941

preferred the option of renting (50 per cent). The remaining 50 per cent equally split between owning and being unsure which they preferred. The survey also asked about preferred interiors. Participants were asked "What kind of kitchen would you really like to have if you could choose?" This question received mixed results. 58 per cent said that they would prefer a kitchen-sitting-room, while 25 per cent said they wanted a larger kitchen.[11] Overall, the participants most wanted to see separate housing (50 per cent) followed by 33 per cent of them wanting a garden.[12] Such questionnaires would inform the government of the housing desires of the people of Stepney. The local Medical Officer of Health was another source of information. In 1939 it was reported "that there were 5,800 underground rooms in the borough not complying with the housing act".[13]

It is not surprising that the people of Stepney, when questioned wanted improvements in their housing conditions. At 14 Commodore Street, for instance it was noted that there was "chaos in the upstairs rooms" and that the front room, which had belonged to the lodger was "now covered with plaster from the ceiling coming down". The front room was also used for the storage of the upstairs furniture with "bedsteads, mattresses and chests of drawers" piled into the room.[14] The destruction of Commodore Street is shown by a report which stated that, of the 80 families who lived in the street until the outbreak of war, only 16 remained by April 1941. Thus a loss of 80 per cent of the population from the street had occurred.[15] As previously, discussed, the council only carried out basic repairs to houses during the war. The council did not have the resources to make proper repairs and the Sanitary Inspectors would not sanction the properties as being suitable to live in. With so many housing issues being raised, improved housing for the post-war era had urgently to be addressed.

As early as 1940, Lord Woolton, who became minister of reconstruction in 1943, had declared: "no power on earth will be able to rebuild the homes at the speed that will be necessary".[16] The programme of slum clearance that had begun in the 1930s was to be continued and completed. Little progress was made in the first eighteen months of the post-war period in relieving the housing shortage and it looked as though the head

---

[11] Ibid. Reel 70 Housing 1938-48 Housing Questionnaire 16 May 1941
[12] Ibid. Reel 70 Housing 1938-48 Housing Questionnaire 16 May 1941
[13] Moye, Andrew, *The LCC's Reconstruction of Stepney and Poplar 1945-1965* thesis, Diploma in Town Planning (Planning Studies No. 5, 1979) p23
[14] MOA TC Welfare and Social Conditions 1939-49 Part 5 op. cit. Reel 70 Housing 1938-48 Housing Questionnaire 16 May 1941
[15] Ibid. Reel 70 Housing 1938-48 Report 14 April 1941
[16] Addison, op. cit. p55

of Aneurin Bevan, Minister of Health and responsible for housing, would roll. Bevan's first solution in the immediate crisis was to patch up war damaged buildings and use prefabs as short-term stop-gap accommodation. However, by the summer of 1946, people were so desperate for their own homes that they began to occupy disused service camps. On 8 September 1946 the Communist Party tried to cause more agitation by occupying a number of blocks of flats in the West End, including the Duchess of Bedford's flat in Kensington. For the government and Bevan this occupation of camps and any other buildings brought relief to the crisis of housing shortages, despite the illegality of such action.

By the mid-1940s, planners in London were looking positively towards the future. During the war any construction that was not for the war-effort had been prohibited. As a result, there was a huge backlog of essential building work once peace was declared. During the conception of the "new" London, there were many analogies between the enticingly blank canvas created by the Great Fire of London in 1666 and the destruction resulting from the Blitz. Christopher Wren's plan of 1666 was revisited and positive steps were taken to ensure that the opportunity the Second World War had created would be seized. In 1666 Londoners were anxious to re-build their homes and get back to work. However, in the post-war period there was a "two-fold task: to repair the ravages of raids and to lay down for the first time effectively wise building standards".[17] *The Economist* argued that:

> It is quite plain now that London must never again develop as London has done in the past, that every new house or office, factory or street can be better contrived than the old ones, and that the implication of London's economy must be a first charge upon the ingenuity of the next generation.[18]

With a mixture of evacuation and bomb damage, it was asserted by Andrew Moye that such circumstances created "a natural break from the past" which provided "an opportunity for the construction of a 'new' East End out of the ruins of the old".[19]

---

[17] "Re-Building London" *The Economist* Vol. 139, 26 October 1940 p513
[18] Ibid. 26 October 1940 p514
[19] Moye, op. cit. p26

The Greater London Plan

The Abercrombie plan for Greater London advocated the creation of ten new or enlarged towns, to siphon away half a million Londoners, as the plan stated:

> The need for decentralisation arises from the twofold desire to improve housing conditions in those areas which are overcrowded, and to reduce the concentration of industry in the London area which has caused an expansion of the metropolis to a size which has become quite unmanageable, and one which has made Londoners a race of straphangers.[20]

This was a long-term plan for improvement, with a view to re-housing people within the next ten years. However, it was expected that the necessary movement of industry would take rather longer than the building of the houses. It was also understood that the creation of new satellite towns would take longer than the expansion of existing centres. The proposed density of population was 100 persons per acre. For the re-housing of London's central area's, such as Stepney, however, it was recommended that a density of 136 persons per acre be adopted. In 1946 the Reith Committee recommended the creation of New Towns with an initial population of 15-20,000. The New Towns Act of 1946 aimed to create twenty new towns with 30-60,000 inhabitants. This was followed by the Towns Development Act of 1952 which advocated the enlargement of selected existing towns.

The County of London Plan

The County of London Plan set out the proposals for reconstruction of the London area. London was overcrowded. It had obsolete and insanitary housing conditions. The area lacked open spaces and an adequate road system. The situation had been exacerbated by the war. The County of London plan stated that London required:

> … now, or within a short term of years, a high degree of reconstruction in conformity with modern accepted standards. Comprehensive replanning schemes have become essential as a means of ensuring satisfactory living and working conditions, and economy in cost.[21]

---

[20] Abercrombie, Patrick, *Greater London Plan 1944* (1945) p30

[21] Forshaw, J. H. and Abercrombie, Patrick, *The County of London Plan 1943* (1943) p99

The reconstruction areas of London were to encompass some 197 acres of predominantly working class housing. Although there had been considerable bomb damage, it was scattered throughout the city. One of the main problems was that many of the surviving terraced houses had been built more than a century before and were now beyond the possibility of economic modernisation. These terraces were classified as slums and had only a limited life expectancy. Such housing had been prevalent in Stepney, and thus only enhanced the desperate need for new homes.

The plan was to encompass all strata of society as the reconstruction areas were classified as "miniature republics in which the planners ... had the opportunity to build from the ground up".[22] In designing the new neighbourhoods Forshaw and Abercrombie stated in the plan that:

> Each community is conceived as containing a number of smaller areas of convenient size to form self-contained, compact neighbourhood units, each equipped with its own schools, local shops, community buildings and smaller amenity open spaces. A convenient size for a neighbourhood unit has been found to contain from 6,000 to 10,000 people.[23]

Also a reform in the road systems was considered, as it would aid the flow of traffic through the area. Industry would be separated from housing areas. Homes would not be uniform. A central shopping area was envisaged containing a large variety of amenities, including shops, a cinema, a theatre and possibly a market. This central area would have good road access and car parking facilities. For built up areas like Stepney, another improvement would be a considerable increase in the size of open public spaces: 4 acres per 1,000 of population. Stepney had 90 miles of streets which were very narrow rendering them inadequate for through traffic. When planners were considering the reconstruction of the area they decided that wider thoroughfares running from east to west were essential. The report by the town clerk noted that:

> In Stepney, industry and housing are very much intermixed. Large portions are used for industry (docks, warehouses, gas and electricity works, breweries, etc.) other portions exist in which industry and housing are mixed and certain portions of the borough are fairly free from industry and are mainly used for residential purposes.[24]

---

[22]Addison, op. cit. p75

[23] Forshaw, and Abercrombie, op. cit. p101

[24] Stepney Borough Council – Scheme 19 Housing Committee Town and Planning Act 1932 Monday 18 June 1934 Report by the Town Clerk LCC/AR/TP/2/156

The County of London Plan's general principles for housing were:

a) All rooms should be of a simple convenient shape
b) There should be separate access to each of the principal rooms in the house from a common entrance hall or landing
c) No room should be arranged so as to serve as a passage
d) The living-room should have a sunny aspect; the larder should be on the shady side
e) In planning the bedrooms account should be taken of the beds and other furniture they are to contain and the intended position of the beds should be shown on the plans
f) The height from floor to ceiling should be 8 foot.[25]

Ideally, a mixture of houses and flats was desired, and in Stepney this was particularly striven for. The Ministry of Health felt that schemes of re-development should encompass as large an area as possible, and that development should ideally take place all at once. If this was not possible, they said that a comprehensive plan with desired completion times should be set in motion.

There were to be three distinct stages to reconstruction:

1) The rebuilding of bomb-cleared sites and land which had already been purchased by the LCC and local authorities for housing purposes, along with the minimum amount of adjacent property in order to make development economic and in conformity with the final plans.
2) The clearance of slum areas and the building of lower density houses, along with communal buildings. At this stage also the layout of new open spaces would be commenced.
3) The completion of reconstruction areas which would provide the inclusion of public open spaces along with the erection of civic centres, etc.[26]

For the Stepney-Poplar reconstruction area the plan was contradictory. Industry was to be relocated and decentralised in order to encourage people to move out of the area and to reduce commuting. However, planners were at pains to limit as far as possible the impact of its re-development measures upon business. In Stepney, the movement of

---

[25] Ministry of Health *Report of the Design of Dwellings sub-committee of the central housing advisory committee appointed by the Ministry of Health and Report of a study group of the Ministry of Town and Country Planning on site planning and layout in relation to housing* (1944) p33
[26] Forshaw, and Abercrombie, op. cit. p103

businesses was possible, and the planners grouped together the "scattered industries into an industrial zone along the line of the Limehouse Cut".[27]

Stepney Borough Council had numerous meetings to discuss the implementation of the County of London Plan. The Borough decided, rather than aiming to house only the 94,000 people mentioned in the Plan, that they would aim to provide housing for a population of 130,000.[28] Another alteration they made to the Plan concerned the amount of open space in Stepney which was to be decreased in order to allow the building of more cottages. Stepney desired to have 60 per cent of the population in 2 and 3 storey cottage properties with small gardens, and only 40 per cent of the population in flats "thus reversing the proposed percentages as contained in the plan".[29] This move was supported by the Reverend R. French who stated that "we do not think that flats constitute a suitable medium for the cultivation of family life, and we are aware from our association with the people, that they themselves greatly disliked the idea of living in flats".[30] The Plan also proposed that the entire area to the west of the Borough, which ran north-south down Vallance Road, New Road and Cannon Street Road, should be devoted to industry.

However, Stepney was not in agreement. The borough council was of the opinion "that some part thereof should be allocated to residential purposes and this, together with the limitation of the area proposed to be allotted for new 'open spaces' would render our proposal for an ultimate total population in the region of 130,000 a practical proposition".[31] Mr Stuttle, who attended a Conference at Stepney along with Mr Forshaw and Professor Abercrombie stated that "… he hoped to take full advantage of war damage and general dilapidation due to the cessation of building repairs to improve Stepney as a place to live and work".[32]

---

[27] The "Municipal Journal" special supplement tells the story of The Lansbury Site: The 1951 Festival of Britain's Live Architecture Exhibition *The Municipal Journal* April 6 1951 p779

[28] LCC Architects Department Town Planning County of London Plan and Scheme 19, Stepney Borough Council, *Report of Special Committee re: "County of London Plan"* dated 10 January 1944 LCC/AR/TP/2/156

[29] Ibid. LCC/AR/TP/2/156 10 January 1944

[30] Clergy of the Stepney Rural Deanery – The Reverend R. French LCC/AR/TP /2/156

[31] LCC Architects Department op. cit. LCC/AR/TP/2/156 10 January 1944

[32] Conference at Stepney 18 September 1941 present Mr Stuttle, Mr Forshaw, Prof. Abercrombie, Mr E. Williams and Mr W. Dougill LCC/AR/TP/2/156

Building Work

One of the first tasks of the post-war era was to repair any unoccupied war-damaged properties thus speedily providing accommodation. It was estimated that eventually "over 60,000 severely damaged dwellings in Great Britain were repaired and made habitable".[33] Five-sixths of these dwellings were in the London area. Stepney's housing problem according to the *East End News* was that: "at present 650 families ... have been bombed out of their homes and 840 families [are] inadequately housed [and] in urgent need of accommodation".[34] There were a number of matters to be taken into consideration as the *East End News* commented:

> We must bear in mind the many thousands all over the country who have been married during the war while in the Forces and who will wish to come back to a home. We must also bear in mind the many thousands whom I mentioned before who have been evacuated and who also wish to come back to the districts where they lived before.[35]

However, in the proposed reconstruction area of Stepney-Poplar, in streets and roads that were designated as reconstruction areas, all repair work was stopped. For example, at 87 Whitehorse Road, a bid for repairs at the cost of £682 was put to the council. They refused permission to carry out the war damage repairs because:

> ... the carrying out of substantial works of repair to this old and obsolete type of property would seriously prejudice the councils planning proposals for the redevelopment for residential purposes of this part of the Stepney and Poplar Reconstruction Area at a fairly early stage.[36]

Refusal to carry out repairs meant likely re-housing of occupants which was followed by the compulsory purchase of the property by the council. This practice gradually cleared the street in preparation for reconstruction. In the case of Woolett Street, too, something similar happened. The council deemed its houses to be:

> 1) ... unfit for human habitation ... by reason of their bad arrangement ... dangerous or injurious to the health of the inhabitants of the area and ... the

---

[33] Holland, Sir Milner, Chairman, *Report of the Committee on Housing in Greater London* (1965) p11
[34] *East End News* 6 April 1945
[35] Ibid. 6 April 1945
[36] 87 Whitehorse Road 23 January 1952 LCC/CL/HSG/2/50

most satisfactory method of dealing with the conditions in the area is the demolition of all the buildings therein
2) ... in so far as suitable accommodation [is] available for the persons who will be displaced by the clearance of the area does not exist, it can provide, or secure the provision of such accommodation in accordance with the requirements of section 42 of the Housing Act 1957 [as] ...
3) ... its resources are sufficient.[37]

The area in question was approximately 0.2 acres in size and comprised eight houses, which included a derelict public house and two vacant homes, all within the council's ownership.[38] Dr J. C. P. Grey, who surveyed the area, stated that the "2 and 3 storey terrace properties ... have many defects including disrepair, dampness, insufficient natural lighting and ventilation, inconvenient sanitary accommodation and inadequate facilities for the storage of food".[39] Grey stated that "... the most satisfactory method of dealing with the conditions in the said area is the demolition of all the buildings therein".[40] In the immediate post-war period a survey of land used in the reconstruction area found that nearly a quarter of the area had been either destroyed beyond repair or seriously damaged. Priority was given to the reconstruction of war-damaged areas in an attempt to alleviate the problems of housing. However, there were "constraints on resources and legislative uncertainty" which made the reconstruction of Stepney and Poplar proceed "more slowly than was intended by the LCC's Town Planning Committee".[41] In December 1948 "the LCC agreed powers of compulsory purchase for about 37.75 acres within the neighbourhood, involving some 1,000 properties in about 370 separate ownerships".[42]

It had been decided during the war that some areas needed to be acquired for post-war housing programmes. In December 1943, for example, a list of sites to be acquired for the proposed post-war housing programme was drawn up and included the East Hill estate extension – Wandsworth; the Briant estate extension – Lambeth; Mermaid Court site –

[37] Lansbury Estate, Poplar and Stepney – General Papers 17 July 1951 to 14 June 1961 LCC/CL/HSG/2/64
[38] To: The Secretary Ministry of Housing and local government, Whitehall from Clerk of the Council 2 July 1958 LCC/CL/HSG/2/64
[39] Report by the Medical Officer of Health LCC Woolett Street area, Poplar Housing Committee 24 March 1958 LCC/CL/HSG/2/64
[40] Official Representation – Woolett Street Area, Poplar to the LCC from John Claude Phillips Grey 24 March 1958 LCC/CL/HSG/2/64
[41] Moye, op. cit. p26
[42] Porter, Stephen, (ed.), *Survey of London Vol XLIII* (1994) p214

Southwark; Ocean Street area – Stepney; St Paul's Way site – Stepney, Devons Road site – Poplar.[43] However, for businesses in East India Dock Road, Chrisp Street, Upper North Street, Canton Street, Jeremiah Street, Southill Street, Woolett Street, Giraud Street and Grundy Street, there was to be a points allocation system:

> One point will be awarded for each year the business has been established up to a maximum of 50; one point for each year the firm has been under the present ownership – even if the business was closed while the owner was in the Services; one point for each year that business was carried out in temporary or adjacent premises because of war damage; 21 points for freehold tenure, and one point for each year of the original term, in the case of leasehold, up to 21.[44]

Through this points allocation system it would be decided which traders would be allocated new shops once the re-development had been achieved. Many residents, however, were disgruntled by the move. One such resident was Mr G. H. Cable of 94 Grundy Street, a tobacconist, confectioner and industrial gloves manufacturer. This was to be the second time that he had been turned out of his premises. The last time the Council had not found him a place and he was not expecting them to do so this time either. He remarked: "No one will employ me. I have to fight for myself".[45]

With areas to be re-developed a new set of crises appeared. In particular two distinctive problems emerged. Firstly, there was the issue of re-assembling the building labour force. Secondly, there was a shortage of building materials. Local authorities were left to deal piecemeal with their individual slum problems. The retrograde rating system worked "in such a way that the local authority with the worst slum districts [was] actually financially penalised by attempting large-scale improvements".[46] Stepney had a large slum clearance problem and the council did not appreciate being penalised for wanting improvements. Rex Pope asserts that performance in house building "compared well with that of the post 1918 period". The completion rate reached nearly 228,000 in 1948 "before the effects of the cuts in government expenditure and timber imports were felt and ... [would force] ... the economic crisis of 1947".[47] However, Sir

---

[43] Post-War Housing Programme 22 December 1943 LCC/CL/HSG/2/50

[44] *East London Advertiser* 29 April 1949

[45] Ibid. 13 May 1949

[46] Anthony, Hugh, *Houses: Permanence and Prefabrication* (December, 1945) p60

[47] Pope, Rex, *War and Society in Britain 1899-1948* (1991) p78

Milner Holland, Chairman of the Housing Committee for Greater London claimed that production grew during this period. 190,000 houses were built by the local authorities, 33,000 houses for the private sector and 4,500 for government departments and other purposes. This took the total to over 227,000.[48]

Progress Reports

The housing progress report contained within the Minute Books for Stepney gives a numeric break-down of the number of men in Stepney employed in the house building trade in the post-war period. Also shown are the different types of housing reconstruction undertaken. These findings can be seen in the charts below.

---

[48] Holland, *Report of the Committee on Housing* op. cit. p12

Table 10-1 LCC Minute Books 1945-1946

Date	24/10/45	01/08/45	07/02/45	02/01/46	06/02/46	20/03/46	12/06/46	17/07/46	TOTAL
No. of extended & complete repairs carried out	1746	2305	3140	1212	779	246	117	152	9697
Total to Date	60273	58527	46479	61485	62264	62540			351568
No. of Dwellings upon which work is in progress	1089	1359	1562	1179	685	682	143		6699
Requisitioned Houses — Houses prepared for Rehousing	94	38		176	94	70			472
Houses in course of repair for Rehousing	205	120		284	276	234			1119
Maintenance works completed	1233	1149		1936	879	973	121		6291
Maintenance works in progress		95		72	87	180			434
Written enquiries answered — Number — War Damage Commission	12	223		151	131	75			592
Land Charges Act	52	26		35	36	25			174
Various	43	11		17	14	7			92
Total	107	260		203	181	107			858

Chapter Ten

Continued…

	Total	Necessitated special inspections						
Landlord & Tenant (War Damage) Acts 1939 & 1941								
War Damage Commission	278		33	67	84		91	3
Land Charges Act	174		25	36	35		26	52
Various	53		7	10	14		8	14
Total	505		65	113	133		125	69
Control of Civil Building Defence General Regulations 1939, Regulation 56A								
No. of Certificates of Repair of War Damage Issued	11		1	1	1	1	1	6
Total	115		24	23	22	10	15	21
No. of Licences and what for	2008		185 for Works by Private Owners	285 for Works by Private Owners	442 for Works by Private Owners	223 for Works under £100	382 for Works under £100	491 for works by Private Owners
No. Refused	279		10	37	38	95	48	51

Stepney and the Festival of Britain, 1951: A Brave New World?

245

Continued…

Ministry of Health Circular 2871

									Total
No. of Certificates - works over £100/General Maintenance			61	33		15	30		139
No. Refused			23	19					42
Temporary Hutments — Uni-Seco Type	Hutments completed	200	190	200	200	200	200	42	1232
	Foundation Completed		7						7
	Hutments in course of erection		3						3
	Total	200	200	200	200	200	200	42	1242
Temporary Hutments — Curved Asbestos Type	Hutments completed	102	44	7	158	198	213		722
	Foundations Completed	75	62	34	72	43	39		325
	Hutments in course of erection	84	121	18	33	45	46		347

Chapter Ten

Continued…

Hutments in course of preparation/not started	39	73	241	37	14	2					406
Type Asbestos Curved											
Total	300	300	300	300	300	300					1800
Men Employed — on repair of houses for requisitioning	1257			1507	1488	1322					5574
war damage repairs to occupied houses/repair of war damage	1505	2915	2130	1432	1413	1088					10483
temporary hutments	264	436	80	129	141	160					1210
Total	3026	3351	2210	3068	3042	2570					17267

LCC Minute Books Volumes 45-49 1944-1950 LCC 78.931

Stepney and the Festival of Britain, 1951: A Brave New World?

247

Table 10-2 LCC Minute Books Volumes 1946-1950

Meeting Date	12/06/46		17/07/46		30/10/46		01/01/47		29/01/47		12/03/47	
Figures for Month	Feb	Mar	Apr	May	Jun	Jul	Aug	Sept	Oct	Nov	Dec	Jan
Repairs to occupied houses in Serial No. 166	325	289	208	175	166	54	45	22	17	7	7	4
Notices of completion sent to Owners	513	441	341									
Vacant houses repaired for occupation	36	35	39	102	57	60	53	55	24	22	7	13
Quoining & rendering flank walls installing additional WC's converting shops to living rooms & other exterior works where necessary to remove danger	_Ends Jul 1947 (see repairs to houses)_											
Tenders for repairs to Vacant Houses, now awaiting consent from Town Planning authority War Damage Commission & Ministry of Health											4	

Tenders for repairs to Occupied houses, now awaiting consent from Town Planning authority War Damage Commission & Ministry of Health												
Maintenance Repairs to Requisitioned Houses and Hutments completed	660	369	478	790	738	838	930	435	620	382	96	94
Temporary Hutments erected for occupation	20	21	19	18	17	7						
No. of Men Employed (average) — On Occupied Houses	1185	599	301	241	196							
On Vacant Houses	982	826	470	490	405							
To Temporary Hutments	129	103	86	78	18							
To Maintenance	935	69	78	79	82							
On Flank Walls etc												
On Site Clearance												
Total	2372	1597	935	888	701							
Building Licences including those for Maintenance — Issues	231	197	157	291	301							
Refused	11	17	19	32	26							
Certificate of Essentiality including those for Maintenance — Issued	17	23	12	32	28							
Refused				2	4							

	War Damage Commission	Land Charge Act	Various	Total
Necessitated special inspection				

Continued....

Meeting Date	30/04/47		11/06/47		23/07/47		29/10/47		04/02/48	18/03/48		05/05/48
Figures for Month	Feb	Mar	Apr	May	Jun	Jul	Aug	Sept	Dec	Jan	Feb	Mar
Repairs to occupied houses in Serial No. 166	3	2	2	1	1	4	1	4	5	6	1	6
Notices of completion sent to Owners												
Vacant houses repaired for occupation	4	18	5	11	11	3	8	7	3	2	2	5
Quoining & rendering flank walls installing additional WC's converting shops to living rooms & other exterior works where necessary to remove danger Ends Jul 1947 (see repairs to houses)	1	4	3	5								

Tenders for repairs to Vacant Houses, now awaiting consent from Town Planning authority War Damage Commission & Ministry of Health										6	6	1
Tenders for repairs to Occupied houses, now awaiting consent from Town Planning authority War Damage Commission & Ministry of Health										6	6	4
Maintenance Repairs to Requisitioned Houses and Hutments completed												
Temporary Hutments erected for occupation												
No. of Men Employed (average) — On Occupied Houses	10	6	11	3	2	23	20	25	6	14	12	18
On Vacant Houses	30	42	43	41	39	14	11	16	21	18	22	28
To Temporary Hutments												
To Maintenance												
On Flank Walls etc	2	8	10	6	4							
On Site Clearance												
Total	42	56	64	50	45	37	31	41	29	32	34	46

Stepney and the Festival of Britain, 1951: A Brave New World?

Building Licences including those for Maintenance	Issued		369
	Refused		32
Certificate of Essentiality including those for Maintenance	Issued		
	Refused		
War Damage Commission			32
Land Charge Act			17
Necessitated special inspection	Various		148
	Total		197

Continued…

Meeting Date	16/06/48		28/07/48		27/10/48		22/12/48		09/02/49		23/03/49	04/05/49
Figures for Month	Apr	May	Jun	Jul	Aug	Sept	Oct	Nov	Dec	Jan	Feb	Mar
Repairs to occupied houses in Serial No. 166	5	1	1	2	1	1	1	4	5		5	2
Notices of completion sent to Owners												
Vacant houses repaired for occupation	1	3	5	6	3			2			2	

Quoining & rendering flank walls installing additional WC's converting shops to living rooms & other exterior works where necessary to remove danger											
Ends Jul 1947 (see repairs to houses)											
Tenders for repairs to Vacant Houses, now awaiting consent from Town Planning authority War Damage Commission & Ministry of Health	1	2	2				3	4	1	1	1	1
Tenders for repairs to Occupied houses, now awaiting consent from Town Planning authority War Damage Commission & Ministry of Health	4	4	6	4	21	18	13	16	9	12	11	14
Maintenance Repairs to Requisitioned Houses and Hutments completed												
Temporary Hutments erected for occupation												

No. of Men Employed (average)	On Occupied Houses	8	6	6	6	4	4	4	12	18	16	19	22
	On Vacant Houses	41	42	58	58	40			16	16	8	14	12
	To Temporary Hutments												
	To Maintenance												
	On Flank Walls etc									12	8	12	8
	On Site Clearance												
	Total	49	48	64	64	44	4	4	28	46	32	45	42
Building Licences including those for Maintenance	Issues	572	548	469	89	75	73	113	74	64	60	46	59
	Refused	25	59	36	5	2	28	7	5	3	2	4	5
Certificate of Essentiality including those for Maintenance	Issued												
	Refused												
	Necessitated special inspection												
War Damage Commission		32	26	20	20	12	16	20	26	30	18	10	14
Land Charge Act		5											
Various		146	101	111	86	47	72	47	53	55	46	25	37
Total		183	127	131	106	59	88	67	79	85	64	35	51

Continued…

Meeting Date	20/07/49			12/10/49		23/11/49		04/01/50	29/03/50		26/07/50				TOTAL
Figures for Month	Apr	May	Jun	Jul	Aug	Sept	Oct	Nov	Jan	Feb	Mar	Apr	May	Jun	
Repairs to occupied houses in Serial No. 166	6	3	6	9	14	6	4	7	1	4	3	5	2	3	1456
Notices of completion sent to Owners															1295
Vacant houses repaired for occupation	2	1	2		1	1					1				611
Quoining & rendering flank walls installing additional WC's converting shops to living rooms & other exterior works where necessary to remove danger															23

Ends Jul 1947 (see repairs to houses)

Stepney and the Festival of Britain, 1951: A Brave New World?

															Total
Tenders for repairs to Vacant Houses, now awaiting consent from Town Planning authority War Damage Commission & Ministry of Health	5	6													40
Tenders for repairs to Occupied houses, now awaiting consent from Town Planning authority War Damage Commission & Ministry of Health	22	19	8	7	5	5	4	9	12	9	9	23	17	27	324
Maintenance Repairs to Requisitioned Houses and Hutments completed															6430
Temporary Hutments erected for occupation															102
No. of Men Employed (average) — On Occupied Houses	29	21	17	32	18	25	36	22	14	20	28	22	18	21	3122
On Vacant Houses	9	7	9	9	4	4									3836
To Temporary Hutments															414
To Maintenance															384
On Flank Walls etc															30

	Total														
On Site Clearance	40	38	28	26	32	22	29	36	22	14	20	28	22	18	21
Total	7826	44	54	72	44	66	31	48	53	64	43	30	62	60	46
Building Licenses including those for Maintenance — Issued	4505														
Building Licenses including those for Maintenance — Refused	378	4	3	7	18	4	8	7	5	12	6	10	1	3	1
Certificate of Essentiality including those for Maintenance — Issued	112														
Certificate of Essentiality including those for Maintenance — Refused															
Necessitated special inspection	6														
War Damage Commission	381	12	8				10	12	4	4	7	7	3	5	4
Land Charge Act	22														
Various	1328	33	22	37	21	9	32	33	31	14	30	18	23	15	36
Total	1731	45	30	44	39	13	42	45	35	18	37	25	26	20	40

Also shown are the number of tenders being proposed, building licences issued, and what needed to be specially investigated. The tables provide almost a month by month break-down of progress in Stepney. Overall, between the end of the war and the middle of 1946 there was an enormous drive towards improving housing. From mid-1946 onwards it would appear that the progress all but ceased. Nationally there was a shortage of labour and supply of goods. This is illustrated by the number of completed repairs shown on the charts. In July 1946 not one man was employed in the borough to do any kind of work on houses. This situation continued until February 1947 when only a handful of men, 42, were employed in housing (see charts). Between February 1945 and March 1946 over 35,000 repairs were carried out and from June 1946 to July 1950 a mere 9,792 repairs were undertaken.[1] In March 1948 there was a noticeable rise in building licences being issued, which included those for maintenance. Although the licences were being issued, the work was not being carried out by the borough workforce as a mere 46 males were employed.[2] Most probably, the LCC or a private company was providing the workforce. In Stepney, after the war, there was an initial surge for repairs in order to accommodate families after which the main focus was on redevelopment and new properties.

Stepney-Poplar Reconstruction Scheme Plans

In all there were eight development areas: 1. The City; 2. Stepney-Poplar; 3. Bermondsey; 4. South Bank; 5. Elephant and Castle; 6. Bunhill Fields; 7. Lewisham Clock Tower; and 8. Woolwich. The majority of the sites had only one or two basic maps that covered the area and showed its planned re-development. However, in the case of Stepney-Poplar, the area was divided into seven maps, showing how extensive the re-development was to be, as it would encompass the entire borough of Stepney. Mr I. J. Hayward, the leader of the LCC said "By 1951 the models, plans and drawings which are on display today will have been translated into the beginnings of a living community in London's East End, the home of the traditional Londoner – the Cockney".[3] He stated that this sense of tradition was to be kept in place through "the use of London stock bricks and purple

---

[1] Totalling the repairs to occupied houses, the number of completion notices sent, vacant houses repaired and maintenance repairs, see above charts
[2] See Table 10-2 LCC Minute Books Volumes 45 to 49, 1946-1950 pp247-256 of this book.
[3] *East London Advertiser* 16 June 1950

grey slates, which have long been the usual building materials for this part of London".[4]

The Festival's Architecture Council had four main reasons for its strong preference for the Neighbourhood Nine Site:

1) ... it had been damaged in the Blitz
2) ... the buildings on the fringes of Neighbourhood Nine were considered quite pleasant and typical for the old East End
3) ... unlike the other schemes, the plans of Neighbourhood Nine had not been finalized
4) ... it was more accessible from the river than any of the other sites, allowing visitors to travel by boat from the South Bank to within a short walking distance of Neighbourhood Nine.[5]

It was claimed that "from a wilderness of narrow streets and mean houses will rise miles of new, wide roads, open spaces and fine blocks of flats – at a cost in millions at present beyond calculation".[6] Also "the scheme for 2,000 acres of Poplar and Stepney ... will be the world's biggest slum-clearance".[7] Six hundred properties had been destroyed or made derelict and a further two hundred properties were to be pulled down. The cost of this work was estimated at £500,000.

The plans of the Comprehensive Development Area No. 2 Stepney-Poplar appeared to live up to these ideals. The main body of the area was residential but throughout are scattered small blocks of shops, to suit the needs of local neighbourhoods. There are also green or open spaces which on pre-war maps were negligible. Towards the city are office blocks and areas of industry, and by the docks a swathe of commerce. Industry also appears as a block in the middle of the development area, although the area's industrial centre was situated in the east of the area. In the map below, the division of Stepney and the proposed use of zones are shown.

The Chairman of the LCC, on the 7 January 1949, formally agreed to the Festival's request that Neighbourhood Nine should be the site for the Live Architecture Exhibition.[8] The grouping of buildings was important from a sociological point of view, according to the *Survey of London*, "a feeling of neighbourliness and social responsibility is much more likely to develop where dwellings are grouped than where they are strung out in long terraces or repetitive blocks of flats". Optimistically it was felt by the

---

[4] Ibid. 17 November 1950
[5] Porter, op. cit. p215
[6] *East End News* 17 December 1948
[7] Ibid. 17 December 1948
[8] Porter, op. cit. p215

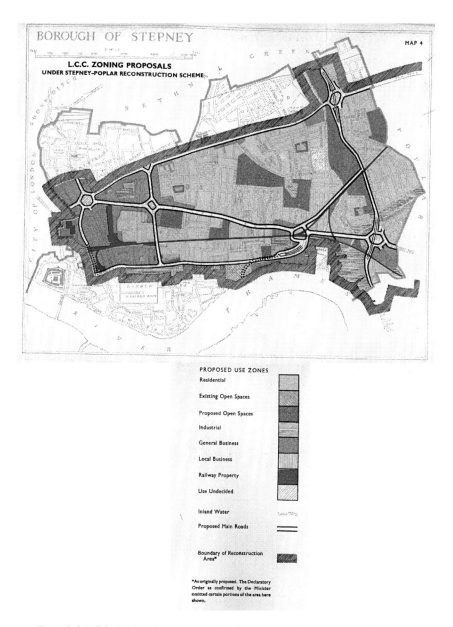

Fig. 10-2 LCC Zoning Proposals under Stepney-Poplar Reconstruction Scheme (Tower Hamlets Local History Library and Archive)

LCC that "children are also more likely to behave well if they are part of a community and if they have their own play space adapted to their needs".[9] Smailes and Simpson argue that the town-planning schemes "enhance[d] the opportunities for community life and promote[d] the social integration of its residents".[10]

It was not until September 1949 that the newspapers reported the "first bricks in the Poplar rebuilding ... will be laid in November".[11] However there were problems, and in 1949 the whole project was put in jeopardy as it was suggested that the "live" architecture exhibition should be abandoned. This was due to two main concerns: firstly, the apparent "slow progress of development", and secondly, the fact that "the government's budget for the Festival was being eroded because of the economic situation".[12] It was reported that:

> Owing to delays caused mainly by the difficult weather for building which ha[d] been experienced throughout the past winter, it ... proved impossible to achieve the degree of completion of the Lansbury redevelopment site which the Festival office regard[ed] as essential for the purposes of their Exhibition of Architecture.[13]

In December 1949 'the Executive Committee of the Festival, "with the greatest reluctance" recommended that the Live Architecture Exhibition "should cease to be a feature of the official Festival of Britain Programme".[14] However, this was not to be so as building work began on Ricardo Street School. It was found necessary for overtime work to begin and instructions were:

> ... given to each of the architects concerned to authorise the working by all operatives whose work contributes to the completion 'target'.[15]

In November 1950 King George VI and Queen Elizabeth visited the Lansbury estate to inspect the progress of the project.

---

[9] Ibid. p219

[10] Smailes, A. E. and Simpson, Gillian, "The Changing Face of East London" *East London Papers* Vol. No. 1 April 1958

[11] *East End News* 13 September 1949

[12] Porter, op. cit. p216

[13] LCC Stepney-Poplar Reconstruction Area – Lansbury Joint Report 9 April 1951 by Controller, Architect, Director of Housing and Valuer and Chief Officer of the Parks Department LCC/CL/HSG/2/31

[14] Porter, op. cit. p216

[15] LCC Stepney-Poplar Reconstruction Area op. cit. LCC/CL/HSG/2/31

Inevitably, there was a last minute scramble to get things ready in time for the first tenants to move in on 14 February 1951. Mr and Mrs Albert Snoddy along with their two children, Albert, aged seven, Jean, aged four, and their pet tortoise, Tommy, moved from No. 6 Yattan Street, Poplar, into a three-bedroom flat in Gladstone House. They paid rent of £1, 9s per week which included their rates. Mrs Snoddy said: "Our new place is just a housewife's dream. There are fitted cupboards and one to air clothes in, a stainless steel sink, [and] hot water tanks". It was speculated that young Albert was disappointed because:

> Ginger the tomcat and Patty, the cocker spaniel [could not] go too. And four chickens may have a new roost tonight!
> The LCC [thought] that flats [were] hardly the place for animals.[16]

It was speculated, in the *Daily Herald,* of the chickens that "The family may celebrate the move with a special dinner".[17] Eventually, the total number of families to be housed in the area comprising the live architecture exhibition was 538. It was expected that "164 dwellings (houses or flats) will be occupied by the time the Festival opens and 440 by the time it closes in the autumn".[18]

The "live" exhibition opened without any ceremony on 3 May 1951. One criticism of the exhibition was that "although the suggested route shown on the plan in the official handbook looked simple to follow, it proved more difficult on the ground, and it was easy to get lost".[19] The cost of the development in the "live" exhibition was £1,725,000. The breakdown of costs was as follows:

---

[16] *Daily Herald* 14 February 1951
[17] Ibid. 14 February 1951
[18] *The Times* 30 January 1951
[19] Porter, op. cit. p218

Table 10-3 Cost of the "live" Exhibition Development

Developments	Cost in £
Housing	825,000
Cardinal Griffin & Ricardo Street School	310,000
Old Peoples Home	66,000
Shopping Centre, Market Place, Public Houses and Clock Tower	270,000
Temporary Shops	21,000
Churches	205,000
Open Space near Trinity Church	11,000
Road Works	17,000
Total	1,725,000

Figures taken from The "Municipal Journal" special supplement which tells the story of The Lansbury Site: The 1951 Festival of Britain's Live Architecture Exhibition *The Municipal Journal* April 6 1951

Of this total the Council bore the cost of £1,400,000. Other sources met the remainder of £325,000.

The exhibition closed on 28 September with as little ceremony as when it had opened. It had attracted 86,646 visitors which would have been equivalent to 580 per day. This was a disappointing figure when "compared to either the 10,000 to 25,000 a day predicted in 1950 or the 8 million people who actually visited the South Bank".[20] Stephen Porter suggests that "although not attracting a great deal of attention in the general press [the] Lansbury [estate] did receive considerable notice in the professional and technical journals".[21] It seems particularly ironic that after the "Live" Architecture Exhibition had finished the Director of Housing sent out a letter to the residents because he "… thought that the tenants and their families might like an opportunity of having the scheme explained to them in general and in particular".[22] A Meeting was held at the Susan Lawrence School, Ricardo Street on 6 December 1951 where the members of the

---

[20] Porter, op. cit. p218
[21] Ibid. p219
[22] Letter from the Director of Housing and Valuer LCC/CL/HSG/2/64

Council and the Architects responsible for the layout answered any questions.

The Lansbury estate at ten years old was still manifestly part of the East End. The pawn shop had adapted a sign-board with three gold balls painted on it, as opposed to real brass balls. The residents also had to adapt. The pawn shop was seen as representing the Lansbury story. When residents returned to their new and strange district the pawn shop had to go with them, as it was an integral part of life for the East Ender. A young wife commented that the Lansbury estate was "giving my little girl a good start ... I dreaded bringing her up in a back to back house with the light on in the kitchen all day and a backyard lavatory to keep the neighbours informed".[23] However, some of the older generation felt that the East End spirit had disappeared. Mrs Flo Camp, a widow of 72, said that "people aren't so sociable, and the kids keep tying my knocker up".[24]

A Brave New World?

In the six years of the Attlee government 79 per cent of all permanent housing was built for local authorities, 3 per cent for government departments and housing associations, and 18 per cent for private purchase.[25] By 1951, the LCC and the Metropolitan Borough Council had made 6,754 homes in Stepney habitable, with a combination of new permanent homes, homes that were re-built and temporary homes. A further 4,159 homes were under construction, as can be seen by looking at the table below:

---

[23] *Daily Herald* 8 April 1961
[24] Ibid. 8 April 1961
[25] Addison, op. cit. p55

Table 10-4 Building Work Completed by 1951

Date	New Permanent LCC	New Permanent MBC	Rebuilt LCC	Rebuilt MBC	Temp (EFM) LCC	Temp (EFM) MBC	Total LCC	Total MBC	Private Building (New & Rebuilt)	Dwellings Under Construction (All Types) Private Building LCC	MBC	
1949	309	351	149	65	238	0	238	416	20	510	724	8
1950	329	813	159	65	238	0	726	878	22	691	262	6
Nov-50	447	1045	174	65	238	0	859	1110	28	780	175	
1951	547	1045	174	65	238	0	959	1110	28	842	175	
Total	1632	3254	656	260	952	0	2782	3514	98	2823	1336	14

LCC = London County Council
MBC = Metropolitan Borough Council
LCC Minute Books Volumes 45 to 49 1944-1950 LCC 78.931

What is clearly evident is that the private sector was marginal in the rebuilding of Stepney. Of the newly built permanent buildings in the area, the borough council was to provide almost double the quantity of homes the LCC provided. The LCC put its efforts into rebuilding or providing temporary accommodation within the borough, as can be seen from the above figures. With a Labour controlled borough council which had promised new homes, efforts were concentrated in this area. Interestingly, in the neighbouring borough of Bethnal Green, the LCC concentrated on building permanent houses and provided 80 per cent of these dwellings.[26] In Poplar, however, the focus in the immediate post-war years was on temporary buildings. The LCC provided 401 temporary structures, while the MBC provided 541 in each year.[27] This difference in approach between Bethnal Green, Poplar and Stepney shows that there was no strict rule on how housing issues were resolved in each borough.

Even with the flood of new building in the area, there were still fundamental problems within some of the existing houses. In 1951 it was established that a mere 21 per cent of Stepney households had piped water, cooking stoves, kitchen sinks, water closets and a fitted bath, whereas in the Administrative County 33 per cent had all five arrangements. 79 per cent of Stepney households had exclusive use of both sink and stove while for the Administrative County it was 83 per cent. 35 per cent in Stepney and 20 per cent in the Administrative County either shared or were without a bath but had piped water, cooking stove, kitchen sink, and water closet. 17 per cent of households had to share or were without sink or water closet. In the case of the Administrative County the figure was 15 per cent. This illustrates the fact that the LCC and the Metropolitan Boroughs still had a long way to go to modernise houses and make piped water, cooking stoves, kitchen sinks, water closets and fitted baths commonplace rather than luxuries.[28] In 3 and 4 bedroom houses, on the Lansbury Estate, bathrooms were to be upstairs and the toilet was to be separate,[29] rather than the toilet being outside and the tin bath coming out in the kitchen once a week. Therefore, with new houses came important improvements.

---

[26] See Table 10-4 Work Completed by 1951
[27] Ibid.
[28] LCC *London Statistics Vol. 1 1945-1954 with comparable figures for 1938* (1957)
[29] Lansbury Estate Stepney and Poplar, Site 7 Plans LCC/HSG/PP/64 - 1950

Stepney Housing

Even after the Festival of Britain, progress still continued. Some eight acres of slums or 300 houses were cleared by the LCC in 1952 as part of the redevelopment of the Stepney-Poplar scheme. It was reported in the *East End News*, that this would displace some 1,288 people at a cost of £300,000.[30] Some locals objected to the upheaval of improvements. Mr M. A. Selwyn, for instance, claimed that developments which involved the "... moving [of] markets and making open spaces in shopping areas was causing a loss of trade in what had hitherto been regarded as a good shopping area".[31] Another resident, a Mr Egan, aired his concerns in the newspapers over being moved to make way for re-development when his house had "only recently had final repairs completed by the War Damage Commission".[32] This example shows the sometimes illogical processes of the re-development.

The LCC's housing scheme for Stepney boasted that 31 Housing Estates and some 5,746 dwellings had been achieved. It also proposed to build a further 2,750 dwellings, thus bringing its total to some 8,500 dwellings in over 50 separate Housing Estates.[33] The planned Ocean Estate was one of the larger post-war developments at approximately 33.5 acres. The estate contained some 1,399 dwellings, of which 1,293 were flats and 106 houses. Part of the site for this estate, approximately 40 acres, was acquired by the Council before the war, and the remainder of the site was secured with a compulsory purchase order. As the borough's official guide suggests "the dwelling sizes illustrate the Council's policy of providing where possible on a single estate the basis for a mixed community". There were:

---

[30] *East End News* 5 December 1952
[31] Ibid. 5 December 1952
[32] *East London Advertiser* 12 December 1962
[33] Stepney Borough Council *The London Metropolitan Borough of Stepney – Official Guide* (1962) p108

1 Room Dwellings.........48
2   "   " 167
3   "   " 605
4   "   " 417
5   "   " 162
49 Shops
7 acres for public open space, nursery school, church, public houses
    etc
½ acre for homes for aged persons
Tenants' club room
Communal laundries furnished with washing machines, gas coppers
    and drying cabinets.

Fig. 10-3 Possible Dwellings on a Single Estate from Stepney Borough Council *The London Metropolitan Borough of Stepney Official Guide* (1962) p108

The area was designed so that houses would "overlook common green spaces where possible, while planted forecourts and gardens [were] proposed for the blocks of flats".[34] Again in *A Survey of Post-War Housing of the LCC 1945-1949*, it is noted that a comprehensive landscaping programme was envisaged to "embrace the re-designing of Shandy Street Recreation Ground close to St Dunstan's Church", showing the priority placed on green spaces as a part of the plans and redevelopment of an area.

Overall since the end of the War there has been considerable reconstruction of the Metropolitan Borough of Stepney as one can see from the table below:

---

[34] LCC *A Survey of the Post-War Housing of the LCC 1945-1949* (1949) p46

Table 10-5 Stepney Reconstruction in the Post Second War Era

Estate	Number of Dwellings
Brokesley Estate	76
Dorian Estate	84
Farrance Estate	143
Fulbourne Estate	52
Newport Estate	70
Ocean Estate	1,399
St Dunstans Estate	78
Stifford Estate	45
Trinity Green	23
Total	**1,970**

Stepney Borough Council *The London Metropolitan Borough of Stepney – Official Guide* (1962) p110

Smailes and Simpson have suggested that "A modest measure of pre-war slum clearance was followed far more effectively by the Blitz, and [that] since 1945 intensive rebuilding has transformed the fabric of the East End within the same lay-out".[35] D. L. Munby in *Industry and Planning in Stepney* wrote that "the fact that the population declined by two-thirds during the war … merely shows what gigantic social revolutions can happen inside the Metropolis without people being aware of their implications".[36] His argument is that, as a direct consequence of the war, one of Stepney's immense problems was addressed, that of overcrowding.

The general reaction, according to Porter, to the first phase of the building of the Lansbury estate was that it was "worthy but dull".[37] Architectural students of the time "were not very impressed". For them it was "all too watered down, Anglicised and compromised".[38] It seems that the visitors were mainly attracted to the "massed choirs and the buildings

---

[35] Smailes, and Simpson, op. cit. p36
[36] Munby, D. L., *Industry and Planning in Stepney* (Oxford, 1951) p4
[37] Porter, op. cit. p223
[38] The Editor, "Lansbury, Poplar 1951" *The Architects Journal* 3 July 1974

further up the river".[39] However, The Editor of the Architects Journal suggests that the Live Exhibition:

> ... strikes a most inspiring note in London's contribution to the Festival of Britain. Whereas the planning and architecture on the South Bank give a hint of an architect's utopia, a world outside economic restrictions, Lansbury shows us the world we can build in spite of these restrictions.[40]

The 1951 development area amounted to approximately one quarter of the whole neighbourhood of 130 acres. The Lansbury estate was to provide homes for 1,500 people. These homes were to take several different forms of council accommodation. The housing developments were to be divided into 5 sites:

No. 1 West
No. 2 Jellicoe & 4 East Armstrong (Jellicoe ended up with both when Armstrong pulled out)
No. 3 Central Bridgwater & Shepherd
No. 5 North Norman & Dawbarn.[41]

This was a deliberate experiment on the part of the Council to find out which particular type of accommodation best suited local residents. This was the first part of the Abercrombie County of London Plan to be put into practice. Unfortunately, as Walter Bor points out in "The Lansbury Neighbourhood Reappraised", there was no follow-up investigation and monitoring of the area. Therefore, no definitive conclusions can be drawn from the original experiment. *The Architects Journal* wrote in the 1970s that:

> The tragedy is that the failure, has been due to lack of powers, labour, materials or finance; the land has been acquired by public authorities and at least half of Stepney and Poplar has been reconstructed; the buildings are there, the money has been spent, but the result is an architectural dog's breakfast.[42]

This was due to a lack of organisation by the technical talent available. There had been a massive team effort for the exhibition but afterwards

---

[39] Ibid
[40] The Editor, "Lansbury: A Principle Put into Practice" *The Architects Journal* 6 September 1951
[41] Porter, op. cit. p215
[42] The Editor, "Lansbury, Poplar 1951" op. cit. 3 July 1974

everyone returned to their own separate ideas. *The Architects Journal* assessed that much of the design was given to private architects on the proviso that they worked within a framework created by the planners. A major problem faced by the architects was the integration of existing buildings alongside new ones. The "aim was to create a neighbourhood where people would like living" but when the area was revisited in the 1970s it was found these plans had sadly failed. The East End was full of disjointed housing efforts upon which individual architects had impressed their own vision, irrespective of the work of others. This had occurred "to such an extent that all their efforts add up to a town planning nothing".[43]

Another problem *The Architects Journal* found, when trying to assess the influence of building such an estate, was the fact that "no specific social and economic objectives [were] defined, such as social mix, employment policies and the role of the private sector".[44] There were no household surveys to ascertain the residents' perceptions of the Lansbury neighbourhood or their level of satisfaction with regards to provisions. Without any records of regular monitoring it is impossible to judge whether the original intentions of the plans were carried out or indeed successful.

However, the comprehensive planning which was pioneered through the Lansbury estate was important because residents were able to be self-sufficient with regards to mobility. Schools, shops, churches, and open spaces were all within easy reach. However, places of employment in relation to homes were not given enough consideration. Local small industries were removed to the east side of the area and provisions were not put in place to deal with the loss of dock employment. This was Walter Bor argues, a negative aspect of the plans. They were, he says, "too exclusively orientated towards providing a purely residential environment with inadequate concern for where the residents would work and how they could get to their jobs".[45]

The land acquisition policy for the Stepney-Poplar reconstruction area suffered from an over commitment on behalf of the LCC to too many concurrent projects. After the initial effort to acquire some 30 acres for the Lansbury estate the rate of acquisition slumped. Having made substantial improvements to some areas the result was escalating land prices which then slowed land acquisitions. If however, all the land had been acquired in the 1940's and 1950's then this state of affairs would not have occurred.

---

[43] Ibid.
[44] Bor, Walter, "The Lansbury Neighbourhood Reappraised" *The Planner* Vol. 64 No. 1 January 1978 p12
[45] Ibid. pp12-3

It is argued, by Bor, that "sight was lost of the scale, complexity and urgency of this task"[46] in that what was being aimed for was like "building a new town within the metropolis".[47] One suggestion made with hindsight, is that the establishment of a Stepney-Poplar Development Corporation might have improved the situation at the time. Such a corporation, which would have had overall power on all aspects of planning and building, could have been composed of elected members of the LCC and the Stepney and Poplar Boroughs. With one body overseeing all aspects of housing redevelopment, a more cohesive area could have emerged. For all the negative points that can be found in neighbourhood development of the period, there are many positives too. Most importantly, overcrowding was reduced. Valuable experience was also gained by planners and officials and some of the ideas that were pioneered in Stepney were to have an influence on a national level.

Conclusion

In conclusion, the question for consideration is whether, during the period examined in this book, Stepney lived up to its motto of *A Magnis ad Moiora* (from great things to greater). One major overall theme has been the politics of the labour movement during the first half of the 20th Century. Stepney saw the rise of three political parties during this period: Labour, Communist, and Fascist. In order to assess the development of Stepney between 1914 and 1951 numerous major events such as the two world wars, the General Strike, the Battle of Cable Street, and the post war elections have been analysed.

At the beginning of the period, Stepney was plunged into the First World War. This was the first all-encompassing war, in the sense that the civilian population remaining in Stepney witnessed aspects of warfare on a daily basis. The Bishop of Stepney at the time, Henry Luke Paget, as well as Arthur Foley Winnington-Ingram, by then Bishop of London, provided a vital link between the war Front and the Home Front. News was passed between the two which helped keep up morale. This would have been the first time that many people would have spent long periods away from the rest of their family. This must have been particularly strange for many Stepney citizens who were used to family members either living with them or close by.

---

[46] Ibid. p13
[47] Ibid. p13

The end of the First World War saw all men, along with women over the age of 30 being given the right to vote. For Stepney, this saw the beginning of an interest and involvement in the political world, which up until that time had been beyond the reach of most people in the area. During the inter-war years, politics was to take centre stage in Stepney. Many second generation Jewish people saw politics as a positive way of integrating into the community. It was also seen as a way of taking up local issues, such as the problems of housing and the "alien" population. Although Stepney became a Labour heartland, the interwar period saw the rise of both the Communist and Fascist Parties. The rise of these parties precipitated numerous major events within the area, such as the Battle of Cable Street and the Rent Strikes of the STDL. These events made national news and have been focused on by other historians[48] studying the Stepney area. Significantly, with these works, the focus has been on a single event, such as the Battle of Cable Street, rather than looking at the development of Stepney as a whole.

In the post-Second World War era, there was a chance for the council to redevelop and modernise the area. It would appear that this was something officials tried to do. Their efforts were hampered, however, and a cohesive area was not the result. However, the fact that it did not develop as a cohesive area could be seen as a testimony to traditional Stepney values and ways of doing things, an assertion of individualism perhaps. Stepney was an individual area made up of a variety of communities simply drawn together by the geographic location. The re-developed area can be seen as a "new town" built on the foundations of Stepney, the borough and its people. After 1961, Stepney no longer existed, as it became part of the all-encompassing East End borough, Tower Hamlets. Today, the old Stepney is lost, and this book will hopefully draw attention to the area once more.

As to the question of whether Stepney succeeded in its motto of going from great things to greater, it can certainly be said that at the beginning of the period covered in this book Stepney was far from being a great or good place. Too much development had taken place too quickly, during an era of rapid industrialisation. The area was squalid. It was to take the bomb damage of the Second World War, and the re-development of the area that

---

[48] For example, Kushner, Tony and Valman, Nadia (eds.), *Remembering Cable Street: Fascism and Anti-Fascism in British Society* (2000); Linehan, Thomas P., *East London for Mosley: The British Union of Fascists in East London & South-West Essex 1933-40* (1996); and Srebrnik, Henry, "Class, Ethnicity and Gender Intertwined: Jewish women and the East London Rent Strikes 1935-40" *Women's History Review* Vol. 4 No. 3 (1995) pp283-299

followed, for Stepney to become an example to others of the form that modern development and building could take. Although, structurally, architects have tended to criticise the area for not living up to the planners' promises, development did resolve one crucial problem for Stepney – the issue of overcrowding. Living conditions for the people improved thanks to the new developments. Throughout the period examined in this book, improvements in housing conditions were one of the council's main targets, but it took the considerable destruction of the area during the Second World War to enable their aims to be finally achieved.

Overall, Stepney introduced a number of significant improvements during the period covered in this book. In time, the diverse communities living in the area at the beginning of the period realised that in order to make significant changes and improvements they needed to work together. The First World War was a catalyst in this respect. The end of the war saw the formation of the Stepney Labour Party, which encouraged unity, for the purpose of political advantage, between the Jewish and Irish communities. Of course, diversity still existed within the political world, as illustrated by the rise of both the Communist and the Fascist parties. However, the labour movement voted tactically in the elections, so that Stepney quickly became a Labour heartland. With Labour representatives for Stepney in Parliament the people of the East End were being represented as many of the MPs came from the same streets as their voters. For example Clement Attlee who lived in Limehouse. The extensive contribution of the Communist party towards the welfare of Stepney was rewarded with the electoral victory of Phil Piratin in the 1945 General Election. This shows that the work of individuals along with party support could have far-reaching consequences.

Peter Hennessy suggests that by 1951 Britain, when "compared to the UK of 1931 or *any* previous decade, was a kinder, gentler and a far, far better place in which to be born, to grow up, to live, love, work and even to die".[49] There had been the establishment of the Welfare State and full employment during the post-Second World War years under the Attlee government. Attlee's rise from Limehouse resident to Prime Minister was one man's journey from great things to greater. For Stepney, with the Festival of Britain choosing the Lansbury Estate as a part of the display of Britain's "contribution to civilization, past, present and future",[50] Stepney was seen - although perhaps only temporarily - as being part of a great

---

[49] Hennessy, Peter, *Never Again, Britain 1945-51* (2006) p454
[50] Festival of Britain op. cit. Pamphlet 18316 p2

national event. Stepney finally had a sense of living up to the motto *A Magnis ad Moiora.*

APPENDIX 1

PARLIAMENTARY ELECTION RESULTS
1919-1951

	1918	%	1922	%	1923	%	1923	%	1924
Stepney					death				
Limehouse	Co. L	59.9	Lab	55.4			Lab	68.5	Lab
Mile End	Co. C	63.2	C	41.0			Lab	41.0	Lab
Whitechapel & St Georges	L	34.9	Lab	40.2	Lab	57.0	Lab	54.0	Lab

	%	1929	%	1930	%	1931	%	1935	%
Stepney				death					
Limehouse	57.7	55.9	55.9			Lab	50.5	Lab	66.5
Mile End	48.5	Lab	47.1			C	56.0	Lab	57.2
Whitechapel & St Georges	58.5	Lab	63.2	Lab	39.2	L	46.5	Lab	54.7

	1942	%	1945	%	1950	%	1951	%
Stepney	death							
Limehouse			Lab	83.8				
Mile End			Com	47.6				
Whitechapel & St Georges	Lab	Unopp.	Lab	83.4	Lab	70.1	Lab	76.5

Craig, F. W. S., *British Parliamentary Election Statistics 1918-1970*

APPENDIX 2

LONDON COUNTY COUNCIL ELECTION RESULTS 1919-1949

Stepney	1919	%	1922	%	1925	%
Limehouse	Prog	35.0	Prog	36.9	Lab	50.7
	Lab	34.3	MR	35.0	Lab	
Mile End	MR	61.5	MR	54.6	Lab	40.8
	MR		MR		Lab	
Whitechapel & St Georges	Prog		Lab	36.5	Lab	59.7
	Prog		Prog	34.7	Lab	

Stepney	1928	%	1931	%	1934	%
Limehouse	Lab	55.9	Lab	49.9	Lab	68.1
	Lab		Lab		Lab	
Mile End	MR	48.3	Lab	51.2	Lab	68.4
	MR		Lab		Lab	
Whitechapel & St Georges	Lab	65.9	Lab	67.3	Lab	71.1
	Lab		Lab		Lab	

Stepney	1937	%	1946	%	1949
Limehouse	Lab	46.7	Lab	79.7	Lab
	Lab		Lab		for
Mile End	Lab	84.6	Comm	53.5	Stepney
	Lab		Comm		
Whitechapel & St Georges	Lab	48.5	Lab	62.1	
	Lab		Lab		

Lab = Labour; MR = Municipal Reform; Prog = Progressive
Willis & Woollard, *Twentieth Century Local Election Results*

APPENDIX 3

STEPNEY BOROUGH ELECTION RESULTS
1919-1949

Stepney	1919	%	1922	%	1925	%	1928	%
	Prog	53.0	RA	50.1	Lab	59.5	Lab	60.4
	Prog		Lab	49.9	Lab		Lab	
Spitalfields West	Prog		RA		Lab		Lab	
	Prog	61.0	RA	80.0	RA	56.5	Ind	58.4
	Prog		RA		RA		Ind	
Spitalfield East	Prog		RA		RA		Ind	
	Lab	38.3	RA	51.2	Lab	76.0	Lab	54.6
	Lab		Lab	48.8	Lab		Lab	
Mile End - New Town	USR	32.3	Lab		Lab		Lab	
	Lab	47.6	RA	59.9	RA	54.0	MR	58.2
Mile End - Old Town	Lab		RA		RA		MR	
North	Lab		RA		RA		MR	
	Lab	45.1	Lab	52.6	RA	50.4	MR	66.0
Mile End - Old Town	Lab		Lab		Lab	49.6	MR	
North East	Lab		Lab		RA		MR	
	Lab	58.4	Lab	40.5	Lab	54.7	Lab	
Mile End - Old Town	Lab		Lab		Lab		Lab	
South East	Lab		Lab		Lab		Lab	
	Lab	45.1	RA	49.0	RA	54.8	MR	53.7
Mile End - Old Town	Lab		RA		RA		MR	
West	Prog		RA		RA		MR	
	Prog	37.5	RA	59.0	RA	52.0	MR	48.5
Mile End - Old Town	Lab	35.3	RA		RA		MR	
South	Lab		RA		Lab	48.0	MR	
	Lab	51.1	Lab	56.2	Lab	59.6	Lab	52.7
Mile End - Old Town	Lab		Lab		Lab		Lab	
Centre	Lab		Lab		Lab		Lab	
	Lab	48.7	RA	54.7	Lab	55.5	Lab	58.4
	Lab		RA		Lab		Lab	
Ratcliffe	Lab		RA		Lab		Lab	

1931	%	1934	%	1937	%	1945	%	1949	%
RA	52.9	Lab	56.5	Lab	80.1	Lab	88.5	Lab	68.5
Lab	42.9	Lab		Lab		Lab		Lab	
RA		Lab		Lab		Lab		Lab	
Ind	52.0	Lab	67.4	Lab	53.2	Comm	60.9	Lab	68.5
Ind		Lab		Lab		Comm		Lab	
Ind		Lab		Comm	38.5	Lab	39.1	Lab	
Lab	56.7	Lab	81.9	Lab	88.9	Unop		Lab	69.0
Lab		Lab		Lab		Unop		Lab	
Lab		Lab		Lab		Unop		Lab	
MR	66.9	Lab	55.9	Lab	52.8	Comm	41.4	Lab	60.3
MR		Lab		Lab		Comm		Lab	
MR		Lab		Lab		Lab	32.3	Lab	
MR	64.9	Lab	62.3	Lab	78.1	Unop		Lab	63.8
MR		Lab		Lab		Unop		Lab	
MR		Lab		Lab		Unop		Lab	
Lab	50.2	Lab	60.4	Lab	60.1	Unop		Lab	94.2
MR	49.8	Lab		Lab		Unop		Lab	
MR		Lab		Lab		Unop		Lab	
MR	56.5	Lab	59.2	Lab	83.4	Comm	64.0	Comm	54.7
MR		Lab		Lab		Comm		Comm	
MR		Lab		Lab		Lab	36.0	Comm	
MR	64.0	Lab	63.9	Lab	64.1	Lab	77.3	Lab	70.9
MR		Lab		Lab		Lab		Lab	
MR		Lab		Lab		Lab		Lab	
MR	51.6	Lab	68.4	Lab	61.9	Lab	77.7	Lab	51.9
MR		Lab		Lab		Lab		Lab	
Lab	48.4	Lab		Lab		Lab		Lab	
Lab	55.1	Lab	62.0	Lab	71.7	Unop		Lab	91.1
Lab		Lab		Lab		Unop		Lab	
RA	48.9	Lab		Lab		Unop		Lab	

Stepney	1919	%	1922	%	1925	%	1928	%
	Lab	67.9	Lab	60.5	Lab	68.1	Lab	68.7
	Lab		Lab		Lab		Lab	
Limehouse North	Lab		Lab		Lab		Lab	
	Lab	59.9	RA	55.8	RA	44.9	RA	37.9
	Lab		RA		Lab	43.5	Lab	36.3
Limehouse South	Lab		RA		Lab		Lab	
	Lab	57.0	Lab	53.0	Lab	62.1	Lab	65.6
	Lab		Lab		Lab		Lab	
The Tower	Lab		Lab		Lab		Lab	
	Lab	63.9	Lab	60.3	Lab	74.1	Lab	45.8
	Lab		Lab		Lab		Lab	
Shadwell	Lab		Lab		Lab		Lab	
St Georges in the East - North (from 1928 divided into North East & North West) — East	Prog	39.1	Lab	41.8	Lab	58.4	Lab	47.0
	Prog		Lab		Lab		Lab	
	Prog		RA	37.1	Lab		Lab	
— West	MR	31.7	Lab				Lab	62.8
	Lab	29.2	RA		Lab	49.8	Lab	
	Lab		Lab		Lab		Lab	
	Lab	51.8	Lab	50.4	Lab	65.9	Lab	61.8
St Georges in the East - South	Lab		RA	49.6	Lab		Lab	
	Lab		RA		Lab		Lab	
	Prog	38.1	RA	72.9	RA	64.4	MR	65.6
	USR	35.9	RA		RA		MR	
Whitechapel East	USR		RA		RA		MR	
	Lab	33.2	Lab	51.0	Ind	50.8	Lab	60.1
	Lab		RA	49.0	Ind		Lab	
Whitechapel Middle	USR	23.6	RA		Ind		Lab	
	Lab	40.1	RA	66.7	Lab	52.1	Lab	54.4
	Prog	36.6	RA		Lab		Lab	
Withechapel South	Lab		RA		Lab		Lab	

1931	%	1934	%	1937	%	1945	%	1949	%
Lab	64.8	Lab	78.1	Lab	69.6	Lab	72.0	Lab	74.3
Lab		Lab		Lab		Lab		Lab	
Lab		Lab		Lab		Lab		Lab	
RA	46.8	Lab	58.4	Lab	60.5	Lab	74.0	Lab	95.2
RA		Lab		Lab		Lab		Lab	
RA		Lab		Lab		Lab		Lab	
Lab	56.6	Lab	63.7	Lab	74.8	Unop		Lab	94.0
Lab		Lab		Lab		Unop		Lab	
Lab		Lab		Lab		Unop		Lab	
Lab	64.9	Lab	88.4	Lab	83.0	Unop		Lab	86.1
Lab		Lab		Lab		Unop		Lab	
Lab		Lab		Lab		Unop		Lab	
Lab	65.5	Lab	81.5	Lab	88.1	Unop		Lab	91.1
Lab		Lab		Lab		Unop		Lab	
Lab		Lab		Lab		Unop		Lab	
RA	52.5	Lab	50.6	Lab	76.9	Comm	52.0	Lab	59.3
RA		Lab		Lab		Comm		Lab	
RA		Lab		Lab		Lab	37.8	Lab	
Lab		Lab	78.0	Lab	88.9	Lab	85.2	Lab	93.2
Lab		Lab		Lab		Lab		Lab	
Lab		Lab		Lab		Lab		Lab	
MR	74.1	Lab	54.5	Lab	59.0	Comm	54.8	Comm	53.8
MR		Lab		Lab		Comm		Comm	
MR		Lab		Lab		Lab	36.3	Comm	
Lab		Lab	58.5	Lab	50.0	Lab	76.9	Comm	51.4
RA		Lab		Lab		Lab		Comm	
Ind		Lab		Lab		Lab		Comm	
Lab	51.4	Lab	57.8	Lab	68.3	I.Lab	61.1	Lab	46.4
Lab		Lab		Lab		Lab	38.9	Lab	
RA		Lab		Lab		Lab		I.Lab	41.3

Key: Ind = Independent; Lab = Labour; MR = Municipal Reform; Prog = Progressive;
RA = Ratepayers Association; USR = Union of Stepney Ratepayers
Willis & Woollard, *Twentieth Century Local Election Results*

BIBLIOGRAPHY

Primary Sources

Bancroft Local History Library (Tower Hamlets, London)
Minute Book of the Air Raid Precautions Committee of Stepney Borough Council 1938-1940
Minute Book of the Council of the Metropolitan Borough of Stepney 1914-1951
Minute Book of the Electricity Supply Committee of the Metropolitan Borough of Stepney 1926
Minute Book of the Housing Committee of the Stepney Borough Council 1914-1951
Minute Book of the Public Health Committee of the Stepney Borough Council 1914-1951
TH/8260 Ramsay, Edith
301. Stepney Borough Council
320.1 Stepney Labour Party
320.4 Stepney Communist Party
321.3 Borough Council Election Results

Dockland Museum Archives (Docklands, London)
Dock Strikes 1945 – Vol. 1

Imperial War Museum (London)
Special Miscellaneous 14: Letter from Isaac Rosenberg to Sydney Schiff 4 June 1915
Women at Work Collection

Lambeth Palace Library (London)
MS 3406 Arthur Foley Winnington-Ingram Papers
MS 3428 Groser Paper

London Metropolitan Archives (London)
Papers referring to Stepney in:
ACC 2417, 3287,
LCC

LCC Government Evacuation Scheme, Directory of London Schools in the
    Reception Area – December 1939
Minute Book of the Commercial Gas Company 1915-1918
Minute Books of the London County Council, Volumes 45-49, (1944-50)

Marx Memorial Library (London)
Piratin, Phil papers

Mass Observation Archives (Sussex)
Diarist 5370 - Masel, Nina Wartime Diary
Masel, Nina - Personal File
Micro-films of Topic Collections

National Archives (Kew, London)
Papers referring to Stepney:
CAB 37
CMD 504
ED 138
FO 383
HD 9011
HLG 7, 52
HO 45, 144, 186
KV 2
LAB 2, 35
MEPO 2, 3
MH 101
MO 207
MT 55
MUN 4, 5
PO 383
RAIL 684

Peoples History Museum (Manchester)
Papers referring to the Stepney Communist Party:
CP/HIST
CP/LON

TUC Archives (London)
Papers referring to the Stepney, in particular the Stepney Communist Party
    in the union papers and the Dock strikes:
HD 6661

HE 551, 557
HX 698

Women's Library (London)
Gertrude Tuckwell Collection

Newspapers and Periodicals
Blackshirts 1936
British Worker 1926 and 1936
Daily Herald 1919-51
East End News 1910-1951
East London Advertiser 1910-1951
East London Observer 1910-1951
East London Pioneer 1936-7
Essex and East London Newspapers Ltd 1976
Essex Newspapers Ltd 1986
Evening Standard 1945
Jewish Chronicle 1914-1951
Jewish Clarion 1950
Lansbury Bulletin 1926
Morning Post 1911
New Statesman 1939-1945
Port Workers News 1949
Punch 1914-1924
Stepney Citizen 1929-1950
Strike News 1926
The Call 1916
The Economist 1940
The Empire News 1945
The Express 1976
The Independent 2007
The Nation 1919
The Times 1910-1951
The Shop Assistant 1920-1930
Weekly Times 1918
Woman's Dreadnought 1914-1917
Workers Bulletin 1926

Maps
Map of Jewish East London. Reproduced by the Museum of the Jewish East End and Research Census from 'The Jew in London 1901' (Guildhall Library, City of London)
Map of Lansbury Estate Stepney and Poplar Site Plans 1950
Map of LCC Development Plan 1951
Map of LCC Zoning Proposals under Stepney-Poplar Reconstruction Scheme
Map of the Borough of Stepney
Map of the positions where Zeppelin and aeroplane bombs landed in London (Collage collection k1237916)
Maps of Second World War Bomb Damage to London (London Metropolitan Archives)
Map of Stepney based on the 1899 London Government Act

Official Publications
(Place of publication is London, unless otherwise stated)
Abercrombie, Patrick, *Greater London Plan* (1944)
Census of England & Wales 1911, 1921, 1931, 1951
Forshaw, J. H. and Abercrombie, Patrick, *The County of London Plan* (1943)
Holland, Sir Milner, Chairman, *Report of the Committee on Housing in Greater London* (March 1965)
London County Council *A Survey of the Post-War Housing of the LCC 1945-1949* (1949)
London County Council, *London Statistics* 1910-1954
Medical Officer of Health for Stepney Report 1939-1945
Ministry of Health, *Report of the Design of Dwellings sub-committee of the central housing advisory committee appointed by the Ministry of Health and Report of a study group of the Ministry of Town and Country Planning on site planning and layout in relation to housing* (1944)
Ministry of Information on behalf of the Board of Education, *The Schools in Wartime* (1941)
Ministry of Labour and National Service – Unofficial Stoppages in the London Docks *Report of a Committee of Inquiry* (May, 1951)
Parliamentary Debates – Commons (1914-1951)

Contemporary Books, Pamphlets and Articles

Anonymous, *An A. A. Brigade at War!* (1944)

Anthony, Hugh *Houses: Permanence and Prefabrication* (December 1945)

Festival of Britain, *The Festival of Britain 1951* (1949)

Harrison, Tom & Madge, Charles, *Britain by Mass-Observation* (2nd Edn 1986 (1st Published 1939))

Hygiene Committee of the Women's Group on Public Welfare (in association with the National Council of Social Service), *Our Towns A Close Up: A Study made during the 1939-1942* (Great Britain, 1942)

Munby, D. L. *Industry and Planning in Stepney* (Oxford, 1951)

Pankhurst, Sylvia E., *The Homefront: A Mirror to Life in England during the World War* (1932/1987)

Peel, C. S., *How We Lived Then 1914-1918* (1929)

Purdom, C. B. *How Should We Rebuild London?* (1945)

Smith, Rev. G. Vernon, *The Bishop of London's Visit to the Front (A. F. Winnington-Ingram Bishop of London)* (1915)

Strachey, Mrs St. Loe, *Borrowed Children: A popular account of some evacuation problems and their remedies* (1940)

Stepney Reconstruction Group *Living in Stepney: Past, Present and Future* (1945)

The Editor, "Lansbury: A Principle Put into Practice" *The Architects Journal* 6 September 1951 pp275-304

The "Municipal Journal" special supplement tells the story of The Lansbury Site: The Festival of Britain's Live Architecture Exhibition *The Municipal Journal* 6 April 1951 pp777-792

The Times, *The Times House of Commons Guide* (1945)

Toynbee Hall, *Living in Stepney: Past, Present and Future* (1943)

Winnington-Ingram, Arthur Foley Lord Bishop of London *Cleansing London* (1916)

—. Sermon preached by, *"They Shall Not Pass"* (Easter 1918)

—. *A Day of God – Five Addresses on the subject of the Present War*

Memoirs and Biographies

Imperial War Museum
Sound Archives IWM Taped interviews
ID Number 20649 Lew Cherley
ID Number 8639 Max Colin
ID Number 10253 Jack Gaster
ID Number 9157 David "Tony" Gilbert

ID Number 16612 Charlie Goodman
ID Number 9479 Solly Kaye
ID Number 11835 Kenny Micallef
ID Number 9341 Louis Kenton
ID Number 20650 Max Levitas
ID Number 10210 Phillip Sherwood Piratin
ID Number 9341 Jack Louis Shaw

Bancroft Local History Library
Mrs G., Tape 31, transcript pp1-4

Books, Journals and Pamphlets
Attlee, C. R., *As It Happened* (1954)
Beardmore, George, *Civilians at War: Journals 1938-1946* (Oxford, 1947)
Bloomberg, Joe, *Looking Back: A Dockers Life* (1979)
Colson, Percy, *The Life of the Bishop of London: An Authorised Biography* (1935)
Finn, Ralph L., *No Tears in Aldgate* (Bath, 1963)
Goldman, Willy, *East End My Cradle: Portrait of an Environment* (1988)
Gosling, Harry, *Up and Down Stream* (1927)
Hartog, Alexander, *Born to Sing* (1978)
Harris, Kenneth, *Attlee* (1982/1995)
Jacobs, Joe, *Out of the Ghetto* (1978)
Janner, Elsie, *Barnett Janner: A Personal Portrait* (1984)
Laurie, Kendrum (ed.), *Sam: An East End Cabinet-maker* (1983)
Lewey, Frank R., (Mayor of Stepney during the London Blitzkreig), *Cockney Campaign* (1944)
Miles, H. E., *Untold tales of Wartime London* (1919)
Paget, Elma K., *Henry Luke Paget: Portrait and Frame* (1939)
Paget, The Right Rev. Henry Luke D.D. Bishop of Stepney, *Records of the Raids* (1918)
Piratin, Phil, *Our Flag Stays Red* (1980/2006)
Ramsay, Edith, *Life in Stepney: World War II 1939-1945* (Pamphlet, 1976)
Reckitt, Rachel, *Stepney Letters: Extracts from Written by Rachel Reckitt, from Stepney during the"Blitz" of 1940-41* (Cumbria, 1991)
Rocker, Rudolf, *The London Years* (California, 2005)
Sokoloff, Bertha, *Edith and Stepney* (1987)
Winnington-Ingram, Arthur Foley, *Fifty Years' Work in London 1889-1939* (1940)

Reference Works

Arnold-Baker, Charles (ed.), *The Companion to British History* (Kent, 1996)
Booth, Charles, *Life and Labour of the People in London*
Cannon, John (ed.), *The Oxford Companion to British History* (Oxford, 1997)
Craig, F. W. S., *British General Election Manifestos 1918-1966* (Chichester, 1970)
—. *British Parliamentary Election Results 1918-1949* (Chichester, 1983)
Finch, Harold *The Tower Hamlets Connection: A Biographical Guide* (1996)
Gardiner, Juliet and Wenborn, Neil (eds.), *The History Today Companion to British History* (1995)
Oxford Dictionary of National Biography (Oxford, 1992)
Smith, Hubert Llewellyn *The New Survey of London Life & Labour* Vol. 3, 4 (1930-1935)
Stenton, Michael, and Lees, Stephen (eds.), *Who's Who of British Members of Parliament Vol. III 1919-1945* (Sussex, 1979)
Thane, Pat, *Cassell's Companion to Twentieth Century Britain* (2001)
Willis, Alan and Woollard, John, *Twentieth Century Local Election Results Vol. 1 LCC (1889-1961) and London Metropolitan Boroughs (1900-1928)* (2000)
—. *Twentieth Century Local Election Results Vol. 2 London Metropolitan Boroughs (1931-1962)* (2000)

Secondary Sources

Books

Ackroyd, Peter, *London: The Biography* (2001)
Addison, Paul, *Now the War is Over* (1985)
Alderman, Geoffrey, *London Jewry and London Politics 1889-1986* (1989)
Alderman, Geoffrey and Holmes, Colin (eds.), *Outsiders & Outcasts – Essays in Honour of William Fishman* (1993)
Andrews, I. O., *The Economic Effects of the World War upon Women and Children in Great Britain* (Oxford, 1921)
Banham, Mary, Firmstone, Christopher, and Hillier, Beris, (eds.), *A Tonic to the Nation* (England, 1976)

Bell, Amy Helen, *London Was Ours: Diaries and Memories of the London Blitz* (2008)

Beckett, Francis, *Enemy Within: The Rise and Fall of the British Communist Party* (1995)

Benewick, Robert, *A Study of British Fascism: Political Violence and Public Order* (1969)

Bevan, Vaughan, *The Development of British Immigration Law* (1986)

Braybon, Gail, *Women Workers in the First World War* (1981)

Brown, Mike, *Evacuees: Evacuation in Wartime Britain 1939-1945* (Gloucestershire, 2000)

Burke, Barry, *Rebels with a Cause – The History of Hackney Trades Council 1900-1975* (1975)

Cable Street Group, *The Battle of Cable Street* (1995)

Calder, Angus, *The Myth of the Blitz* (1991)

—. *The People's War: Britain 1939-1945* (1993)

Castle, H., *Fire over England* (1984)

Cox, Jane, *London's East End: Life and Traditions* (1994)

Davis, John, *A History of Britain 1885-1939* (1999)

Davis, Mary, *Sylvia Pankhurst: A Life in Radical Politics* (1999)

DeGroot, Gerard J., *Blighty: British Society in the Era of the Great War* (1996)

Dorril, Stephen, *Black Shirt: Sir Oswald Mosley & British Fascism* (England, 2007)

Eatwell, Roger, *The 1945-1951 Labour Government* (1979)

Eksteins, Modris, *Rites of Spring: The Great War and the Birth of the Modern Age* (1989)

Fegan, Thomas, *The 'Baby Killers': German Air Raids on Britain in the First World War* (Great Britain, 2002)

Feldman, David and Stedman-Jones, Gareth (eds.), *Metropolis London: Histories and Representations since 1800* (1989)

Fielding, Steven, Thompson, Peter and Tiratsoo, Nick, *England Arise!* (Manchester, 1995)

Fishman, William J., *East End Jewish Radicals 1875-1914* (1975)

—. *The Streets of East London* (1979)

Gilbert, Bentley B., *British Social Policy 1914-1939* (1970)

Glinert, Ed, *East End Chronicles* (2005)

Green, J., *A Social History of the Jewish East End in London 1914-1939: A Study of Life, Labour and Liturgy* (Wales, 1991)

Grieves, Keith, *The Politics of Manpower: 1914-1918* (Manchester, 1988)

Hannam, June and Hunt, Karen, *Socialist Women: Britain 1880s to 1920s* (2002)

Harrisson, Tom, *Living Through the Blitz* (1976)

Hennessy, Peter, *Never Again, Britain 1945-51* (2006)

Hinton, James, *Women, Social Leadership and the Second World War: Continuities of Class* (Oxford, 2002)

Holloway, Gerry, *Women and Work in Britain Since 1840* (2005)

Holmes, Colin, *Anti-Semitism in British Society 1876-1939* (1979)

Holman, Bob, *The Evacuation: A very British Revolution* (Oxford, 1995)

Hopkins, James K., *Into the Heart of the Fire: The British in the Spanish Civil War* (California, 1998)

Howell, David, *Attlee* (2006)

Hylton, Stuart, *Their Darkest Hour: The hidden history of the Home Front 1939-1945* (Gloucestershire, 2001)

Inwood, Stephen, *A History of London* (1998)

Johnson-Marshall, Percy, *Rebuilding Cities* (Edinburgh, 1966)

Keating, P. J., *The Working Class in Victorian Fiction* (1971)

Kershen, Anne J. (ed.), *London: The Promised Land? The Migrant experience in a Capital City* (1997)

Kingsford, Peter, *The Hunger Marches in Britain 1920-1939* (1982)

Kushner, Tony, *We Europeans? Mass-Observation, 'Race' and British Identity in the Twentieth Century* (England, 2004)

Kushner, Tony, and Valman, Nadia (eds.), *Remembering Cable Street: Fascism and Anti-Fascism in British Society* (2000)

Laybourn, Keith, *The General Strike Day by Day* (Gloucestershire, 1996)

Linehan, Thomas P., *East London for Mosley: The British Union of Fascists in East London & South-West Essex 1933-40* (1996)

Lyman, Richard W., *The First Labour Government 1924* (1958)

Mandle, W. F., *Anti-Semitism and the British Union of Fascists* (Great Britain, 1968)

Marwick, Arthur, *The Deluge* (1991)

Marrin, Albert, *The Last Crusade: The Church of England in the First World War* (USA, 1974)

Mason, Anthony, *The General Strike in the North East* (Hull, 1970)

McCallum, R. B. and Readman, Allison, *The British General Election of 1945* (Oxford, 1947)

Morgan, Kenneth and Jane, *Portrait of a Progressive: The Political Career of Christopher, Viscount Addison* (Oxford, 1980)

Morgan, Kenneth O., *Britain Since 1945: The People's Peace* (Oxford, 2001)

—. *Consensus and Disunity: The Lloyd George Coalition Government 1918-1922* (Oxford, 1979)

Morris, Margaret, *The British General Strike 1926* (Pamphlet – General Strike Series No 82) (Great Britain, 1973)

—. *The General Strike* (England, 1976)

Mowat, Charles Loch, *Britain between the Wars 1918-1940* (Cambridge, 1987)

Palmer, Alan, *The East End: Four Centuries of London Life* (2000)

Panayi, Panikos (ed.), *Minorities in Wartime* (Oxford, 1993)

—. *The Enemy in Our Midst: Germans in Britain during the First World War* (Oxford, 1991)

Pelling, Henry, *The British Communist Party – A Historical Profile* (1958)

Phillips, Jim, *The Great Alliance: Economic recovery and the problems of power 1945-1951* (1996)

Pope, Rex, *War and Society in Britain 1899-1948* (1991)

Porter, Stephen (ed.), *Survey of London Vol. XLIII* (1994)

Pugh, Martin, *The Evolution of the British Electoral System 1832-1987* (1994)

—. *"Hurrah for the Blackshirts!"* (2005)

—. *The Making of Modern British Politics 1867-1945* (Oxford, 2002)

Robb, George, *British Culture and the First World War* (Hampshire, 2002)

Robins, Keith, *The First World War* (Oxford, 1984)

Rogers, Colin, *The Battle of Stepney. The Sidney Street Siege: Its causes and consequences* (1989)

Rose, S. O., *Which Peoples War? National Identity and Citizenship in Wartime Britain 1939-1945* (Oxford, 2003)

Rumbelow, Donald, *The Houndsditch Murders and the Siege of Sidney Street* (1988)

Rust, William, *Britons in Spain: The History of the British Battalion of the XVth International Brigade* (1939)

Russell, C. and Lewis, H. S., *The Jew in London* (1900)

Scaffardi, Sylvia, *Fire Under the Carpet: Working for Civil Liberties in the 1930s* (1986)

Schweitzer, Pam, Andrew, Andy and Fawcett, Pat (eds.), *Goodnight Children Everywhere: Memories of Evacuation in World War Two* (1990)

Shepherd, John, *George Lansbury* (Oxford, 2002)

Shepherd, John, and Laybourn, Keith, *Britain's First Labour Government* (2006)

Skidelsky, Robert, *Oswald Mosley* (1981)

Srebrnik, Henry Felix, *London Jews and British Communism, 1935-1945* (Essex, 1995)

Stepney Borough Council, *The Metropolitan Borough of Stepney – Official Guide 10th Edition* (1962)

Sykes, Alan, *The Radical Right in Britain* (Hampshire, 2005)

Taylor, A. J. P., *English History 1914-1945* (Oxford, 1965)

Taylor, Robert, *The Trade Union Question in British Politics* (Oxford, 1993) Thom, Deborah, *Nice Girls and Rude Girls: Women Workers in World War One* (1998)

Thompson, Paul, *Socialists, Liberals and Labour: The Struggle for London 1885-1914* (1967)

Thorpe, Andrew (ed.), *The Failure of Political Extremism in inter-war Britain* (Exeter, 1989)

Timmins, Nicholas, *The Five Giants: A Bibliography of the Welfare State* (1995)

Titmuss, Richard M., *Problems of Social Policy* (1950)

Watkins, Stephen, *How East Enders won the Battle of Cable Street* (THN, May) Press Cuttings (1991)

Weightman, Gavin and Humphries, Steve (eds.), *The Making of Modern London 1815-1914* (1983)

White, Jerry, *London in the 20th Century* (2001)

—. *Rothschild Buildings: Life in an East End Tenement Block 1887-1920* (1980)

Wicks, Ben, *The Day they took the Children* (1989)

Wing, Sandra Koa (ed.), *Mass Observation Britain in the Second World War* (2007)

Wilson, Trevor, *The Myriad Faces of War: Britain and the Great War 1914-1918* (Cambridge, 1986)

Winslow, Barbara, *Sylvia Pankhurst* (1996)

Winter, J. M., *The Great War and the British People* (1985)

Worley, Matthew, *Labour, Inside the Gate* (2005)

Wrigley, C. J. (ed.), *A History of British Industrial Relations Vol. II: 1914-1939* (Sussex, 1987)

—. *David Lloyd George and the British Labour Movement* (Sussex, 1976)

—. (ed.) *Warfare, Diplomacy and Politics – Essays in Honour of AJP Taylor* (1986)

Wybrow, Robert J., *Britain Speaks Out 1937-1987 – A Social History as Seen Through the Gallup Date* (1989)

Ziegler, Philip, *London at War 1939-1945* (Great Britain, 1995)

Articles

Bagwell, P. S., "The Triple Industrial Alliance, 1913-1922" in Briggs, Asa and Saville, John, (eds.), *Essays in Labour History 1886-1923* (1971) pp96-127

Fishman, William J., "Allies in the Promised Land: Reflections on he Irish and he Jewish in the East End" in Kershen, Anne J. (ed.), *London: The Promised Land? The migrant experience in a capital city* (England, 1997) pp38-49

Gillespie, James, "Poplarism and proletarianism: Unemployment and Labour politics in London 1918-34" in Feldman, David and Stedman-Jones, Gareth (eds.), *Metropolis London: Histories and Representations since 1800* (1989) pp163-188

Harmer, Harry, "The Failure of the Communists: The National unemployed Workers' Movement, 1921-1939, A Disappointing Success" in Thorpe, Andrew (ed.), *The Failure of Political Extremism in inter-war Britain* (Exeter, 1989) pp29-48

Harris, José, "Some aspects of social policy in Britain during the Second World War" in Mommsen, W. J. (ed.), *The Emergence of the Welfare State in Britain and Germany* (1981) pp247-262

Kershen, Anne J., "Immigrants, Sojourners and Refugees: Minority Groups in Britain, 1900-1939" in Wrigley, Chris (ed.), *A Companion to Early Twentieth-Century Britain* (Oxford, 2003) pp137-151

Kushner, Tony, "Jew and Non-Jew in the East End of London: Towards an Anthropology of 'Everyday' Relations" in Alderman, Geoffrey and Holmes, Colin (eds.), *Outsiders & Outcasts – Essays in Honour of William Fishman* (1993) pp32-52

Linehan, Thomas P., "Fascist Perceptions of Cable Street" in Kushner, Tony and Valman, Nadia (eds.), *Remembering Cable Street: Fascism and Anti-Fascism in British Society* (2000) pp23-30

Macnicol, John, "The evacuation of schoolchildren" in Smith, Harold L. (ed.), *War and Social Change – British Society in the Second World War* (Manchester, 1986) pp3-31

Panayi, Panikos, "Dominant Societies and Minorities in the Two World Wars" in Panayi, Panikos, (ed.), *Minorities in Wartime* (Oxford, 1993) pp3-20

Smith, Elaine R., "Jews and Politics in the East End of London, 1918-1939" in Cesarani, David, *The Making of Modern Anglo Jewry* (Oxford, 1990) pp141-162

Thurlow, Richard, "The Failure of British Fascism 1932-40" in Thorpe, Andrew (ed.), *The Failure of Political Extremism in inter-war Britain* (Exeter, 1989) pp67-84

Wrigley, Chris, "The State and the challenge of Labour in Britain 1917-1920" in Wrigeley, Chris (ed.), *Challenges of Labour, Central and Western Europe 1917-1920* (1993) pp262-288

Journal Articles

Alderman, Geoffrey, "M. H. Davis: The Rise and Fall of a Communal Upstart" *Jewish Historical Studies* Vol. XXXI 1988-1990 pp249-268
Bor, Walter, "The Lansbury Neighbourhood Reappraised" *The Planner* Vol. 64 No. 1 January 1978 pp10-14
Bullock, Nicholas, "Re-assessing the Post-War Housing Achievement: the Impact of War-damage Repairs on the New Housing Programme in London" *Twentieth Century British History* Vol. 16 No. 3 2005 pp256-282
Bush, Julia, "East London Jews and the First World War" *London Journal* 6 *1980* pp147-161
Cesarani, David, "The East London of Simon Blumenfeld's Jew Boy" *London Journal 13* 1987 pp46-53
Devey, Ernest, "Forest Gate Under Zeppelin Raid" *Cockney Ancestor* No. 16 Autumn 1982 pp18-20
Dewey, P. E., "Military Recruiting and the British Labour Force during the First World War" *The Historical Journal*, 27, 1 1984 pp199-223
Douglas, Jay, "The Attlee Government" *Contemporary Record* Vol. 2 No. 4 Winter 1988 pp23-24
Douglas, Roy, "The background to the 'Coupon' election arrangements" *The English History Review* Vol. April 1971 pp318-336
Holton, Sandra Stanley, "The Suffragist and the 'Average Woman'" *Women's History Review* Vol. 1 1992 pp9-24
Hunt, Karen and Worley, Matthew, "Rethinking British Communist Party Women in the 1920s" *Twentieth Century British History* Vol. 15 Nov 1 2004 pp1-27
Kingsley-Kent, Susan, "Remembering the Great War" *Journal of British Studies* 37 January, 1998 pp105-10
Knowles, Kenneth, "The Post-war dock strikes" *Political Quarterly* July-September 1951 Vol. xxii No. 3 pp266-287
Lee, Roger K., "Planning and Social Change in East London" *East London Paper* Vol. 14 No. 1 April 1972 pp25-43
Macfarlane, L. J., "Hands off Russia: British Labour and the Russo-Polish War, 1920" *Past and Present* Vol. 38 No. 1 1967 pp126-152

Phillips, Jim, "The Postwar Political Consensus and Industrial Unrest in the Docks, 1945-55" *Twentieth Century British History* Vol. 6 No. 3 1995 pp302-319

Rubinstein, William D., "Henry Page Croft and the National Party 1917-22" *Journal of Contemporary History* 9 1 1974 pp129-48

Smails, A. E. and Simpson, Gillian, "The Changing Face of East London" *East London Papers* Vol. No. 1 April 1958 pp31-46

Smith, Elaine R., "Class, ethnicity and politics in the Jewish East End, 1918-1939" *Jewish Historical Studies* Vol. XXXII 1990-1992 pp355-369

Srebrnik, Henry, "Class, Ethnicity and Gender Intertwined: Jewish women and the East London Rent Strikes 1935-40" *Women's History Review* Vol. 4 No. 3 1995 pp283-299

—. "Communism and Pro-Soviet Feeling Among the Jews of East London, 1935-45" *Immigrants and Minorities* Vol. 5 1986 pp285-304

The Editor, "Lansbury, Poplar 1951" *The Architects Journal* 3 July 1974 pp23-42

Welshman, John, "Evacuation and Social Policy During the Second World War Myth and Reality" *Twentieth Century British History* Vol. 9 No. 1 1998 pp28-53

—. "Evacuation, hygiene and social polity: the Our Towns Report of 1943" *Historical Journal* 42, 3 1999 pp781-807

Winter, J. M., "Britain's 'Lost Generation' of the First World War" *Population Studies* 31 1977 pp449-466

Woolven, Robin, "The London Experience of Regional Government 1938-1943" *The London Journal* Vol. 25 No. 2 2000 pp59-78

Worley, Matthew, "Building the Party: Labour Party Activism in five British Counties between the Wars" *Labour History Review* Vol. 70 No. 1 April 2005 pp73-95

Theses

Bush, Julia Frances, *Labour Politics and Society in East London During the First World War* PhD thesis (1988)

Connelly, M. L., *The Commemoration of the Great War in the City and East London 1916-1919* PhD thesis (1995)

Gillespie, James, *Economic and Political change in the East End of London during the 1920s* PhD thesis (Cambridge, 1983/4)

Godley, Andrew, *Enterprise and Culture: Jewish Immigrants in London and New York 1880-1914* PhD thesis (1992)

Moye, Andrew, *The LCC's Reconstruction of Stepney and Poplar 1945-1965* Diploma in Town Planning thesis (1979)

Mullings, Margaret Mary, *The Left and Fascism in the East End of London 1932-1939* PhD thesis (London, 1984)

Tyler, Paul, *Will Crooks MP, Local Activist and Labour Pioneer: Poplar to Woolwich 1852-1921* PhD thesis (2003)

Srebrnik, H., *The Jewish Communist Movement in Stepney: Ideological Mobilisation and Political Victories in an East London Borough 1935-45* PhD thesis (Birmingham, 1984)

Film Sources

ITV1 Carlton *Scenes of Crime* 15 November 2001

Internet Sources

British Broadcasting Corporation World War Two People's War Website

Oxford Dictionary of National Biography (Oxford University Press, online edn.)

INDEX

Italic pagination indicates illustrations, tables etc.